THE SCREENPLAYS OF

LINA WERTMÜLLER

THE SCREENPLAYS OF

LINA WERTMÜLLER

Translated from the Italian by Steven Wagner
Introduction by John Simon

THE SEDUCTION OF MIMI
LOVE AND ANARCHY
SWEPT AWAY
SEVEN BEAUTIES

WARNER BOOKS

A Warner Communications Company

CONTENTS

INTRODUCTION

Lina Wertmüller is the first woman to have become an internationally recognized filmmaker, and that in itself is a remarkable achievement. Film buffs can, of course, name other female directors—Dorothy Arzner and Germaine Dulac (totally mannish though they were), Ida Lupino and Leni Riefenstahl, and one or two others. Yet Dulac is remembered chiefly for having directed Antonin Artaud's only produced filmscript (misdirected, Artaud claimed), and Arzner and Lupino made nothing of significance. Riefenstahl did make two important films, but they were documentaries, and she was backed by Adolf Hitler on a grand scale; clearly, a somewhat special case.

In Italy, only one other woman director gained more than cursory notice: Liliana Cavani, best known for *The Night Porter,* a piece of ineptly made, pretentious kitsch. This brings us back to Wertmüller as the first woman really to make it big in film directing: though she already has a substantial *oeuvre* behind her, one feels that she barely has begun to tap her creative funds. The present collection brings together her four most important and successful screenplays, although her very first effort, *The Lizards* (*I basilischi*, 1963), is nothing to sneeze at. The quartet of films represented here is in no sense a tetralogy, yet, as we shall see, it is held together by strong thematic links.

To begin with some biographical data: Lina Wertmüller was born some forty-eight or nine years ago Arcangela Felice Assunta Wertmüller von Elgg Spanol von Brauchich (at least that is the way she wrote it out for me; I can't vouch for the spelling). Although descended from a German-Swiss baronial family, there is nothing in the least aristocratic or Swiss about her, and she doesn't speak a word of German. She springs from solidly bourgeois Roman parents—is considered, in fact, a prototypical Roman—and turned Socialist and bohemian. She was a hellion in school, and, following in the footsteps of a slightly older hellion, Flora, ended up in drama school. Eventually, there was to be nothing in theater that she did not try her hand at; above all, she directed and wrote plays, one of which, later on, was to prove very successful and had in it a young man with whom Lina was to form an extremely fruitful artistic fellowship—Giancarlo Giannini.

After dramatic academy, Lina joined the controversial puppet troupe of Maria Signorelli; afterward, through her friend Flora, now married to Marcello Mastroianni, she met Fellini, who let her be an assistant on 8½. This did not satisfy Lina's needs for very long; she soon quit in order to make a documentary about Fellini directing 8½. When Fellini finished, she spirited away many of his technicians—including that brilliant cinematographer, the late Gianni di Venanzo—to Sicily, there to shoot her own first film. *I basilischi* did quite well, as did also her next picture. She worked with success in television, too. Nevertheless, she was unable to raise the money for her next film, and so returned to the theater, working briefly even for the popular musical-comedy team of Garinei and Giovannini. She then met the painter Enrico Job (who has since switched to conceptual art and other forms of extreme modernism, but was at that time still doing quite nicely with brushes and canvas) and married him, gaining not only a husband but also a gifted set and costume designer for her future works. And she kept going to the movies—ravenously—sometimes consuming five films a day.

When she finally came back to making her own films, it was with renewed assurance and with a much greater technical facility or, if you prefer, cinematic sense. After *The Seduction of Mimi*, whose real title is *Mimi the Metallurgical Worker Wounded in His Honor*, there could be no doubt that she belonged to the movies and the movies to her. Her camera had acquired that true fluidity so absent from her second film, *Let's Talk About Men* of 1964. I wonder how clearly she even remembers that one now. She tends to wear a necklace with little plaques bearing the titles and dates of her works; that is how she knows just what she has done and when.

Mimi is the first Wertmüller film in which her main theme comes clearly to the fore. That theme is, simply, politics and sex or love. Politics and love or sex (sometimes it is more love than sex, sometimes vice versa) are the poles between which her comedy-dramas evolve; one of the films, *Love and Anarchy*, even has them in its title. It is not, however, a mere oscillation or even antagonism between these poles that concerns her most; rather, it is a matter of interpenetration: the way love or sex becomes politicized, and politics sexualized. So Mimi's Communism has much to do with the fact that it enables him to have an affair with the sexy Communist Fiore; his troubles begin when he begrudges equality to his wife whom he does not even particularly care for and allows his alleged conjugal rights to get the better of his political enlightenment. Of course, avenging one's marital "honor" by whatever absurd means is also a form of social politics, however misguided.

It is in bed, while sexually dominating his frightened little wife, that Mimi tells her he forbids her to vote for Cannamozza. When the timid soul, neglected by the gallivanting Mimi, emancipates herself socially, and thus politically, she, too, is able to take on a lover, if only briefly. So love and politics mingle. But when Mimi finds out that his wife is pregnant by another man, the poles fly apart: "Communist, Communist, my arse. I'm a cuckold, that's what I am."

But the polarity becomes even more perspicuous in the next film, *Love and Anarchy*. Here the peasant-turned-anarchist Tunin is caught between his political duty to kill Mussolini and his love for the little whore Tripolina, or between love of heroic death, which the former would lead to, and love of life and woman—between a politicized passion and a natural one. Yet a perhaps even more spectacular dilemma takes place within the bosom of Salomè, who, as a dedicated anarchist, is truly committed politically, and, as an experienced prostitute, is equally committed to sex. But also to love, for Salomè loves Tunin, and loves him with two different loves: the old love for her boy-fiancé whom the Fascists killed—a love that, after years of whoring, is rekindled in her in all its innocence and sweetness by Tunin; and a new love, the fanatical, politicized love of an Electra for her Orestes who will execute the slaying that will bring about revenge, justice, liberation—the love of one divinely inspired avenger for another who is the instrument of her holy wrath.

It is between these two loves that Salomè must choose in the end, and it is the former that wins out. The choice is hard, and proves destructive even while attempting to be salutary. And when Tunin proceeds to shoot the policemen who have come to the brothel without even knowing of his existence, it is difficult to say just what his motives are. Partly, it is a misunderstanding—fear that they are out to get him; partly, it is impotent rage at having missed his chance to destroy the tyrant; partly, it is the sense of political mission and duty to his dead friend—even if it is to be only a much lesser assassination; but partly, I am sure, it is also a misplaced desire not to look like a failure and coward to the two women who love him, and both of whom, in different ways, he loves. Love and politics have become thoroughly entangled, with dire consequences.

In *Swept Away* (or, properly, *Swept Away by an Unusual Destiny on the Blue Sea of August*), sex and politics become still more palpably interwoven. In the beginning, Donna Raffaella, who is clearly less than fulfilled in her marriage, uses power—a political force—as a substitute for happy sexuality and love. Thus she bullies her male companions on the yacht with clever political arguments and endless disputation that make her feel a quasi-sexual superiority; this is even more obvious in the way she torments the staff, particularly Gennarino, with capricious commands peppered with condescending or downright insulting remarks—capitalist domination of the working-class steward, from which she derives a protophysical satisfaction. The sunbathing near-nudity in which she and her woman friends expose themselves to the male staff's view may be the most glaring example of the sexualization of power. Yet it is not as if the Communist Gennarino were perceived as innocent by Wertmüller. He uses sexual domination as a source of power, as indicated by his angry remark about capitalist husbands, "These bastards will ruin our women! Who's going to wash our underwear in the future?"

Later, on the island, when Raffaella, initially out of hunger but later out of all kinds of sexual needs (some normal, some possibly masochistic), becomes, first, Gennarino's slave, then his slave-concubine, and finally his mistress-wife, Gennarino's political superiority over her has been slowly infiltrated by genuine passion and love, just as her involuntary, impotently raging submission has changed into purring submissiveness: satisfied servitude in which the servant knows her master's domination to be exceeded by his dependency, indeed love. Politics has become sexualized and even, to coin a word, lovified.

Seven Beauties, which I consider Lina's finest film so far, also hinges on a curious blending of sex (this time decidedly without love) and politics: Pasqualino's ability to seduce—if that is the word for it—the horrible camp commandant is what, most likely, saves his life. Ironically, though the film's score is partly by Wagner, who is most famous for his *Liebestod* music, what goes on in the movie is the exact opposite of a love-death—a sex-survival. In this chronicle of the ludicrous, pathetic, and horrendous progress of an uninnocent Candide, sexuality is seen as the means for survival *par excellence*. But that survival is an equivocal, questionable achievement at best.

The key speech here is, of course, the one in which the Commandant sneers at the "subhuman Mediterranean larvae" that even in the dismal circumstances of extreme exhaustion and starvation can "find the strength to get an erection," and get it, what is more, vis-à-vis a monster of murderous repulsiveness. "You'll be the ones who are left, you tiny, slithering worms" with "no ideals or ideas." Anyone who in the light of such utterances thinks that Wertmüller is exalting the Pasqualinos of this world, has to be as obtuse as Dr. Bruno Bettelheim, the eminent child psychiatrist, in his notorious attack on *Seven Beauties* that filled endless pages in *The New Yorker*.

Worm as an image—or, if not image, term of abuse—keeps appearing in these Wertmüller films. Significantly, Pasqualino was already called a worm by the pimp Totonno, an insult that struck him as worse than the preceding "bastard," and was to be the beginning of his ordeals. When, at the climax of his grotesque misadventures and calamities, the Commandant, too, calls him a worm, things have come full circle; the worm has not so much turned as returned to his initial worminess in its fullest manifestation. When Tunin, in *Love and Anarchy*, bewails his failure most bitterly, he cries out, "I'm worse off now than if I were dead, I'm nothing but a crawling worm!" In *Swept Away*, when Raffaella feels the greatest loathing for and rage against Gennarino, she exclaims, "You're a worm!" and, a little later, "Disgusting worm!" The term, or metaphor, seems to combine political and sexual implications. It is certainly a symbol of the lowest, most spineless kind of creature, the very one that makes totalitarianism and social exploitation possible. But "worm" has sexual connotations, too: the wiggling, slimy, disgusting yet fascinating creeper is a standard phallic symbol, at least where sex is viewed from a puritanical or otherwise hostile position. The worm is phallic and, because of its very lowness on the biological scale, survives. And survival is not only a biological, but also a political phenomenon.

It is also something morally ambiguous, something toward which Wertmüller takes a fundamentally ambivalent stand. This ambivalence is what makes her films so rich: the realization that nothing in life is simple—black or white, this or that. Always there is a precarious happiness in these movies, part delightful, part untenable, unable to endure. It is always confronted with a postponable but inescapable choice between alternatives of which neither is wholly right, wholly happy, or even wholly wrong.

That, too, is what these films are about: Mimi basking in the amoral delights of a double life with wife and mistress, and a double politics—

espousing Communism because of its heroic stance and alleged just-
ness, but also staying on the good side of the Mafia and handsomely
benefiting from it; Tunin, finding a brief, undreamt-of felicity in the
complementary loves of a strong maternal whore and a gentle, daugh-
terlike one—a preposterous ménage in an absurd setting that obviously
cannot last; Gennarino and Raffaella having to choose between a "perfect" relationship that, however, means her giving up the amenities of
high society, and his forgoing the satisfaction of knowing for certain
that this woman would choose him above all others, rather than be his
out of mere expediency under the unnatural (or are they natural?) circumstances of the island. Whether Raffaella and Gennarino signal the
ship that could rescue them, or whether they don't, something must be
given up—realize it or not—forever.

The terrible difficulty and inexorable necessity of choosing become
most evident in *Seven Beauties*, where there is, on the one hand,
Pasqualino, the vermiculate survival artist who will plead insanity, join
the army in a disastrous war, copulate with a vicious hippopotamus, kill
his best friend—do anything to live. On the other hand, there are the
decent Francesco, the unnamed Socialist condemned to 28 and a half
years in prison, and Pedro the anarchist, champion of "man in disorder," all of whom make heavy, or indeed supreme, sacrifices for a
cause: Socialism, anarchy, human dignity. And just as there was no
clear answer to the dilemma between love and politics, there is no
simple solution here. Pedro is surely right to choose death; still, to die,
to die like that? Pasqualino is surely wrong to survive at all costs; still,
only where there is life is there hope for learning and growth. Yet
Pasqualino, at any rate, is incapable of that, as his deleteriously garbled
version of Pedro's lesson demonstrates. Still, there may be some good
in just being alive, even in a sinister travesty of what it is all about;
Carolina, the purest character in the film, sings a song that begins,
"You must go on living and not give a damn." No easy solutions, then;
perhaps no solutions of any kind; yet, ironically, people who attack
Wertmüller do so most often on account of her allegedly facile or
primitive choices, which they, in their simplicity, do not realize that
Wertmüller never advocated.

What Lina Wertmüller is very much against, in all of her films, is, in
fact, patterns: a narrow, constricting order or tradition or discipline.
She is clearly in wholehearted sympathy with Pedro and his gospel of
"man in disorder," which is echoed by the convicted Socialist who
yearns for the pre-Fascist times: "Bless those days of disorder, of
strikes. . . ." The idea is perfectly encapsulated in the title of one of

Lina's lesser films, which the U.S. distributor vulgarly changed to *All Screwed Up*, but which really reads *Everyone in Place, Nothing in Order*—for the best kind of order, Lina feels, is a kind of disorder exhibited even by the Wertmüller-Job apartment: a kind of inspired clutter, man and woman in cozy, creative disarray.

Trouble in life, these films are saying, always stems from some antiquated notions of rules to live by, really existential clichés—whether it is the "place" of men and women in society, or the "place" of social classes in the hierarchy, or the code of "honor" by which one is supposed to behave. It is the macho mentality of the Italian middle- and lower-class male, for instance, that triggers the mechanism that undoes a Mimi or a Gennarino, as fanatical feminists who attack Wertmüller for her supposed antifeminism have been unable to note. Even Pasqualino's gross misunderstanding of Pedro's message, turning it into an imperative for nonstop begetting, must have something to do with male chauvinism, which is ultimately only one of several destructive patterns. Well might Wertmüller have exclaimed with Amy Lowell, "Christ! What are patterns for?"

Most insidious of these patterns is the outmoded sense of honor, the one that starts Pasqualino Settebellezze on the road to condign ruin, the supreme indignity of the concentration camp; that gets Mimi into a mock duel that turns out to be real; that does not permit Tunin to grasp the fact that he is a frightened little man who should run away with Tripolina; that makes Gennarino Carunchio return the million lire in the form of a ring he proudly labels "a divorce ring" meant to launch Raffaella's definitive departure from her husband, but that proves, ironically, the emblem of her divorce from him. The ring is "an enormous topaz surrounded by diamonds . . . a horrible-looking ring with a cheap setting"—in other words, a pattern, a proletarian's notion of patrician taste, and a sure indication to Raffaella that Gennarino and she are worlds, or at least patterns, apart. And poor Gennarino and his wife are out even of a well-deserved million lire. As Fiore says in a letter to Mimi: "Today little Mimi asked me what the word honor meant. I told him that it was a very stupid thing."

However, nothing being simple in Wertmüller's world, there is also something sublime about this honor that makes Tunin cry out, "There comes a time when you say, 'Enough!' The day when you feel you've got to do something positive." What, then, is it that mediates between the excesses of honor, which are too much for most of us, and the excesses of compromise with everyday indignities, which get to be too much for all of us? It is a sense of humor. Or, as Salomè puts it, "Life is so shitty that if one doesn't have a good laugh now and then, it just isn't worth living. . . ."

It is, of course, vastly inadequate for an appreciation of Wertmüller, or any other true filmmaker, to concern itself solely with words and ideas, and ignore the visual aspects, hard as it may be to deal with them in any context other than an illustrated lecture. What makes Wertmüller so remarkable is the combination of her sights and sounds, but the former can be fully appreciated only by seeing her films, for which the reading of these screenplays, however instructive and pleasurable, is no substitute.

Wertmüller's films are full of images, rhythms, juxtapositions, cross-cuttings that bespeak the master. Take, for instance, the soiled whiteness of the quarries near Catania where we see Mimi first and last. A fateful vehicle is arriving in the opening shots, bringing disastrous politics into his life; another, equally fateful, vehicle is departing in the last shot, taking love out of his life and leaving him a tiny, prostrate figure, a measly black grain in a grainy whitish landscape. Or take the confrontation with the Mafia boss: what a masterstroke it was to place it on a rooftop terrace with the view of the city below, and the old man sitting, as it were, on top of the world. Or consider the inspired absurdity of *La Traviata* on the soundtrack while Mimi mimes his wooing of Fiore across the roaring traffic of Turin. The sonorous incongruity brilliantly objectifies the emotional absurdity. Or what about the reference to Turks in the dialogue that then comes comically to life as Mimi sneaks a Fiore swathed in heavy black veils, worthy of an odalisque abroad, into Catania?

And what about the seduction of Amalia Finnochiaro, staged with a kind of accelerated action and shot in part with a distorting lens to achieve Rabelaisian dimensions of the grotesque—pushing farce to its farthest reaches and forcing it to reveal its woeful, disturbing underside. But I particularly like the way part of the story is told in voiceover by Mimi who is, in fact, narrating one of his letters home. The action on screen duplicates what he is saying, i.e., writing. Now we cut to his naively trusting wife reading out the latter part of the same epistle as the rest of the family is listening. Next, as we still hear the wife's trustful voice reading about Mimi being too busy for any kind of social life, we see him popping into bed—a regular practice, apparently—with his lusty landlady. The state of affairs has been conveyed wittily, concisely, and highly cinematographically.

What remains with us most indelibly from *Love and Anarchy* is the contrast between the bits of dazzlingly marmoreal, austerely inhuman Fascist architecture and the gaudily overdone but campily enjoyable décor of the "disorderly house"—the brothel that is the true breeding ground of man in disorder. Even the plethora of freckles dreamed up for Tunin's face is a small visual *coup:* it is the nearest thing to measles, or the sickness of idealism, that isolates this peasant dreamer from the rest of the world. And there is that extraordinary set of scenes in which Spatoletti, Fiore, Tripolina, and Tunin go to the country, where the changes of locale and illumination, the variations in pacing between sequences involving the two pairs of lovers, the abrupt switches of mood are exhilarating to experience. Enrico Job's set design performs miracles; the brothel bathroom alone is a triumph of misplaced luxury mocking emotional squalor.

Or consider how ingeniously Wertmüller manipulates her hero and heroine in their tiny boat in *Swept Away*. Recall, even earlier, the shot with which she introduces Gennarino: a hatch opens part way, just enough to allow the enormous rotundities of Giannini's eyes to beam their disapproval at Raffaella's shenanigans. Then there is the magnificent choreography of Gennarino's sexual assault on Raffaella, the chase across the dunes, complete with leaps and tumbles, that is both brutal battle and impassioned wooing. And how about that extraordinary closing sequence in which Gennarino and his wife become grudgingly, wordlessly reconciled over who is to carry the suitcase, and the camera switches from a lateral tracking shot in which the warring spouses stomp across our field of vision to an extreme long shot from behind where the couple wanders off in seeming serenity toward the vanishing point? Clearly, a movement leading out of the frame toward one side is something unresolved and disturbing, whereas absorption into the horizon at the center of the frame has a calm finality about it.

Concerning the tremendous visual achievements of *Seven Beauties* I have written at length elsewhere (*New York* magazine, February 2, 1976), and I wish to add here only that this is Lina's shortest script; words have been compressed and action is often allowed to unfurl in purely visual terms, whether outrageously comic or morally outrageous, indeed monstrous, with the monstrous in cruel ways travestying the comic.

Wertmüller adds to her keen cinematic sense the valuable lessons she gleaned from the theater; think, for example, how touchingly she stages the first love scene between Tripolina and Tunin—there is something theatrical in the best sense in the way she has the girl whorishly bragging as she undresses Tunin, yet at the same time, innocent as she still is and moved by his utter innocence, crying. There is a feeling of close work with her actors in all those very humane, sexy but unsalacious bedroom scenes—of the director moulding a scene as fine stage directors do. And the repartee crackles with the tempos and inflections of high theatrical comedy. Much, in fact, has already been written about the arduous, thorough, even despotic way Wertmüller has worked with such performers as Giannini and Mariangela Melato.

Finally, like most great directors—and like the greatest of all, Bergman—Wertmüller is her own writer. She turns out whopping good plots and dialogue that can be very poignant or funny, or even both at once. But I am still more impressed by some of her monologues where, in a couple of pared-down sentences made up of a few denuded words, something essential is caught in all its terrible, shining simplicity. I shall cite two examples among many.

Consider, first, Salomè's desperate *cri du coeur* to the indifferent crowd as the police mercilessly beat and then drag off Tunin: "It is for you that he was doing this, you bastards! For you who are slaves and don't know it! He was young and he had a heart of gold and he wanted to help you pigs." I find something ineffably lovely about that last sentence. There is something lyrical about the very irrelevance of that "young," being there only as a romantic sob; there is something curiously touching about that "heart of gold," usually ascribed to whores in second-rate books and movies, but here spoken *by* a whore about someone else; there is something awesome about that achingly direct, "He wanted to help you," followed immediately by that pitifully childish little insult, so hopelessly inadequate to the situation, "you pigs!"

And now take another *de profundis*, the invective Gennarino hurls at the helicopter in which Corrado is taking away Raffaella forever: "You fucking traitor! You slut! Damn the day I believed in you! I knew I shouldn't trust the rich, because the rich will always screw you in the end! Industrial slut! You're leaving me all alone . . . alone!" The camera angle, from the helicopter's point of view, emphasizes the abandoned lover's puniness, and the words are a marvel: a man unused to amorous grief is finding only the vocabulary of lowlife insult with which to express it. Then, "Damn the day I believed in you," which sounds like an inverted echo of Petrarch's "Blessed be the day, the month, the year" when the poet met Laura. After which the plebian turns, pathetically, into a Communist throwing comic-strip Marxism at his vanishing beloved. Bravely and foolishly he denounces the rich who'll always screw you in the end (though this one stopped screwing him in the end), then hits upon the ridiculously inept, and therefore heart-breaking, epithet of execration, *"Industrial* slut!" Then even this semblance of ideological outrage collapses and the pure, personal agony breaks through in "all alone . . . alone." It is so sad and beautiful, and made so much more sad and beautiful by being also ludicrous.

Yet Lina Wertmüller, this woman who brings to film what is best in film, theater, and literature, is attacked by so many, so maliciously or stupidly. One American woman critic is clearly jealous of her success; another one cannot make Wertmüller's ironic humanism square with some narrow concept of militant feminism. The eminent Dr. Bettelheim accuses her of exalting Pasqualino's values, which she plainly does not do; and of misrepresenting the alleged reality of concentration camps, which (even assuming that Bettelheim uniquely possesses it) is not the issue at all. The artist has the right to use even the death camps as a metaphor, to reimagine or reinvent them to suit his or her vision. If that vision is authentic, if it makes points about life that we can believe and respect, the niggling verisimilitude of details is unimportant. Art, after all, is neither reportage nor historiography; it has at its disposal truths even beyond those of child psychiatrists who were once actually camp inmates.

In Italy, where the film world is predominantly Marxist, Lina's anarchic Socialism appears to many movie people to be politically irresponsible. But the canons of Marx can bind Wertmüller no more than those of Bettelheim. She just goes from strength to strength, and is already becoming mythic—even on Long Island. There, not long ago, on the marquee of a movie theater you could read "LINA WERTMULLER'S 8½." How Fellini's ephemeral assistant will blush when she reads this: her revered master's work being ascribed to her, her reputation eclipsing his. Eclipsing, no; but, in due time, equaling? I can't see why not.

JOHN SIMON

1
THE SEDUCTION OF MIMI

THE SEDUCTION OF MIMI

CAST

Mimi	Giancarlo Giannini
Fiore	Mariangela Melato
Rosalia	Agostina Belli
Signora Finocchiaro	Elena Fiore

CREDITS

Written and Directed by	Lina Wertmüller
Producers	Daniele Senatore
	Romano Cardarelli
Assistant Director	Giovanni Arduini
Music	Piero Piccioni
Cameraman	Blasco Giurato
Editor	Franco Fraticelli
Art Director	Amedeo Fago
Set Director	Emilio Baldelli
Costume Designer	Maria Bono
Sound Engineers	Mario Bramonti
	Antonio Bramonti

Running time: 89 minutes

The first American showing of THE SEDUCTION OF MIMI was on June 19, 1974 at the 68th Street Playhouse in New York City.

SCENE 1

(A road in Sicily—exterior—daytime. A gigantic, sun-drenched quarry. Titles. A dark car with five men in it drives up the road. Five ominous-looking men, with distinctive Mafioso traits. The most somber-looking one occasionally checks the road ahead. Each one of the men is hiding something under his jacket—it could very well be a machine gun or some other type of weapon. The car comes to a halt. Farther up the road, in the quarry, we see a group of sweating men busy working. The car doors fly open and the men pour out of the car. The doors are in the way, and we can't clearly see what they are carrying. Suddenly, instead of the expected machine-gun blast, we hear a scratchy tune being played over a loudspeaker. Music. The four men start shouting into their megaphones. We now realize the true mission of the "would-be killers." Leaflets are thrown into the air and the wind carries them over to the workers. The men's words become more audible.)

VOICES: For the well-being of the humble and the defeat of the arrogant, vote for Carmine Cannamozza . . . Cannamozza!

(The scratchy campaign slogans reach the tired, sweaty workers, who stop to listen.)

VOICES: Workers! For a future of well-being, Cannamozza is your man, vote for freedom, vote for Cannamozza! Workers . . . do you know who Cannamozza is?
MIMI: A son of a bitch, that's who he is!

(The voice belongs to a young man with an enormous head of hair and an awe-inspiring mustache. He is Mimi Mardocheco. The car drives away as we hear the national anthem being played over the loudspeakers. The other workers laugh, but their laughter soon dies out. Hovering over them at the top of the quarry is the caretaker, with a Basque beret on his head and a gun slung over his shoulder. The men go back to their work. The caretaker has a cruel expression on his face.)

CARETAKER: Don't forget, if you are disrespectful to Carmine Cannamozza you are being disrespectful to Don Calogero. Be sure not to forget that when you go to the polls tomorrow!

SCENE 2

(Sulfur deposit—interior—daytime. Mimi is sitting on a huge mound of sulfur. He whistles, trying to attract Pasquale's attention. Pippino and Mimi's brother Vito walk in.)

PASQUALE: What?

MIMI: Cannamozza's men came to the quarry today with their slogans and leaflets.

PASQUALE: We'll talk about it later on. As soon as I finish work, I'll come back . . . wait for me outside.

(Mimi comes down off the sulfur hill. Vito runs over to him.)

VITO: Mimi, Mimi, I found a butt, can I try smoking?

(Vito puts the butt between his lips. Mimi tries to take it away from him but Vito foresees the move and hides the cigarette butt behind his back.)

MIMI: Here, with all this sulfur! We'll blow ourselves sky high! I'll keep it for you.

(Vito raises his head defiantly.)

VITO: Nnnnoooo!

MIMI: What, you don't trust your own brother?

(Vito smiles and gives him the butt.)

VITO: I trust you.

(Mimi puts it behind his ear, showing Vito that he has another butt in the same place.)

MIMI: This one is yours, and this one's mine. We'll smoke them later on. Don't worry, your brother will teach you everything you need to know.

(Pippino looks in.)

PIPPINO: So what's new?

MIMI: It's out of the question. I don't want to give my vote to Cannamozza, but I wouldn't want to get into any trouble.

PIPPINO: So that's how these bastards keep you under their thumbs . . . with fear. Vote for whoever the hell you please! What can they take away from you? You've got nothing to lose.

MIMI: My work . . .
PIPPINO: In the quarry? With the pittance they pay you? You call this a good job?
MIMI: No.
PIPPINO: So . . .
MIMI: You're right.

(*Mimi whistles to his brother, who slides down the sulfur hill.*)

MIMI: Fuck!

(*The three walk away.*)

SCENE 3

(*Mimi's house—interior—nighttime. "Uncle" Cicciu Mardocheco, Mimi's father, is sitting in the middle of the room being bathed. By taking a bath, Cicciu means putting his feet into a basin of hot water, his pants rolled up, and his arms in a basin on either side of him, his sleeves rolled up over his elbows. As always, he wears his Basque beret and a cigar butt is firmly clenched between his teeth. The effect is that of a bored emperor on his throne. Three women bustle around him, pouring water in the basins and generally serving him. They are Maria, his wife, and her two spinster sisters, Rosa and Celeste, who are as attached to their brother-in-law as a dog to his master. In a corner we see Mimi, the spitting image of his father, his feet in a basin of water being washed by his wife, Rosalia. His trousers are rolled up, the beret is on his head, and a cigar is firmly held in his mouth. Vito watches the whole scene, amused. Uncle Cicciu looks at his son with disgust.*)

UNCLE CICCIU: Mule! Idiot, presumptuous ignorant animal! Secret vote? In this place? Those people know how many hairs you have up your ass! They know everything!
MARIA: My son, I promised them six votes from our house . . . and six votes we must give them.

(*Maria goes to fetch some water.*)

CELESTE: That's right. Cicciu Mardocheco is a man who keeps his word, and if he promised to do this, he must do it. . . .
ROSA: We don't want to find him lying in the street with his liver in

one hand and his heart in the other and his. ears crossed on his chest like a bow tie do we?

(A lot of coming and going from the stove, where the water is being heated for the various bowls. A yell breaks through the steam.)

CICCIU: Judas be damned! You trying to boil me?

(The women fetch a basin of cold water.)

MARIA: Cicciu, did you burn yourself?
CICCIU: Goddamn it, you burned me, you ugly idiot! I'd like to know why we must have all this spring cleaning before the elections? Do you have to have clean feet to vote? Shit!

(The fat, dark-skinned Rosa is scrubbing her master's feet vigorously.)

ROSA: What's this guy's name that we have to vote for?
CELESTE: You're a real fool! It's been three months since Don Calogero told us he had committed himself to this Cannamozza fellow.
MIMI: What I don't understand is why we have to vote for him just because Don Calogero has committed himself.
ROSA AND CELESTE: Of course!
MIMI: Well, I don't want to give him my vote!
ROSA AND CELESTE: Why not?

(Mimi has a stubborn expression.)

MIMI: Because I don't like him!
CICCIU: You don't like him? Well, you don't have to get engaged to him! Vote for him and that's that!

(Mimi's stubborn expression)

MIMI: Nnnnnno!

SCENE 4

(Uncle Cicciu's house—Mimi's and Rosalia's bed. Interior—nighttime. The family is asleep. Behind the curtain which separates them from the rest of the family, Mimi is making love to Rosalia. He's trying to turn her on. He's putting body and soul into the operation. Rosalia puts up with it, but chews on the corner of the pillow to stop herself from moaning too loud.)

ROSALIA: Awooo!

(Mimi blows in his wife's ear.)

MIMI: You like that? Tell me you like it.

(Terror is written all over Rosalia's face. She's worried that the others might hear them. She takes the corner out of her mouth.)

ROSALIA: Quiet, or they'll hear us!

(Mimi peeks around the curtain to see if everything is all right.)

MIMI: Blood of Christ! Woman, what can they hear if they're all asleep?

(Mimi is really annoyed by his wife's attitude and fear. The large room is just like a dormitory. Uncle Cicciu lies snoring in the large bed with his wife. The two sisters snore as well. Mimi draws back the curtain and kneels over his wife once again. Rosalia opens her eyes wide, then offers herself up as a sacrifice. Mimi looks at her rather disinterestedly.)

MIMI: Rosalia, you're the wife, you've got to help, you've got to say something!
ROSALIA: Well, I've got nothing to say! What do you want me to say?
MIMI: Whatever you please.

(Mimi tries again, but Rosalia's pained expression irritates him.)

MIMI: You still have that frightened look! You look like a goat on the way to the slaughterhouse. You take all the joy away from the act . . . that's why we have no children. . . . It's all your fault! If you could only see your face!

(Rosalia is about to cry.)

ROSALIA: Well, don't look at me.
MIMI: Then who am I supposed to make love to, the cushion? It's as if you were sacrificing yourself. Shit! *Do* something! What kind of a woman are you?

(Rosalia's lips tremble. She starts to cry.)

ROSALIA: I'm ashamed . . .
MIMI: Now we have to put up with a flood of tears! Rosalia—screw you!

(*A furious Mimi turns his back to her. Rosalia shoves the pillow corner back into her mouth to stifle the whimpers. Suddenly Mimi turns around.*)

MIMI: And I forbid you to vote for Cannamozza!

SCENE 5

(*Square in the town—exterior—daytime. Men and women dressed in their Sunday best are walking across the village square heading for the polls. Close to the church and the inn is the door to the school that is serving as the polling station. Two policemen are standing on guard. Next to the police are some men leaning against the wall checking the people going in to vote. They are definitely Mafiosi. Among the men we see Ntoni, one of Don Calogero's men whom we noticed earlier by the quarry. Mimi is standing in front of the Communist Party headquarters with Turi, Vito, and Pasquale. Pippino is handing them lemon grenadines, which he serves from his colorful Baroque cart. The group watches the comings and goings in the square.*)

From a nearby terrace Don Calogero watches the square. He is comfortably seated in a wicker chair and surrounded by various friends who watch the scene with somber expressions.)

PIPPINO: Don't be intimidated by Don Calogero's men. They're there simply to frighten people.

(Three large birthmarks can be seen on Don Calogero's cheek.)

PASQUALE: The vote is secret!

(Mimi looks at his friend rather skeptically.)

PASQUALE: Vote for the left, and no one will ever know.

(Mimi looks up at Don Calogero. Mimi looks back at Pasquale.)

MIMI: It's secret, huh?
PASQUALE: Very secret.

(Uncle Cicciu and the four women appear at one end of the square. Mimi makes up his mind and joins his family. Linking arms with Rosalia, they walk into the polling station.)

SCENE 6

(*Village street—exterior—daytime. A very long, narrow street meanders between the low houses. Mimi Mardocheco walks briskly down the street, his jacket slung over his shoulder. It's early morning. From the other end of the street we see Ntoni walking toward him. As he comes abreast of Mimi, he calls out to him.*)

NTONI: Mimi Mardocheco!
MIMI: My most humble respects.
NTONI: I wanted to inform you that you might as well forget about going back to the quarry. There's no more work for you, now or ever! It's all over between you and us.

(*Mimi turns white.*)

MIMI: Why?
NTONI: Well, I know why and you know why—so we don't even have to discuss it.

SCENE 7

(*Communist Party headquarters—interior—daytime. A pale Mimi is talking to Pasquale in the Communist Party headquarters.*)

PASQUALE: Oh, no!
MIMI: You told me the vote was secret, didn't you?

(*Pasquale hunches his shoulders.*)

PASQUALE: Well, I suppose it just isn't all that secret.

(*Mimi walks away absolutely furious. He's made up his mind.*)

SCENE 8

(*Seafront and village square—exterior—daytime. Mimi strides along angrily.*)

MIMI: There's no work for me! I can't find any work! Fucking son of a castrated bull, frigging slut!
FISHERMAN: Mimi, what's wrong? What the hell's the matter with you?

MIMI: The matter is that they won't even hire me to sweep horse shit, that's what's the matter!

(*Vito appears from a side alley and joins his brother. Mimi starts shouting.*)

MIMI: Don Calogero is going to be the death of me!
FISHERMAN: So what?
MIMI: There's no work for me now, and there never will be!

(*A bricklayer falls in behind him.*)

MIMI: I'm going to go to Turin!
BRICKLAYER: Oh, don't be stupid!
MIMI: Fucking country! Full of bastards!
BRICKLAYER: Come and work down at the docks, that's what I do. I'll find you some work.
MIMI: They don't want me there either. Well, up theirs!

(*Mimi gives a rude gesture to the entire village, hidden behind the low stone walls of their houses.*)

MIMI: Off to Turin!

(Pippino is riding his three-wheeled cart. Mimi continues his rantings.)

MIMI: In Turin they pay the workers well and even the owner of Fiat takes off his hat to them! People who work in Turin are free and respected!

(Pippino grabs him by the arm as he stamps away angrily.)

PIPPINO: So you're going to let them get away with this? We've got to win our respect and our freedom right here in our hometown, not in Turin.

(But Mimi won't listen to reason. As he continues his march, he shouts back at Pippino.)

MIMI: No, I won't! I'm going to Turin! At least there aren't any Mafiosi there and you don't see any murderous faces like that one!

(He points to Ntoni, who is looking down at them from Don Calogero's terrace.)

SCENE 9

(Streets of Turin—exterior—daytime. Mimi is enveloped by fog. He looks as if he were trapped in a bottle of milk. The traffic is unbelievably chaotic. Cars, more cars, traffic policemen, hordes of people. Mimi's mind is dulled by the commotion. He's upset and terrified, but at the same time his nostrils are wide with excitement.)

A TENOR (off camera: from the opera *Il Trovatore*):
"We have arrived. This is the land where the political prisoners weep. . . . Ah! This is where the poor man was brought to."

(Mimi drags his enormous suitcase through the city traffic. The Mafiosi are here as well. Ntoni's face follows him, but it really isn't Ntoni's face, it just looks the same. Everything is different here except for the Mafia—and that for which it stands is probably here as well.)

SCENE 10

> (*Garage—interior—daytime. Three men are sitting on an impro- vised office on top of a small truck. In front of the truck is a group of poor devils who have just arrived in the city busy giv- ing their names and addresses to a bookkeeper. Salvatore Tri- carico is a powerful, elegant man, something like Cannamozza, the candidate.*)

SALVATORE TRICARICO: Okay, my friends, let's be honest and we'll be good friends for life. Now, then, are you registered with any party, union, or association?
VOICES: No sir, no sir . . .
SALVATORE TRICARICO: Very good, because if you were looking for insurance, nine-to-five hours and the like, I couldn't offer you any work. I can only help those who want to work without busting our balls. . . .

> (*Mimi is in this group. Mimi can hear the tune of the national anthem, "Brothers of Italy," ringing in his ears. His look focuses on the three beauty spots on Tricarico's cheek. He, like Don Calogero, has the mark. Is it a secret society? A Sicilian trait? The Mafia? A sign of God? Terror washes over him as he stares at the enormous birthmarks on the man's cheek.*)

SALVATORE TRICARICO: Very well, then, tomorrow morning you guys start working at six. You'll be paid double what they gave you in Sicily for a day of threshing. Five hundred sparkling lire an hour. If you've nowhere to stay Mr. Papagiovanni will set you up at the Hotel Trinacria . . . two hundred lire a bed. We're all members of the Sicilian Brotherhood Organization, and we consider ourselves your brothers. But you must do as we say, and above all be discreet, don't advertise, do I make myself clear? I'm doing you a favor and I would be most upset if one of you were to do something which might annoy me . . . clear? Let's go now.
PAPAGIOVANNI: Come on, let's move it! Let's have the first guy up here to give his name to the bookkeeper. Move it!

> (*The poor devils line up to give their names.*)

SCENE 11

(*Building site—exterior—daytime. Up in a highrise under construction. Bricklayers walking around. Mimi, an old worker, and a young painter called Nicola are whitewashing the walls, standing on a scaffold.*)

MIMI: Hey there, how are you?
WORKER: Look, friend, here in Turin we wear paper hats to protect our hair from the paint.

(*The worker hands him a paper cap. Mimi takes off the handkerchief which he had tied around his head and puts it on. In the meantime the old worker takes a piss over the edge of the scaffold. Papagiovanni, acting as foreman, inspects the progress the men are making.*)

PAPAGIOVANNI: What the fuck are you doing? We don't pay you to pee during working hours, pee during your break . . . come on, boys, work!
MIMI: Can't a man even piss in peace in this place?
WORKER: Don't listen to that prick-face, just piss as long as you like.

(*Nicola smiles.*)

NICOLA: I'd love to have a piss right now, right on his head!

(*He starts laughing so loudly that he suddenly loses his balance and falls off the scaffold.*)

SCENE 12

(*Another part of the site—exterior—daytime. Salvatore Tricarico is busy studying some plans when he hears Nicola's shout as he falls, and the screams of the other workers.*)

SHOUTS (off camera): Help! Help! Someone fell!
SALVATORE TRICARICO: What the fuck's going on here?

SCENE 13

(*Open space in the building site—exterior—daytime. Nicola's body lying facedown on the ground. Mimi and a group of other men are running toward the body.*)

MIMI: Nico! Nicola!
PAPAGIOVANNI: Is he hurt?
MIMI: How the hell do I know, he looks dead to me.

(Papagiovanni helps Carmelo turn the body over. Nicola is dead. From the other end of the open space a group of men run toward the scene of the accident. Tricarico looks at the young man's face. He utters a terrible curse.)

TRICARICO: Damn our bad luck, fucking bitch! Shit!

(He gives Papagiovanni a sign. Papagiovanni in turn whistles to another man. Suddenly a brisk operation goes into effect. Orders are given.)

PAPAGIOVANNI: Give me a hand!
TRICARICO: Come on, boy, give him a hand. Let's go boys, we're going back to Turin, work is over for the day!

(In the meantime Tricarico has made sure that Nicola is really dead. While the other men are directed toward a small bus, Mimi, Papagiovanni, and one of Tricarico's men lift Nicola's body. Tricarico orders a van to back up to them.)

TRICARICO: Let's go, let's move it, the Sicilian contingent stops work right now!

(They lift the body into the van. Papagiovanni, Tricarico, and another man get into the front seat. Mimi hasn't had the time to get out of the back of the van.)

SCENE 14

(A highway—exterior—daytime. The van speeds along the highway.)

SCENE 15

(Van—interior—exterior—daytime. Nicola's body is jostled around the back of the van as it speeds along the highway. Mimi is sitting beside him. He raps on the glass partition between him and the front seat.)

MIMI: There's no point in rushing to a hospital, he's dead.

(Tricarico and Papagiovanni turn around in surprise.)

PAPAGIOVANNI: What's he doing here, who let him on?
TRICARICO: Hey, what the hell are you doing there?
MIMI: I was in the back when the car sped off, and I didn't have a chance to get out.
TRICARICO: Shit, who asked him to come along?
PAPAGIOVANNI: I didn't ask him!
TRICARICO: Damn it!

SCENE 16

> *(Highway—exterior—daytime. The van comes to a stop. Tricarico and the other men get out, open the back door of the van, and start taking out Nicola's body. Mimi is getting nervous and tries to stop them.)*

TRICARICO: Hurry, let's try and get him out of the way as quickly as possible.
MIMI: What the hell are you doing?
TRICARICO: Look, all we did was give him some work, just like we did you. It isn't our fault he fell off the scaffolding. Come on, hurry! Shit, we don't even know his name.

> *(Mimi butts in forcibly.)*

MIMI: I'll tell you what his name is. Nicola Sparano. Who's going to feed his family?

> *(The men start getting angry.)*

TRICARICO: What do you take us for, the Salvation Army? Hurry, now that there aren't any cars.

> *(Mimi holds on to the body.)*

MIMI: No, you've got to think about his family, or else . . .

> *(Mimi realizes, to his horror, that as Papagiovanni pins his hands behind his back the driver has pulled out his pistol. He turns white as a sheet and feels his legs giving way.)*

TRICARICO: See, you're in a lot of trouble.

> *(Mimi is terrified as he steps slowly out of the back of the van.*

He feels trapped. The three Mafiosi stand in front of him. A car drives by on the highway.)

TRICARICO: Watch it, you guys! Get back in!

(Papagiovanni quickly lifts the back door to hide the body while Tricarico moves over to Mimi, pretending they are having an amicable conversation. The car drives by. Taking advantage of the situation, Mimi starts running after it. He dashes along the highway, trying to catch the attention of the driver.)

MIMI: Stop! Stop!
PAPAGIOVANNI: Where are you going?

(The car comes to an abrupt halt. Mimi jumps in and the car speeds off, right in front of the Mafiosi's surprised faces.)

TRICARICO: He must not return to the hotel in one piece!

(As he climbs back into the van he looks menacingly after the other car.)

SCENE 17

(Large garage—interior. Tricarico waits impatiently, leaning against his Mercedes. A car drives into the garage and Mimi is thrown out by our thugs. He tries to escape, but they quickly catch up with him.)

PAPAGIOVANNI: Catch that son of a whore, don't let him get away!

(They drag him over to Tricarico. Mimi is a pale figure surrounded by the four Mafiosi. Tricarico's expression is truly frightening, but even though Mimi is scared out of his wits, he fights desperately for his life.)

MIMI: You guys better be careful with what you do to me, because I'm not like Nicola. If I disappear there are people who will come looking for me, and they'll teach you a lesson.
THUG: Let's bump him off right away.

(Papagiovanni shakes his head.)

PAPAGIOVANNI: I'll take care of him.

(Tricarico stops him.)

TRICARICO: Who the hell is this frigging bastard?

> (*Tricarico grabs Mimi by the arm, then pushes him violently against a car.*)

TRICARICO: Speak up! Are you threatening me? Tell the truth, were you sent by the syndicate?

> (*Mimi hasn't quite understood, but he's ready to put all his cards on the table.*)

MIMI: What syndicate? No, I wrote to my wife, a special delivery letter, and I gave her your names and everything else I knew.

> (*Tricarico laughs.*)

TRICARICO: So you wrote to your wife? It shows that you aren't really experienced, my boy. I'm not scared of your threats.

> (*Tricarico's tone becomes very menacing; his voice is distinctly Mafioso.*)

TRICARICO: You know, in this city there are so many traffic accidents and the reason for them is the number of cars . . . so, what's one more accident? Am I being clear? And, oh, by the way, since you gave your wife my name I will remember to send her a wreath of flowers to place on your coffin! Take him away!

(The other men grab him and throw him back into the car. He is terrified; his brain works a mile a minute looking for a way out.)

MIMI: You better watch out. My wife is Don Calogero Niggio's godchild. I told her to go see Don Calogero if anything happens to me. I also told her to tell him that he should look for Salvatore Tricarico.

(Tricarico stops and looks at him carefully.)

TRICARICO: Is he the same Niggio from Colleone?
MIMI: His cousin.

(Tricarico smirks and moves up to him defiantly. At that moment Mimi would rather be looking down the barrel of a gun than be subjected to Tricarico's deadly eyes.)

TRICARICO: Leave him. Tell me something . . .

(He walks around Mimi, still staring at him intensely.)

TRICARICO: Why is it that a member of the Niggio family is in Turin in your condition?

(Mimi's chin trembles uncontrollably, but his eyes manage to stay fixed on those of the Mafioso.)

MIMI: Well, I never wanted to bother them, but now that the occasion has arisen . . .
TRICARICO: Okay, I want to believe you. But you could have told me right away who it was that sent you here. . . . Salvatore Tricarico has always had great respect for the Niggio family.
MIMI: Well, I really didn't know you and I just wanted to keep to myself.
TRICARICO: I would have done the impossible to help you.

(Mimi can't believe his ears. Mimi's brain is working double-time.)

MIMI: Well, if I'm not too late I would like a job at either the Fiat or Pirelli plant. A nice comfortable position.

(Tricarico bursts into laughter.)

TRICARICO: Pirelli or Fiat, huh? Okay, we'll see. Even though you behaved like a fool, I want to do you this favor. I believe your story and before the evening is done you'll find yourself working in a factory.

(Tricarico climbs into his car.)

TRICARICO: Listen, my boy . . . remember that if you're trying to be smart I'm going to make you regret it until the day you die!

SCENE 18

(Entrance to a factory—exterior—daytime. The gates open. The workers arrive in their cars, bikes, motorcycles, buses, and mini-buses. The sirens blow and a hundred and twenty thousand workers are on their way to work. The enormous industrial machine begins operating. Mimi is part of the multitudes.)

SCENE 19

(Factory complex—interior—exterior—daytime. Mimi is in the factory. Assembly line, great machines which bring to mind the monsters of mythology. Shots of the factory.)

MIMI'S VOICE (off camera): Dear wife . . . I would like you to know that for the past month I have been working in a factory and that I am no longer simply Mimi Mardocheco, but Mimi Mardocheco "the metallurgist," which is an entirely different matter.

(Mimi has been transformed from a member of the subproletariat to the proletariat.)

MIMI'S VOICE (off camera): . . . I now have my insurance, and I am eligible for all the benefits—in other words, everything is fine and I can hardly believe it! At first I must admit I found myself a bit lost in the middle of this "inferno" . . .

(We see him by the assembly line putting spark plugs together.)

MIMI'S VOICE (off camera): . . . then I realized that the people were all Sicilian and from Calabria and they were more lost than I was. You won't believe this, but it took me more than a week to come across a native Turinese . . .

SCENE 20

(Communist Party headquarters—interior—daytime.)

MIMI'S VOICE (off camera): There are plenty of fine people here.

(Shots of a group of workers gathering after working hours.)

MIMI'S VOICE (off camera): I have made some good friends and they've taught me a great deal of things about politics and the plight of the worker.

SCENE 21

(Beer cellar—interior—nighttime. A group around a table drinking beer and discussing politics. We hear Duilio's voice.)

DUILIO: Politics, my dear Mimi, isn't something that should be part of the individual. Politics is a part of life! Just imagine . . . you go out and buy a pair of shorts. There's politics in that, you know? You see, by deciding which pair you're going to buy you help the process by which the "bosses" screw us constantly.

SCENE 22

(Party headquarters—interior—daytime. A meeting of the factory workers. Banners declaiming the plight of the worker. Mimi handing out leaflets and talking to a group of workers.)

MIMI'S VOICE (off camera): . . . I can just imagine my father's face. Perhaps it's better I tell him myself than have someone else do it. Not only did I join a union, but I'm now also a member of the Communist Party!

SCENE 23

(Uncle Cicciu's house—interior—daytime.)

CICCIU: Shit, I knew he would get himself into trouble up north . . . he'll end up in jail! Communist, my ass, he's a hunk of shit!

(Uncle Cicciu shouts his head off. We see all the women gathered around Rosalia as she reads the letter out loud.)

MOTHER: My poor boy, he's ended up in the unions.

CELESTE: Relax!
ROSALIA: I don't understand all this. What are trade unions?
CELESTE: They're subversive organizations!
ROSALIA: Really?
CELESTE: Yes, isn't that true, Cicciu?

(The mother tries to calm Uncle Cicciu down.)

MOTHER: Don't choke, Cicciu . . . poor boy, God only knows what'll happen to him.
CICCIU: In jail, that's where he'll end up!
MOTHER: Virgin Mary, please help him! Lord, look after him!

(Vito grabs the letter out of Rosalia's hands.)

VITO: Show me, let's see what else he says.

(Rosalia takes it back.)

ROSALIA: Stop it, let me read. "Now, my dearest wife . . ."

SCENE 24

(Small hotel—interior—evening.)

MIMI'S VOICE (off camera): . . . I must say no to your coming here. . . .

(We see a tired Mimi walking down the hall. He walks into a tiny, depressing room, takes off his jacket, and walks out again.)

MIMI'S VOICE (off camera): . . . Things are very expensive, especially housing and especially for us Southerners who are looked upon like animals by these northern sons of bitches. I live in a furnished room . . . a grim existence and certainly not the place for a wife to have to live . . .

(Mimi walks in the door opposite his. We see a Turinese woman sitting in bed wearing a nightgown and reading a comic book. As soon as she notices Mimi she takes off her glasses and moves over, making room for him.)

WOMAN: Hey, here's the Latin lover! We going to have a grand fuck? Hurry up, I have to get up at seven tomorrow morning!

(Mimi rapidly removes his socks, shirt, trousers, and underwear and shuts the door.)

MIMI'S VOICE (off camera): All my love—your husband Mimi.

SCENE 25

(Communist Party headquarters—interior–exterior—daytime. Mimi is making a public accusation before a committee of workers. He is recounting his past experiences.)

MIMI: They greet you at the station and take you off to some dump where they make you sleep all together like pigs. They pay you a few stinking lire because they know you have to accept it or starve. If anything happens to you at work they just throw you in the street as if you were a dog. I saw it with these very eyes. . . .
VOICES: Right! Tell it like it is!

(Mimi's friend is clearly the chairman and is gathering information on the abuse of the Southerners in order to turn it over to the authorities. He is disgusted by Mimi's story.)

DUILIO: Stories like Mardocheco's must end, more than twenty-five thousand construction workers, working without insurance! We must put an end to this . . . an end to piecework. We must turn them over to the authorities, but in order to turn them over we must have their names . . . and the trouble is that the poor devils that work under those conditions don't want to turn their bosses over because they're scared. Fear is like a drug, it shows you what isn't really there instead of showing you reality.
UNION MEMBER: One moment . . . silence . . .

(The man has a strange face. The strangeness consists in the fact that he resembles Don Calogero and Salvatore Tricarico.)

UNION MEMBER: Silence. Mimi Mardocheco is a comrade and *he* certainly isn't scared.

(Mimi is struck by that similarity and especially by the fact that the man has the very same three beauty marks on his cheek that the others do.)

UNION MEMBER: That group you worked for—the Sicilian Brotherhood—who was their leader?

(Besides the union member we see a group of thugs who also have a strong resemblance to Don Calogero's and Salvatore Tricarico's men.)

UNION MEMBER: Who was behind it, then, his name!
MIMI: His name?

(Mimi hesitates. In a split second we see an ancient fear in his eyes. Fear, prudence, reticence. These make up the fertile ground into which the Mafia has sunk its ancient roots.)

MIMI: I'm sorry, but I can't remember that son of a bitch's name. If I knew it I would certainly tell you.

SCENE 26

(A street in Turin—exterior—daytime. We are at the enormous open-air market in Turin. A light golden mist envelops the market. Accompanied by the notes of La Traviata, Mimi walks through the crowds. Two young girls are selling their "ideological" wares sitting by the sidewalk. Hippie sweaters, blowups, and posters of a political nature. Mimi is fascinated by the girl selling the sweaters. He removes his wedding ring and prepares for the attack.)

SOPRANO (off camera: from *La Traviata*):
  "Ever free my heart must be
  "As I flit from joy to joy.
  "I want my life to glide
  "Along the paths of pleasure.
  "May the dying or dawning day
  "Always find me in haunts of
  "Mirth and to ever new delights.
  "May my thoughts soar and fly."

(Mimi is a classical example of the Latin lover. His look is coaxing, tempting, flattering, menacing, caressing, and promising. The girl looks at him amused.)

TENOR (off camera: from *La Traviata*):
  "Ah such love so tumulous
  "Out of the heavenly universe
  "Mysteriously from on high
  "Come sorrow and gladness to the heart. . ."

(Mimi moves up to the girl and inspects a sweater. A car suddenly pulls up beside the stand. Four or five young men leap out and start beating up the girls as well as poor Mimi, who has gone to their aid. They are obviously Fascists, and wielding their billy clubs they give all three a hearty beating. The thugs disappear as quickly as they appeared. Passers-by help the girls and the unfortunate Mimi, who is rather the worse for wear.)

SCENE 27

(Beer cellar—interior—daytime. The girl who was selling the sweaters is sitting with Mimi in the beer cellar. Cheerful and very talkative, she eats her eggs with a wholesome appetite. We get a first glimpse of her beautiful lively eyes. Mimi is in a trance.)

FIORE: Pigs! Sons of bitches, that's what they are. They even had knuckle-dusters! Shit! I was scared out of my pants . . . want some more?

(The waiter is serving her some more fried eggs, which Fiore divides between herself and Mimi.)

FIORE: Here you go. Last week they came as well and beat us up, we even tried to call the police but there's never one around when you need them.

(Fiore eats hungrily and talks incessantly with her mouth full. Mimi gazes at her with his most seductive look. His bottle-green eyes eat her up. His intentions are very clear.)

FIORE: Nowadays if the police can avoid any trouble you can be certain they will, and besides, I'm sure they're happy the Fascists beat us up. You know what they told us to our faces the last time this happened? They said, "Why don't you go sell hot chestnuts instead of political posters, that way no one will bother you." . . . Unbelievable, isn't it?

(Fiore smiles.)

FIORE: My name is Fiore, what's yours?

(As though he were an Arab seducer, Mimi gazes at Fiore through half-veiled eyes. In an attempt to give himself some airs, he slips his cigarette into a holder and lights up.)

MIMI: Carmelo Mardocheco.
FIORE: Shit, what a name!

(Fiore smiles.)

MIMI: Well, I was born on the Feast of the Virgin from Carmine, any-how my friends call me Mimi.
FIORE: So they call you Mimi? Judging from the day you were born you should be called Lucia.

(Fiore laughs. Mimi's face has turned to stone. The "man of honor" feels he is being made fun of.)

MIMI: What's so funny?
FIORE: Nothing, really . . . boy, what a face! You didn't get offended did you? You really are a peasant!

(Mimi smiles at her nicely and pretends he hasn't heard.)

MIMI: No, I'm not offended, but you mustn't call me names.
FIORE: Good. By the way, you're a comrade, aren't you? Stop being so formal!
MIMI: Thank you for allowing me the privilege! Fiore . . . are you a comrade as well?
FIORE: What a question! Of course I am, but I have my own particu-lar views. I used to be a Trotskyite, but now . . .

(Mimi looks at her. He doesn't have a clue what a Trotskyite might be but he doesn't want to show his ignorance.)

MIMI: Tro . . .?
FIORE: Trotskyite, that's lefter than the left.
MIMI: Ahh! There is nothing lefter than the left wing. . . . The only true left wing is made up of the eight million workers belonging to the Communist Party.

(Fiore starts laughing.)

FIORE: Well, all right. But anyhow, at the moment I really don't belong to anything in particular. You see, before I decide what party I should join next, I'm waiting for something to happen. On the one hand there are those who are planting bombs, on the other they're all on strike. We're all left-wingers, but instead of being united we're fighting among ourselves. . . . Look, it might just be that because I'm a simple person, my grandmother was a farmer, that I need much more explaining from these parties. One man shouldn't exploit another man. That's a basic truth. As for the rest, I'll just sit around and wait for something to happen.

(*Mimi hasn't really been listening. What the hell is she talking about politics for? This person in front of him, this Fiore, is a tasty morsel. His only thought is that this woman must be his.*)

FIORE: Listen, in the past hundred years the ruling classes had to give up a lot, didn't they? I don't believe that Russia is going to turn into another United States. There the individual is swallowed by industry, by machines, and by commerce, just like Italy. I don't believe it. What about you . . . what do you think about these things?

(*Mimi wasn't expecting the question and he's taken off balance.*)

MIMI: Me, well, I . . . I really wouldn't know.

SCENE 28

(*A park—exterior—daytime. Mimi and Fiore walk close to each other through the fog. The enchanted setting reminds one of a frozen milk bottle. Mimi is taken by the romance of the moment and looks at her hungrily. Fiore talks incessantly.*)

FIORE: So I said to her, "Dear mother. I just don't want to stay here in Gallarate and end up like you, a simple schoolteacher. I'm sorry . . . I'll take a few things with me, and I'll try my luck in Milan . . . 'bye!"
MIMI: Did you find what you were looking for?
FIORE: Shit, did I find it? You've got to be joking. I ended up as a clerk in a department store. It just isn't in my nature. Anyway, the whole job ended rather badly . . . but let me continue.

That worm—my boss that is—calls me in one day and sees that I have Mao Tse-tung's *Little Red Book* in my bag. He takes it out, shuts the door, comes over to me and puts his hand on my ass . . . that prick! He smiles and says to me, "How 'bout it, gorgeous? Either you give me a piece of ass or I'll fire you for being an anarchist." I gave it to him . . . right in his filthy face!

(*They're walking along the river. She still doesn't stop talking, and Mimi looks at her like a beast nearing its prey, ready to pounce. He walks very close to her, and it is obvious he has no interest in what she is saying.*)

FIORE: It's so pretty here, it reminds me of Hyde Park. It's like one of those places in films where people get murdered . . . you know, what the hell are those people called? Ah yes, sexual maniacs! Why are you looking at me like that? You're frightening me!

(*As a matter of fact, his face is quite frightening as he looks at her.*)

FIORE: You look like you've got a bellyache! You haven't really got a bellyache have you? It could have been that cold beer, sometimes it has that effect.

(*Mimi shakes his head.*)

MIMI: No . . . it's all your fault.
FIORE: My fault?

(*Mimi nods his head solemnly.*)

MIMI: I'm sorry, sorry comrade, but would you mind if I kissed you?

(*She looks at him curiously, thinks about it for a while.*)

FIORE: Well . . .
MIMI: Please, I beg of you.

(*Mimi feels sick with anxiety. At last she says yes.*)

FIORE: Well, if you say pretty please . . .
MIMI: Pretty please . . .

(*Slowly and very excitedly he moves closer to her, kisses her lightly, then very passionately. Suddenly he is like a wild bull. Fiore wasn't expecting this attack and loses her balance, falling to the ground. He's on her like a shot, ignoring her protests. He is like a madman.*)

FIORE: Don't, you bastard! You son of a bitch, don't! You're hurting me!

(*After a few moments of wild fighting, Fiore manages to sink her knee where it does the most damage, and Mimi lets out a scream. Fiore gets up angrily.*)

FIORE: Pig! Nice ways you people have! Peasant! They come to the city and think they can take advantage of the first woman they meet . . . scum! I was nearly raped by a peasant, can you imagine! Don't you dare try it again, because I'll crack your head open. First you ask for a kiss . . . pretty please he says . . . then it's carnal violence! Go to hell, why don't you, you scum bag!

(Fiore turns her back on him and starts walking away. Mimi stops her, but gently this time.)

MIMI: I'm sorry, but it wasn't violence, it was passion. Forgive me, Fiore, but I lost all control, I just couldn't resist the temptation, my senses got the better of me. Violence . . . that wasn't violence, I would never dare be violent. In the past I've had quite a bit of luck with ladies . . . but with you, my beautiful Fiore, things are different. I like you more than anyone else I've ever liked. You can't turn me away, Fiore, you just can't!
FIORE: I'm going to . . . what the hell do you take me for, huh?
MIMI: You won't have me?
FIORE: Right!
MIMI: Why not? Did someone tall you things about me?
FIORE: To me? Who the hell do you think you are? I've never seen you in my life before!
MIMI: Fiore, tell me the truth! Did someone tell you I was married?
FIORE: Can you believe this? As if the whole world comes up to me and talks about you! Look, you slob, I really don't give a shit about your marriage. As if that would matter to me anyhow. I don't even agree with the sacrament. In any case, married or bachelor, it's all the same to me . . . my reason is different. I believe in love, it's a very serious matter to me. . .
MIMI: Well, do I look merry to you? I'm deadly serious . . . at first I wasn't quite sure, I didn't understand, I think I fell in love with you the instant I set eyes on you.
FIORE: You did? Well, I didn't, so there!

(She walks away and Mimi chases her, walks along the river, and eventually reaches the main path through the park.)

MIMI: Fiore, Fiore! Wait, I never believed in love, I thought it was a silly thing that only happened to women. But now I find it's breaking my heart.
FIORE: Well, I'm terribly sorry for you, but my heart is still in one piece.
MIMI: What does your refusal mean? I thought you liked me at first.
FIORE: Yeah, but liking you doesn't mean I love you.
MIMI: I'm sick, I'm suffering! After all, what's it to you? Do it as a favor.

FIORE: Are you crazy? As if I would do it as a favor! These aren't things one does out of kindness. And besides, I'm a virgin.

(Her words really upset him because the Sicilians attach the greatest importance to virginity. He can't believe his ears.)

MIMI: Virgin, I don't believe it!

FIORE: Yes, my dear, I'm a real honest to god virgin. Get that look off your face or I'll slap you! He's another of those creeps who doesn't believe me.

MIMI: Well, my compliments—but didn't you say you were a comrade or a . . . Tro . . . Tro . . . Shit, how the hell do you say that word?

FIORE: Trotskyite. So what, it doesn't mean one is automatically a whore, you know?

MIMI: Whore? I would have never dared call you that! It's just that things are so different up here in the north and I just don't know where I stand any longer.

FIORE: Damn it, all I seem to do is have to explain to people how I feel. Most of the time they don't believe me, and when they do, then they want to see some concrete proof!

MIMI: I'm sorry, really I am.

FIORE: They've been bothering me about this forever. Am I nuts? Am I frigid? Shit, it's my own business how I feel . . . right? I don't believe in marriage but I do believe in love, and I want to do it only with the man I feel I love, when the time comes. Even if I have to wait for the next fifty years. Am I making myself clear? Otherwise it seems to me a filthy thing to do. Okay, then, you peasant, you know something? With you there isn't a chance in hell. Now get the hell out of here, piss off, go to hell!

(Fiore turns around and walks away. Mimi is annihilated by her words but finds the strength to react.)

MIMI: Idiot, *you* go to hell!

SCENE 29

(A street in Turin—exterior—daytime. Fiore and her friend Violetta are still in the same place on the traffic island in the middle of the street. Mimi looks at her lovingly. Using his eyes and a few gestures, he courts her. Prelude to La Traviata.)

SCENE 30

(Parks and streets of Turin—exterior—daytime. The camera travels through the snow and fog covering the streets and parks of the city. Prelude to La Traviata. *Mimi and Fiore walk romantically together. Mimi alone and unhappy. Pain—love—winter.)*

SCENE 31

(Fiore's apartment—interior—daytime. Mimi is desperate.)

MIMI: This insane love of mine has reduced me to a state where I don't give a damn about anything at all anymore! If I'm really a man I have to end it here and now even though I don't know what the consequences might be. Fiore, don't say anything, nothing—please . . . I apologize if I don't look at you, I just can't . . . you see, I believe you are right, Fiore, I believe that a woman should give herself only to the man she loves. . . .

(The attic apartment is spacious and flooded with light. A blow-up of Lenin dominates the room. Bundles of colored wool wherever you look. Even though he is so upset, Mimi continues to analyze the situation.)

MIMI: I feel that you really don't love me, because when I look into your eyes and see them staring blankly I know there is no place for me in them. . . . I think of you dreaming at night, and I know that you don't dream of me.

(Fiore sits down on the enormous bed.)

MIMI: You see, Fiore, you can't love me, because if you did you wouldn't be hurting me this way. Unfortunately you don't love me and I must carry the weight of this great love alone. It's all so pointless . . . and therefore, Fiore, Mimi Mardocheco bids you farewell, and you will never hear his name again.

(Fiore is beautiful and gentle.)

FIORE: What are you saying? I do love you.

(Mimi looks up. He isn't quite certain he has understood.)

MIMI: What?

(Fiore reaches out for him.)

FIORE: See, you've done it! Now you'll tell me that in the end the man who perseveres wins.

MIMI: Fiore, I didn't understand what you said before . . . what was it you said?

FIORE: Come . . . goddamn it, come here . . .

(*Mimi can't believe his ears. He feels faint.*)

MIMI: My god! Fiore . . . Fiore . . .

FIORE: You heard right, I said I loved you.

MIMI: Listen, if this is your idea of a joke, it would kill me!

FIORE: Who the hell is joking, goddamn it? I've really fallen for you, you bastard. I want you in the same way you want me . . . that's why I kicked out my roommate, and now this house is yours . . . if you want it.

(*Mimi's eyes begin swelling up with tears. He moves closer to her, his knees buckling.*)

MIMI: Fiore!

FIORE: Now wait a minute, be careful.

(*Fiore stares at him seriously.*)

FIORE: Look, this is something very serious to me, do you understand? It's important to me because for me—well—for me, it's either everything or nothing at all.

MIMI: Of course, certainly . . .

FIORE: Listen carefully. We must get things straight and then we'll be friends forever. Look, if you so much as touch another woman—and that goes for your wife as well—you will never see me again. As long as our love lasts I want it to be perfect . . . if not I would rather not start anything. Now swear . . .

MIMI: Swear? Of course I'll swear to it, I swear!

> (*Mimi is falling apart. Fiore is moved as well. She slowly starts removing her clothes.*)

FIORE: Well, then, what are we waiting for?

> (*Mimi sits down next to her and rests his head on her lap. He breaks into tears.*)

MIMI: It's like a dream.

FIORE: My sweetest love . . . my pussy cat . . . Mimi, come on.

> (*Fiore hugs him lovingly.*)

MIMI: Fiore—little flower—as soon as I get over this I'll tear you to shreds.

SCENE 32

> (*Attic apartment—interior—nighttime. Fiore and Mimi are lying naked in bed. Mimi is very tense and clearly miserable. Gradually it becomes apparent that he has "struck out." Fiore smiles and embraces him.*)

FIORE: So what, what's the problem? Come over here. What does it matter? Aren't you happy anyway?

MIMI: Yes, very happy . . . I'm going to kill myself!

FIORE: Oh, come on, why?

MIMI: Because if I'm unable to make love to you, then it's better that I kill myself!

FIORE: Come here, you silly thing, listen to me.

> (*Fiore hugs him and brushes against him sexily.*)

FIORE: Isn't it lovely here? Listen to the rain falling. It's you and me

. . . alone. Don't be so upset, please. You know something? I've never been like this before . . . I mean naked . . . in the arms of a man . . . I think it's fabulous.

(*She strokes and hugs him, but Mimi is really desperate.*)

FIORE: I never imagined it to be so wonderful, so sweet—what more is there to it?

(*She caresses him gently and finally Mimi feels something stirring. The beast wakes up and he throws himself on her. His manhood proclaims victory and so Fiore finally discovers what was missing, the pain and pleasure of love.*)

SCENE 33

(*Fiore and Mimi's bathroom—interior—daytime. Clearly months have gone by. Mimi has tidied up his mustache and is wearing a hair net to flatten out his hair. He is just finishing his morning ablutions and is combing his mustache as he whistles an aria from* La Traviata.)

MIMI (singing): "Mysterious . . . mysterious and different . . ."

SCENE 34

(*Attic apartment—interior—daytime. Mimi walks into the large room, wearing a strange outfit, a multicolored sweater over his pajamas. He makes sure Fiore is still asleep. As he drinks his coffee he reads a letter from his wife, which he had kept hidden in his work jacket.*)

ROSALIA'S VOICE (off camera): My dear husband, I want to tell you with this letter that your father refuses to pay for my trip to Turin and therefore I have had to start looking for work to pay for it myself.

SCENE 35

(*Laundry—interior—daytime. We see Rosalia working with a group of other women in a large commercial laundry. The women are members of the "new" and "old" Sicily, brought together by modern industry.*)

ROSALIA'S VOICE (off camera): . . . The woman writing you is no longer plain Rosalia Mardocheco, but Rosalia Mardocheco, "worker," which, as you pointed out, is an entirely different matter. I'm a super-fast laundry lady. The personnel here is entirely made up of women, so you needn't worry.

> (*Rosalia is very changed. She no longer wears the black shawl and has cut her hair and wears a cute dress with a slightly gaudy pattern on it. She has a relaxed and casual air about her. During their break we see Rosalia lighting up a cigarette, taking a deep drag and letting the smoke out awkwardly.*)

ROSALIA'S VOICE: . . . I would also like to tell you that I now smoke . . .

SCENE 36

> (*Street in Sicily—exterior—daytime. Rosalia is using a bobby pin to keep her skirt from blowing all over the place.*)

ROSALIA'S VOICE: . . . Ellenuzza has taught me to ride a mo-torbike . . .

> (*Rosalia takes off on a motorbike.*)

ROSALIA'S VOICE: I immediately became an excellent driver, and if you will allow it I would like to buy one for myself on the installment plan. I won't even begin to tell you what your father thinks about all this.

> (*We see Rosalia driving by, her legs crossed as if she were sitting in an armchair. The motorbike passes right in front of Uncle Cicciu, who looks at her disgustedly. He shakes his walking stick menacingly at her.*)

UNCLE CICCIU: One can see your thighs, you revolting slut!

SCENE 37

> (*Attic apartment—interior—daytime. Mimi's face intent on read-ing Rosalia's letter. Fiore wakes up without Mimi noticing.*)

FIORE: Hey, Mimi, what the hell are you wearing on your head?

> (*Mimi quickly hides the letter. He picks up his demitasse cup and goes over to sit on the edge of the bed.*)

MIMI: You really must have more respect for me, Fiore, respect! You understand?

(*She takes a sip from his cup.*)

FIORE: I just don't understand you, you have such lovely curls. What's this fixation you have with straight hair?
MIMI: Why, don't you like it?
FIORE: Come on, can't you see you look just like Donald Duck's cousin?

(*He throws himself on the bed and tries to embrace her.*)

MIMI: Yes, that's exactly who I am, Donald Duck's cousin.

(*Fiore tries to get away from him.*)

FIORE: No, you look ridiculous like this, stop it!
MIMI: Donald Duck's cousin!

(*Suddenly he becomes serious and threatening.*)

MIMI: Look, you're a woman and you musn't concern yourself with men's fashions. You were born to knit and make these ridiculous sweaters you force me to wear.

FIORE: Oh, stop it!

MIMI: And besides that, you were born to make love!

(*He jumps on top of her once more, trying to pin her down.*)

FIORE: No, wearing that silly hair net I just won't let you!

MIMI: Don't I remind you of Rudolph Valentino?

(*Fiore breaks away from him.*)

FIORE: No, and besides it's ten o'clock.

(*Smiling, she slides off the bed.*)

FIORE: Today there's the builders' demonstration, and I don't want to miss it.

(*Mimi looks at her strangely.*)

MIMI: And why don't you want to miss the demonstration?

FIORE: Well, we can't just ignore our comrade builders, can we? They say there's going to be some thirty thousand of them marching. Think how beautiful it's going to be! Thirty thousand builders all parading in the square!

(*Mimi is somber.*)

MIMI: I'm a metallurgist, and I'll only march in the square with the metallurgists!

FIORE: Well, my bugsy boo, I'm going to go and march with them!

MIMI: Bugsy boo, my fucking ass!

FIORE: What?

MIMI: You're a metallurgist's woman and you're not going to march with the builders. You should sympathize only with us and not with them! You don't even know them! Comrade builders, my ass! Thirty thousand Sicilian and Calabrese criminals who will just be there to take advantage of the situation to squeeze a few buttocks . . .

(*Fiore gives him a teasing look. She looks lovely in her multicolored dressing gown.*)

FIORE: You wouldn't perhaps be jealous of thirty thousand builders, would you?

MIMI: What's that got to do with it? I'm against this demonstration from a political standpoint!

(*Fiore is on the bed. She looks at him with an amused and loving expression.*)

FIORE: Out with it! Admit it, you're embarrassed to admit that you're just plain jealous!

(Mimi looks at Fiore, then throws himself on top of her and turns her over.)

MIMI: What can I do? When I think of a bunch of bloody builders all staring at your ass I feel my blood run cold!

FIORE: It isn't a good thing for a Communist to be so jealous, you know. Look, I can't be expected to go out wearing a veil around my face like Turkish women.

MIMI: Turks? what was wrong with those poor Turks? The whole world criticizes the Turks, but I think the Turks were a fine race, with their ideas pretty well sorted out! That's why they conquered the whole world! Of course, with their veiled women waiting for them at home they could go fight without any worries!

FIORE: You really are nuts, aren't you! You're lucky I'm so much in love with you! Come on then, Mr. Sheik. This is your harem, and I'm your little sultana . . .

(She lifts the sheet to cover her face and starts a belly dance. Passionately Mimi embraces her.)

FIORE (singing): Lalalalalalalala!

MIMI: The young sultana, now my Fiore is going to play my very own sultana. You're so beautiful, you're so beautiful! Wearing all these colors you remind me of a butterfly—a sexy butterfly. You're so pretty, how am I going to screw you today?

(The phone rings. She continues to laugh and tease him as he answers the phone.)

MIMI: The phone is ringing . . . the telephone! Hello, hello! Stop tickling! This is Mimi Mardocheco, hello . . . Catania?

(Mimi is suddenly pale and very nervous. Fiore stops fooling around.)

MIMI: Rosalia!

SCENE 38

(Attic apartment—interior—daytime.)

FIORE: You pig . . . you can keep your fucking TV set!

(Mimi is handing her a tiny television.)

MIMI: Wha . . . ?

(Mimi tries calming her down, but she won't listen to reason and disappears through the colorful curtains separating the room.)

FIORE: I don't give a shit . . . what the hell do you think I'm sending you to Catania to see your wife in order to get a television out of you? You great pig of pigs!

(They chase one another through the colorful draperies.)

MIMI: It's been more than a year since I've been home. All I need is three days.
FIORE: Yeah, three days and three nights.
MIMI: Well, not really, because two will be spent on the train.
FIORE: So? One night in bed with a woman!
MIMI: But she's my wife.
FIORE: I don't care, she's still another woman, isn't she?
MIMI: Fiore, how many times must I tell you that Rosalia isn't a woman . . . she could be my aunt.

(Fiore pushes him toward the bed and trips him onto it. She's beautiful, jealous, and aggressive.)

FIORE: Well, screw you and your aunt, you Sicilian prick! You're not going to Catania, get that straight in your head. You're nothing but an ugly peasant! As long as you talk about leaving there's no eating and sleeping in *my* house, do you hear me?

(Fiore undresses him and then herself. She's in a hurry and Mimi is amused.)

FIORE: We're going to make love now, and I'm going to teach you a lesson. . . . I'm going to squeeze it all out of you, I'm going to destroy you. You'll look like a wet rag by the time I'm finished with you. You'll never ask to make love again. Catania? I won't let you go to Catania, you and I are going to make love until your damn mustache falls off!

(Mimi laughs.)

MIMI: Fiore, stop it . . . that tickles!

SCENE 39

(Attic apartment—interior—nighttime. Fiore's face and her hair catch the reflections from the lamp covered by one of her color-ful scarfs. Mimi lies next to her, looking at her, totally spent.)

SCENE 39B

(Attic apartment—interior—daytime. Their night of passionate love can be seen reflected in their eyes. Gentleness and adora-tion can be seen in Mimi's eyes as he looks at his smiling Fiore.)

FIORE: I wonder what your wife's expression would be if she were to see me right now . . . poor thing . . . no, what I'm trying to say is that here I am, about to give birth to your child, and the poor thing was never able to give you one. . . .

(Mimi's hand is resting on her six-month-pregnant belly.)

MIMI: A wife doesn't mean a thing, it's love that produces children!
FIORE: Shit, go tell that to all those poor unwed mothers who made it with a one-night stand and now they're burdened with a baby. Chil-dren come when you least expect them.

(A great commotion can be heard outside. Fiore hears it.)

FIORE: Hey, what the hell's going on out there?

(Mimi gives her a tired look.)

MIMI: Oh, it's the same old thing, a demonstration, a parade.
FIORE: Poor boys, out there with all this snow! Why don't you ever tell me what the comrades are doing anymore? I haven't got any idea of what's happening, how is the fight against the "masters" going?

(Mimi doesn't answer her question. He's too involved in his new role. He strokes Fiore's enormous belly.)

MIMI: There, he just kicked . . . he kicked, my little iddy biddy googoo . . . sleep, sleep just like a birdie in its nest . . . little Mimi, beautiful little Mimi, sleep. Don't worry, your father will look after you, buy you a nice T.V. and then . . . and then . . . a tricycle.
FIORE: Listen to him, the baby isn't even born and you're already conditioning him to this consumer society. What do you want, that before teaching him how to walk and read, we let him get his driver's license?

MIMI: My son must have everything he can. I want to give him everything I never, never had—my son will be a king.

SCENE 40

*(Banquet room in a restaurant—interior—daytime. A bottle of
champagne is uncorked. A group of friends is celebrating Mimi
II's baptism. Along with Fiore and Mimi there is a priest, some
friends of Fiore's, a couple of old people, and one or two cou-
ples. Pictures are taken, flashes explode. Mimi is overexcited as
he pours out the foaming liquid.)*

MIMI: Drink, it's champagne!
VOICES: To his health, best wishes!
MIMI: This is top-quality champagne, French to be exact. I'm going to
get another bottle from below. Today I'm not worrying about money, I
have a child! Be right back!

SCENE 41

*(Back room and main room of the Gran Caffé—interior—day-
time. Mimi goes downstairs, smiling, but suddenly finds himself
in the midst of a group of terrified people running in all directions. Shouts and gunshots. The people running away are shouting at each other. Mimi doesn't understand what's going on.
People flee in terror. He looks into the main room and realizes
he has made a big mistake. He is face to face with a Mafia show-
down, in true traditional style. A hand of steel grabs Mimi.
Someone is trying to shield himself behind Mimi's body. It's
Papagiovanni, Tricarico's right hand. Collapsed beside a table
we see the inanimate body of another of Tricarico's "gorillas."
Tricarico is standing by the café entrance, a cruel, proud, and
calm expression on his face as he shoots wildly at two other
Sicilians who are trying to escape. Tricarico's merciless shots
quickly finish off everybody. The victims are drilled full of holes
and blood is gushing everywhere. Mimi is immobile. Using Mimi
as a shield, Papagiovanni tries to take advantage of a moment's
pause to reach the exit. Mimi tries to say something, but no
sound comes out.)*

TRICARICO: This is for you, Papagiovanni!

(Luckily, as he is being dragged off, Mimi trips on an over-turned chair. As he falls we hear the shots which find their mark in Papagiovanni's body. Tricarico stands there calmly with the guns still smoking in his hands. He prods Papagiovanni's body with his foot, and Mimi slides away like an eel. Tricarico shakes his head and points his pistol at Mimi, who is trembling as if he has a high fever.)

MIMI: No, don't shoot, I didn't see a thing! Please, please don't—I didn't see a thing, I'll be quiet, please don't, I beg of you!

(Tricarico has no time to waste.)

TRICARICO: Mimi Mardocheco, I'm sorry.

(He pulls the trigger. We hear the distant wail of the police sirens. The shot goes off at the very instant Mimi falls to the floor in a faint.)

SCENE 42

(Back and main room of the Gran Caffé—interior—daytime. Suddenly the room is full of policemen. The captain of police is

leaning over Mimi. Fiore and their friends are there as well, holding smelling salts under his nose. Mimi has a wound in the very middle of his head.)

FIORE: Mimi, darling, Mary Mother of God! Mimi!

(As he opens his eyes he sees a swaying sultana in front of him, but it's only for an instant.)

MIMI: What happened?
CAPTAIN: He's come to, good! Well, you were lucky, young man, you got away with it, a mere surface wound. Don't worry, madame, it's nothing at all.
FIORE: Are you sure he's all right?
CAPTAIN: Give him a brandy.

(The four victims are covered up with sheets and the police begin gathering information.)

CAPTAIN: Young man! Come on, young man!

(Mimi comes to.)

CAPTAIN: Okay, then, we'll have a few brief questions immediately. So then, we thought you were dead! Good evening, Your Excellency . . .

(A plain-clothes big shot walks into the café, probably the chief of police.)

CAPTAIN: This time we have an eyewitness who survived!

(Mimi notices to his horror that the chief of police has three beauty marks on his cheek, and the policemen accompanying him have an uncanny resemblance to Tricarico's men who have just been murdered.)

SCENE 43

(The birthmarks scene. As in a nightmare, Mimi relives all the experiences involving people with three birthmarks: Don Calogero—Tricarico—the trade unionist.)

SCENE 44

(Main room of the Gran Caffé—interior–daytime. Mimi adopts the ancient Sicilian expression of silence.)

CAPTAIN: Young man, tell us how it happened. You saw the murderer, didn't you?
MIMI: No, I'm afraid not, I have nothing to say. You see, I walked in and just fainted.
CAPTAIN: But what about the murderer, can you describe him?
MIMI: Nope, sorry, can't help you at all. . . . I don't know anything and besides I'm not feeling too well.

SCENE 45

(Factory—interior—daytime. Mimi is standing at the assembly line. He is extremely fast. We see him working on a piece of machinery with such dexterity that we finally see how he has been conditioned to being a superproductive worker. From another assembly line Duilio is giving him a disgusted look. During a break Duilio and two other union members walk up to Mimi.)

DUILIO: Hey, Mardocheco, we're still expecting you at the union meetings.
SANDRO: Leave him be, he's trying to get ahead, he's gone over to the other side!
MIMI: What other side?
LELLO: On the side of the bosses!

(Mimi turns on him like a viper.)

MIMI: What the hell are you going on about? Very well, yes I'm trying to do the best I can. . . . I have a child to think about.
DUILIO: Fuck it, we've all got children. It's just that some fuckers mind only their own business and other people think of their companions. Have a good day.

(A manager walks by and walks toward Mimi.)

MANAGER: Mardocheco, you're going to be through on the twenty-fifth. Your application for a transfer has been approved. You'll be going to head a group down in Catania, in the new refinery.

(Mimi turns white as a sheet.)

MIMI: What application? I never asked for a transfer.

(The manager walks away.)

MANAGER: Well, who did?

SCENE 46

(Personnel office—interior—daytime. One of the personnel officers is showing Mimi his application. Mimi is pale.)

PERSONNEL OFFICER: Young man, is this or is this not your signature?
MIMI: How can it be? I never signed this. I swear it on my son's head.

(The officer is annoyed.)

PERSONNEL OFFICER: Listen my boy, don't think we faked your signature. I assure you we didn't. If you have your own reasons for not wanting to go back to Catania—well, that's your own business. As for us, we already have a replacement.
MIMI: Oh . . .
PERSONNEL OFFICER: You see, as far as we're concerned, you're already in Catania.

(Mimi stands there looking like a fool.)

SCENE 47

(Taxicab—the streets of Catania—interior—exterior—daytime. A mysterious black car with curtains in the back travels through the streets of Catania. Fiore carefully draws the curtains and we see shots of the city from the cab.)

FIORE: It's really such a beautiful city . . .

(Mimi angrily draws back the curtains.)

MIMI: You fool, do you want everyone to see you?

(Mimi's entire family is crowded into the taxi. They are moving. Mimi's outfit is quite odd. He is wearing an enormous pair of sunglasses and a Basque beret pulled down low on his forehead. Fiore and the child are wrapped up in the black shawls often worn by Turkish women. They, too, wear enormous sunglasses.)

FIORE: Darling, don't you think we're being a bit overcautious?

> (*Having pulled back the curtains, Mimi proceeds to bundle up Fiore and Mimi II even more. We can hardly see them anymore. Fiore is dying of heat.*)

MIMI: You really don't believe me when I tell you if that wife of mine sees us she's going to shoot . . . now cover up.

> (*Mimi points to the driver, then leans closer to Fiore and whispers.*)

MIMI: Here the walls have ears as well . . . especially when it's a delicate matter like this.

> (*The car continues its journey through the city.*)

SCENE 48

> (*A square near Fiore's and Mimi's house—exterior—daytime. The taxi stops, pulls up near a large building on the outskirts of the city. Mimi steps out quickly. He pushes Fiore back into the car and closes the door. With a mysterious air about him, Mimi beckons to the driver. As soon as he has made sure that indiscreet eyes aren't spying on them he opens the car and, with the help of the driver, unloads it. Mimi and the driver carry the luggage to the entrance of the building. He pays the man, takes one last look around, and finally lets Fiore and the child get out, covering them completely with the shawl and shielding them with his body.*)

SCENE 49

(Fiore and Mimi's house—interior—daytime. They are busy settling into their new house. Mimi is unpacking while Fiore looks on with Mimi II in her arms.)

FIORE: Goochie, goochie boo boo . . . goochie goo . . .

(The doorbell rings. Mimi looks worried.)

MIMI: Who could that be?
FIORE: I don't know.

(Fiore goes to the door.)

FIORE: Who is it?
VOICE (off camera): Is Mr. Mardocheco there, please?

(Mimi becomes pale. He's nervous. Fiore looks at him. Mimi walks over to the door, then motions to Fiore that he isn't home.)

MIMI (whispering): No, I'm not here, I'm not in for anyone, tell him, tell him, go on!
FIORE: No, he isn't here—who is it?
VOICE (off camera): Doesn't matter. Just tell him that the head building contractor wants to see him.

SCENE 50

(A terrace on a new building—exterior—daytime. A large terrace. Blinding, white, sun-drenched sheets hanging up to dry. At one end of the terrace a table with construction plans on it. A beach umbrella. A man wearing a Panama hat. The man is looking at the apartment complex below. He is the head building contractor. Once again it's the same Mafia face. Mimi worriedly looks at the three birthmarks on the man's right cheek. The man talks to Mimi slowly without looking at him.)

HEAD CONTRACTOR TRICARICO: My cousin, Salvatore Tricarico, asked me to look after you. We never forget our friends.

(Suddenly Mimi understands.)

MIMI: So he was the one that got me transferred down here. Why? What's he got against me? Wasn't it enough that he shot me in the head?

(Tricarico looks at him affectionately.)

TRICARICO: It was a mistake and I apologize on his behalf. He just didn't know how far he could trust you. You've proved yourself to be a man of honor, and that's why you were transferred. Here you can start a new life and have a brilliant career . . . you'll work at the refinery . . . the man in charge here has been warned that you're one of us.

(Mimi raises his chin. He tries to give himself some courage.)

MIMI: But that's just it! I don't want to have anything to do with you people! I'm different, I believe in honest people and in the working classes.

(Tricarico still doesn't look at Mimi, but continues in a paternal tone.)

TRICARICO: For the record, my dear boy, I've always worked. Do you think that all this can be achieved with words alone?

(He points to the brand-new complex visible from the terrace.)

TRICARICO: You see, this has been a lot of honest, hard work for the poor people!

(Mimi turns red.)

MIMI: Please . . . don't mention the poor people. You . . . you've been using the poor people . . . the poor! Exploiting them, that's what! How else could you have built all this? I'll tell you—by burning the orange groves so you could build this monstrosity, where for a stinking two-room apartment and kitchen you have to put down a 900,000 lire deposit. And what about the elections? We know how they're rigged, especially down here. But, you're the real slaves! Slaves of the masters!

(Tricarico snaps at him. He raises his adderlike eyes and points his stick at Mimi's neck. Even though he is speaking gently, there is enormous power in his voice.)

TRICARICO: The ones you refer to as our "masters" in fact are our slaves. Did you ever think of that? You asshole! Don't you try pulling the wool over my eyes, I know what stuff you're made of. You had the opportunity to blackmail Salvatore Tricarico but you wouldn't turn him over to the police or the unions. You know why? Because deep inside you know that you can trust us and can't trust the police. So you're on our side and not on theirs . . . remember that!

(Tricarico pulls himself together.)

TRICARICO: And forget that left-wing ideology . . . Communist dream worlds . . . that's not for you or for our people. We need real masters down here. We have to put things back into place.
MIMI: What the hell do you want, a political coup?
TRICARICO: There's no need for that. You see, anyone with a bit of know-how can easily take over a situation. What do we need? A handful of professionals . . . two or three months of bag snatchings, robberies, rapes . . . a few bombs to be blamed on the anarchists . . . a little bad publicity against our enemies in Rome . . . and it's done. People will run to us begging for protection and some order, and we'll give it to them.
MIMI: Great system!
TRICARICO: These are political systems. I told you, we need masters down here. When the time comes we'll need young men like you who can be trusted.

MIMI: No, don't count on me. Scratch me off your lists—I'm off.

(*Mimi turns to leave. Tricarico's men gather around Mimi menacingly. Tricarico speaks to him sweetly, just like an uncle would.*)

TRICARICO: Listen, lad . . . I suffer from sciatica and I can't bend over. . . . I dropped a coin . . .

(*Slowly he pulls out a hundred lire coin and throws it on the ground ostentatiously.*)

TRICARICO: Do you think you could pick it up for me?

(*Mimi feels the full force of the provocation. He glances at Tricarico, who is looking at him sweetly. In those gentle eyes we see all the criminal irony of the man and all his evil wisdom. Their eyes meet. Never has Mimi met a more determined look.*)

TRICARICO: I'm asking you as a special favor . . .

(*Mimi bends over and picks up the coin.*)

TRICARICO: Good-bye . . .

(*Suddenly Mimi throws the coin down into the street, turns his back, and walks away.*)

SCENE 51

(*Refinery complex—exterior—daytime. Pippino is standing with Mimi's brother, Vito, in front of his colorful cart. They look at this futuristic city made up of tubes with awe. A group of workers walks out and Pippino calls to them.*)

PIPPINO: Can we come in and say hello to Mimi Mardocheco?
WORKER: No, it isn't allowed.

(*Vito looks at Pippino disappointedly.*)

VITO: They won't let us in?
PIPPINO: Afraid not . . .

(*Mimi's group makes its way through the hundreds of thousands of entwined tubes. Mimi reminds us of a sergeant controlling his squad, inciting it to work better and faster.*)

MIMI: So, are we a bunch of lazy peasants or what? Step on it!

(*Two of the workers are offended by his tone.*)

FIRST WORKER: Hey, foreman, what is this, the army?
MIMI: You stay right in your place!
SECOND WORKER: And you just watch your step. I hate bossy "sergeants."

SCENE 52

> (*Mimi's and Fiore's house—interior—nighttime. They have just finished making love and Mimi is lying in bed completely exhausted. Fiore makes sure the baby is asleep.*)

FIORE: Mimi II is fast asleep . . . darling, where would you like me to put Lenin?

> (*Fiore points to the poster of Lenin temporarily placed at the head of the bed.*)

FIORE: Want me to put it on the bed, huh?
MIMI: He's giving me such filthy looks, shit, he always looks at me accusingly. He's getting on my nerves, you know. Take him away, put him far away . . . wherever you want as long as it's far from here!
FIORE: Okay.

> (*Fiore begins to sew.*)

FIORE: You know, Sicily really is beautiful . . . and the people, oh, I love them and the children as well, they look just like little olives, enormous dark eyes, but I've never seen such poverty, I suppose it's really up to you, well, you people who have traveled to the north, to bring back some culture . . . you've broadened your horizons and you can help these poor people to fend for themselves.

> (*Fiore turns to look at Mimi, who is half asleep.*)

FIORE: Darling, come on, you've got to go home.

> (*Mimi looks at her in desperation. He yawns loudly.*)

MIMI: Holy mother of God!

> (*Pushed by Fiore, Mimi gets out of bed.*

SCENE 53

(Uncle Cicciu's house—interior—nighttime. Mimi is very pale as he lies beside Rosalia in Uncle Cicciu's house. He lifts his arm and makes a gesture in the air as if he were saying "I can't take it anymore!")

MIMI: Rosalia . . .

(Rosalia leans worriedly toward him.)

ROSALIA: Darling, are you all right?
MIMI: Exhaustion . . . I'm sorry . . .

(Rosalia is wearing a sexy outfit. Her hairdo and everything about her show that she has been preparing herself for this important night. The fact that Mimi is not feeling well has put the poor woman into a state of agitation.)

ROSALIA: Shall I get you some vinegar?
MIMI: No, be quiet, I don't want them to hear you, if they do, they'll start getting worried. Poor people, it's been a while . . . I've been sick for some time now . . . I'm really sorry for you, because I'm unable to perform my "duty."

(Mimi gives her his most hateful look.)

MIMI: Weak, I'm so weak . . .

(Rosalia sighs.)

ROSALIA: I don't care, honestly, all I want you to do is swear to me that while you were in Turin you didn't cheat on me. . . .

(Mimi gives her a sick smile.)

MIMI: Me? Not even in thought. I was always surrounded by men.

(Mimi yawns.)

MIMI: Just like in the war, always surrounded by men!

SCENE 54

(Block party on a terrace—exterior—daytime. A Sunday afternoon dancing party in honor of St. Torquato. Almost all the men and women of the block are gathered on the terrace. A por-

table record player churns out a constant flow of scratchy sounds. A table with a young boy selling beer, Coca-Cola, and lemonade. The group of people gathered is a fascinating mixture of the traditional, archaic, and modern industrial peasants. We are made aware of the different factions by the diversity in clothing and in the dancing. Men dance with men and women with women. Mimi looks at them in a superior and paternal way. He watches the peasants dance with an Anglo-Saxon smile on his face. He lights a cigarette. Rosalia is dancing with Elena. Somehow Rosalia seems to have matured. Her initial shyness has given way to a slightly mysterious, teasing, and provocative look. Mimi looks around and sees a friend down below in the street. He waves to him.)

SCENE 55

(Alleyway near the terrace where the party is being held—exterior—daytime. The friend returns the greeting and walks away. Mimi is up there on the terrace and doesn't understand.)

SCENE 56

(Party on the terrace—exterior—daytime. Pippino makes his way through the guests to greet Mimi.)

PIPPINO: Hey there, Mimi!
MIMI: Pippino, Pippino, it's wonderful to see you again!

(They embrace like two brothers. Rosalia and Elenuzza continue dancing together.)

ELENUZZA: Your husband looks all right to me . . .
ROSALIA: Well, how should he look?
ELENA: Well, I thought . . . .
ROSALIA: Don't think. It's better . . .
ELENA: Is he still suffering from "exhaustion"?
ROSALIA: Unfortunately . . . it seems to have become a permanent thing.
ELENA: You poor woman, having to cope with a husband like that!

(*Mimi is with his old friend.*)

MIMI: I've got to tell you everything. It's some story!
PIPPINO: Were you part of the autumn strikes?
MIMI: More or less.
PIPPINO: It would be great if you came to speak with the comrades down here so they could hear a different side.

SCENE 57

(*Alleyway near the terrace—exterior—daytime. Mimi's friends are standing in the alleyway. They are faced with a problem.*)

LENTINI: Well, aren't we even going to say hello?
ANGERI: We've got to . . . at least go up and say a few words.
PASQUALE: I'm not going. These sexual matters are very delicate. It may just be gossip, but sooner or later it's bound to come out into the open.

SCENE 58

(*Party on the terrace—exterior—daytime. Pippino and Mimi are working their way through the crowd.*)

PIPPINO: Come on, let's go over to the headquarters.
MIMI: No, I can't today, but I promise that I'll come on my first free Sunday.
PIPPINO: Well, okay, but don't disappear again. We'll wait for you, Mr. Metallurgist!

(*Pippino waves good-bye and walks away. Mimi feels odd. He looks around at the guests. The long sideburns, sagging buttocks swaying to Afro-Cuban rhythms. Mimi has the distinct feeling that everyone is looking at him. He is very aware that all his friends are acting coldly toward him, and decides to find out what the reason is. He walks over to another of his friends, Turi. Turi looks worried. They exchange a few words.)*

MIMI: What do you mean, nothing?
TURI: Nothing . . . stupidities . . .
MIMI: What stupidities?
TURI: Not here—when we're all alone . . . these things can't be discussed in public.
MIMI: Well, I've got time.

SCENE 59

(Alleyway—exterior—daytime. Mimi is in his car insulting Turi. Behind the car doors we hear Mimi's voice insulting his friend.)

MIMI: You fucking bastard pig!

(Pasquale and the other friends face Mimi, who has leapt out of the car and is now looking at them with hatred.)

MIMI: You dared? You dared say that about me? Me? Mimi Mardocheco? Nice friends! He confessed, you know. He told me what you had the courage of saying about me. Pigs! Who was it that started it? Who?

(The friends realize that Mimi's anger could easily get out of hand. They look around. They want to avoid a scandal. Luckily there is no one in the street. Vito is the first to speak up.)

VITO: It was Pasquale.
PASQUALE: I'm innocent! It was Elena who started the story. She was the one who told us that Rosalia was looking for a potion to help cure your weakness.
MIMI: So the gossip mongers started saying that I was in fact pretending exhaustion for other reasons?
CENTAMORE: That's it. And so some people thought some bad things about you.
PASQUALE: The reason being, that in sex anything is possible.
MIMI: I never would have thought that you would take me for a fagot! A puff! A queer! Pigs!
TURI: Look, I swear, Mimi, I never believed it!
MIMI: Shut up! Silence! This affront should be sorted out with pistols

at dawn! But I'm a civilized man, unlike you worms. Get in the car, get in!

(*He opens the door for his friends.*)

TURI: What do you want us to do?
MIMI: Silence! Get in the car. Cocksucker? No one ever called me that!

SCENE 60

(*A square near Fiore's and Mimi's house—exterior—daytime. The car has come to a halt in the square. Mimi and his friends step out furtively. Mimi is being extremely careful.*)

MIMI: Is anyone following us?
PASQUALE: No . . . don't worry.
MIMI: I warn you, I want you to forget what you are about to see. If you don't a life could easily be lost.
PASQUALE: Whose?
MIMI: Can't say. Now listen carefully. This is a very delicate matter, we musn't be seen, let's split up into groups of two.

(*They start walking furtively. Mimi steps into the doorway of his building.*)

PASQUALE: Silence!

SCENE 61

(*Fiore's and Mimi's house—interior—daytime. Fiore sits in a chair with Mimi II like a Madonna and Child as the others sit around sipping coffee.*)

MIMI: Love is a word whose meaning completely escapes you! We were bowled over by a passionate, romantic, and sensuously erotic love. A love so strong, in fact, that it could lead to my divorce! Actually, in this precarious situation I should have had a divorce, but the reason I didn't was because of you!
PASQUALE: Our fault?
MIMI: Yes, your fault. Your primitive way of thinking! Rosalia is a wonderful woman, but which one of you idiots would marry a divorced woman?
PASQUALE: Well, if she were American, yes—but never a Sicilian.

SCENE 62

> *(Square—exterior—daytime. Pasquale and Felice watch Mimi's car passing by. Their eyes are full of admiration.)*

PASQUALE: Boy, Mimi really is quite a man. He's a metallurgist, he's got a car, a wife, a son, and a concubine. What more could one want?

> *(Felice says good-bye to Pasquale and walks away.)*

FELICE: See you.
PASQUALE: 'Bye.

> *(Elena appears on the doorstep and motions to Pasquale. She has a very serious expression on her face. Pasquale moves up to her.)*

ELENUZZA: Pasquale, listen . . .
PASQUALE: What is it?
ELENA: Something awful has happened . . . it's a disaster!

SCENE 63

> *(Refinery complex—exterior—daytime. During a break Mimi notices Pippino, Elena, and Pasquale on the other side of a fence trying to catch his attention. Mimi leans across the tubings.)*

MIMI: Hey, Pippino!
PIPPINO: Mimi, we have to talk to you! Can you come out and talk? It's a very delicate matter.
PASQUALE: Very delicate!

SCENE 64

> *(Countryside—automobile—exterior—daytime. Shots of an empty expanse of land as far as the eye can see. Mimi's car is parked in the middle of this deserted wasteland. Mimi offers cigarettes to everyone.)*

MIMI: Well, then, what have you got to tell me?

> *(An embarrassed silence. Elena doesn't know where to start.)*

ELENA: It's delicate, a very delicate thing . . .
PASQUALE: Very delicate, yes . . .

MIMI: Well, what is it?

PASQUALE: Mimi, you're a man of the world. You've been places, seen things, you know the ways of the world. . . .

MIMI: Out with it, what are you talking about?

PIPPINO: What Pasquale is trying to say is that circumstances have made you neglect certain duties . . . certain material and moral duties . . .

MIMI: What are you referring to?

ELENA: Rosalia . . . your wife . . .

MIMI: In what way?

PIPPINO: Poor thing, you left her alone. First you were up north, then you came back, but still you neglected her. You had things to do and you always left her alone.

MIMI: So what's she looking for, companionship?

PIPPINO: No, it's just that . . .

(Carmelo is worried that they might be saying too much.)

MIMI: Come on, out with it. Did Rosalia send you? Did she tell you stories about me?

PIPPINO: No, it's just that your wife . . .

PASQUALE: She's sad.

PIPPINO: She feels neglected.

PASQUALE: Upset and miserable.

PIPPINO: Pasquale, shut your mouth! As I was saying, she feels neglected, you know, she has no children, and . . .

MIMI: Without children? Well, was it my fault they never came?

ELENA: Well, no . . . you were exhausted . . .

(Mimi looks at Elena, who is turning red and is getting worried. He turns to Pippino and Pasquale.)

PIPPINO: Well, simply, your wife just hasn't been terribly happy . . .

(Mimi thinks he has understood Elena's mission.)

MIMI: I'm sorry for Rosalia . . . I love her, really. She's always been a good wife . . . a hard-working woman . . . and for a Sicilian she's a modern woman. On the other hand—well—Rosalia isn't really . . . shit, I don't want to get into intimate matrimonial problems, but . . . let's just say she's a calm woman, yes, calm. So now she feels lonely? Well, what does she want, a child?

PASQUALE: No.

ELENA: No.
MIMI: What do you mean, no?
PASQUALE: She's already pregnant.
MIMI: Wha . . .
ELENA: Three months pregnant.

> (*Mimi doesn't move. The cigarette butt dangles loosely from his lips.*)

PIPPINO: Well, it happened and now you know. But you're an intelligent man, a metallurgist, a Communist . . . you've got your own faults! So, don't you start behaving like a Sicilian! The time has come to settle things, divorce or no divorce. Above all, no tragedies. With mutual admiration and understanding. Anyway, it's better this way for you, isn't it? You can show us all how one should behave in these situations . . . civilized and level-headed.

> (*Mimi looks as if he has just been hit by lightning. He can hardly utter the words, but finally they come out.*)

MIMI: Who was it?
ELENA: When the poor thing went to driving school some guy fell in love with her. She fought it, but you . . . you were . . . exhausted. He insisted, she gave in and it happened. Only once, mind you, but it happened.

> (*A sudden shudder runs through Mimi's whole being like a volcano before it erupts. The boiling lava slowing rises and finally bursts forth in a violent eruption:*

MIMI: Whooooooooore!
> (*Mimi is furious and dangerous. He reminds us of Uncle Cicciu. The whole car shakes from his anger. He grabs a wrench and dashes out of the car as the others try to hold him back. He starts running down the deserted road, shouting his terrible threats to the sun. Pippino steps out of the car as well.*)

MIMI: Slut! You bring shame to the Mardocheco name! Whore! I'll rip her heart out and make her eat it!

(*Pippino calls to him to come back. He runs after him.*)

PIPPINO: A Communist doesn't behave like this!
MIMI: Fuck you! Communist, Communist my ass. I'm a cuckhold, that's what I am!

(*Mimi is totally insane now. But he does realize that it will take him a lot longer to get home if he goes on foot.*)

MIMI: What am I doing going by foot?

(*Mimi goes back to the car, still clutching his wrench.*)

PIPPINO: Mimi, wait, wait!
MIMI: Now, right now! I have to kill that ungrateful cheating bitch immediately!

(*Mimi takes off. Pippino stands in the middle of the road. He tries to make Mimi stop.*)

PIPPINO: Mimi, stop! Stop!

SCENE 65

(*Rosalia's mother's house—interior—daytime. The door flies open and Mimi storms in, furious and extremely fierce-looking.*)

VOICES (off camera): Mimi, stop! What are you doing? Stop!

(Rosalia is alone, bundled up in her black outfit, crying. She looks up at him, then turns her gaze away and with an odd sound starts to cry again. Mimi glares at her.)

MIMI: Why, you bitch? Why did you drag the name of the Mardochecos through the mud like this? My mother's name! Ahhhhh!

(With a leap he is on top of her, trying to grab her by the throat. But he can't get to it because her enormous shawl is in the way. He tries to remove it as Rosalia turns pale with terror.)

ROSALIA: Are you trying to kill me?
MIMI: Yessireee, my name must be cleansed of this deed! Fuck this shawl, take this thing off!

(Like a lamb ready to be sacrificed, Rosalia bravely removes her shawl and looks at her husband.)

ROSALIA: It is right! I dishonored your name and I must pay for it! You're right, Mimi, you're right!

(She offers her white throat like a queen on the guillotine. Mimi is incapable of acting now that she is willingly offering her life. He tries to tighten his grip around her throat but is unable to.)

MIMI: Don't say I'm right, goddamn you, don't agree with me you slut! If you don't react I just can't do anything . . . you ugly cheating sow!

(As he pulls her by the hair, Rosalia doesn't fight back. It is this very passiveness which irritates Mimi more than anything because he finds himself unable to really inflict any significant injury on her.)

MIMI: I've got to kill you! I can't live as a dishonored man, can I?
ROSALIA: No, you can't!

(She bursts into an uncontrollable torrent of tears.)

MIMI: Can I spend the rest of my days a cuckold?
ROSALIA: No, you can't!
MIMI: Lowly slut! Confess before you die! Tell me how it happened!
ROSALIA: I went for my license.

(Mimi is trembling with anger.)

MIMI: Yeah, a license to walk the streets, huh?

ROSALIA: No, a driver's license! And you see . . . well . . . there was this man, wearing a uniform . . . he was a customs officer . . . Brigadier Amilcare Finocchiaro . . .

MIMI: How did it happen?

ROSALIA: He always had some honey sweets and he would offer them to me.

MIMI: So, he offered you candies and you offered him pussy?

(*Rosalia is offended.*)

ROSALIA: How dare you? He fell in love with me! In love! He always sang that romantic song . . . "the heart is just a gypsy." I tried to resist him, but the more I resisted the more he sang. Finally the morning the town councilor was shot—you remember the town councilor they found walled up in cement?

MIMI: What the fuck do I care about the town councilor walled up in cement? Where did it happen?

ROSALIA: In the cab of a crane.

MIMI: The cab of a crane!

ROSALIA: Well, he was on duty guarding a building site when it started to rain, so we went to look for shelter and that was the only place.

MIMI: So, my wife gets herself pregnant in the cab of a crane! I'll have to kill this son of a bitch immediately! Where is he?

ROSALIA: No, Mimi, don't do it! There are too many innocent people involved.

MIMI: Why, I suppose he's married?

ROSALIA: Yes . . .

(*Rosalia looks down.*)

MIMI: And I suppose he's got children as well . . .

ROSALIA: Five . . .

MIMI: Well done, Rosalia! What kind of cheating is this? A customs officer; he's got five children; you do it in a crane; and—worst of all—his name is Amilcare! You've really let me down!

ROSALIA: He was so kind . . . especially when he found out about your "misfortune."

MIMI: What misfortune?

(*Mimi is all ears.*)

ROSALIA: You know, your illness . . . your . . . weakness.

MIMI: My weakn . . . Oh, so you went and told him all our most intimate secrets?

ROSALIA: No, he had heard it from somewhere else. . . . I tried to deny it, you know, so you wouldn't lose face, but then one day he took me to the movies and we saw the film *Handsome Anthony* and I just had to confess it all to him. . . .

    (Mimi is overcome by his anger.)

MIMI: So, not only do they take me for a cuckold, but I'm considered a fag as well. So that son of a bitch, that prick in uniform, thinks that since the husband's a poof he can do what he pleases! Well, I'm not a fag and the first reason why I haven't had any carnal relationships with you is because you make me sick . . . and secondly, you might as well know about it . . . well, I have a woman, a beautiful woman with whom I make love maybe ten or fifteen times in a row, day or night . . . and we love it! Fagot! I'll give you fagot! And what's more, she bore me a child, a boy, beautiful as the sun!

    (Mimi barely manages to avoid the plunging fish knife.)

MIMI: A knife!

    (Once the words have sunk in, Rosalia doesn't waste time, she throws herself onto Mimi. A complete transformation from the pitiful woman she was a few minutes ago to a raving witch. Her eyes are falling out of their orbits.)

ROSALIA: You bastard, I'll eat your heart!

    (Fingernails flashing, she throws herself on her husband. She is quite determined to kill him. Mimi shouts for help.)

MIMI: Not my hair! Stop it, not my hair!

ROSALIA'S MOTHER (off camera): Help, help, they're killing my daughter!

    (The door flies open and Rosalia's mother walks in followed by some people.)

MIMI: Help! She's the one killing me!

SCENE 66

(Lawyer's office—interior—evening. The two plaintiffs are standing before a lawyer. On one side we see Mimi with Pippino, on the other Rosalia with her mother. The lawyer is trying to find a satisfactory solution for the couple.)

LAWYER: And, in conclusion, my client could agree to recognizing the child if Mrs. Rosalia Mardocheco, née Capuzzo, will agree to the adoption of Mr. Mimi Mardocheco's and Miss Fiore Meneghini's offspring.

(Mimi is very tense and is avoiding Rosalia's eyes.)

ROSALIA: Why?

(Rosalia is very pale and her expression is mean.)

LAWYER: Now, let's be practical, madame. It would be a wise move if this situation were legalized in view that there *may* be a separation. In other words . . . if you adopt your natural child you will then have to recognize your husband's child.
MIMI: Never! That son of a whore will never have my name!
ROSALIA: Oh, yes, he will! That'll teach you, you'll lose face in front of the whole world, you'll be the butt of everybody's jokes!
MIMI: Disgusting pig!
ROSALIA: I'll never give him the pleasure of giving my consent to his child . . . his child is a bastard, and will remain a bastard!
MIMI: You bitch!
ROSALIA: My child will be called Mardocheco! The whole world will laugh at you!
MIMI: No way, he won't ever have a name because I'm going to kick both of you to death!

(He attacks his wife as the people present try to hold him back.)

MIMI: I'll kill you, kill you!

(She protects her belly and provokes him by pointing to her swelled stomach.)

LAWYER: Please, let's be calm, calm down!
ROSALIA: Mardocheco! Amilcare like his true father and Mardocheco like you!

(She laughs like a shrew.)

SCENE 67

(Street of Catania—exterior—daytime. Mimi is walking along one of the main streets of the city with Pippino following close behind. Mimi looks like a madman. He talks, gesticulates, is distraught. Standing in front of them we see one of those men who when they turn to you to bid good morning make you feel as if he had just threatened your life. Definitely a hired killer. Cautiously the killer walks up to Mimi and Pippino. He stops and looks expectantly.)

MIMI: In this bloody city people never mind their own business!

(The killer nods to Mimi the moment Mimi notices him.)

KILLER: A mutual friend of ours told me you have been the victim of, let us say, an unfortunate mishap. You must demand satisfaction! He has asked me to be at your complete disposal.
MIMI: To do what?
KILLER: Well, that's for you to tell me. As soon as you've made up your mind you'll let me know. As far as practical matters are concerned, you needn't worry—I'm a professional!

(Mimi and Pippino are pale as they listen to the man. Pippino hasn't understood a thing but Mimi knows very well what the man is referring to.)

MIMI: Tell whoever sent you that I don't need a thing. Let's go, Pippino!

SCENE 68

(A small public park in Catania—exterior—daytime. Mimi and Pippino walk along a path. Mimi is desperate. The killer following them closely. Pippino is terribly nervous.)

PIPPINO: Are you sure it was Salvatore Tricarico who sent him?
MIMI: Who the hell do you think it was, Santa Claus?

(Mimi sits on a bench.)

MIMI: That's all we need, a killer. Rosalia would certainly deserve it, that's for sure. Did you see her at the lawyer's office? What a bitch! She wants to take it out on Mimi II.

(Pippino has taken his mind off Mimi's marital woes and is completely absorbed by the strange character who has been following them.)

PIPPINO: He hasn't let us out of his sight for a moment. Are you aware of who Salvatore Tricarico is? He's the one who unionized the "skilled workers." . . .

MIMI: My son! My son! The son of that uniform fucker growing up in my house, bearing my name! The whole world laughing behind my back! A cuckold, that's what I am!

PIPPINO: As I was saying . . . you do know who Salvatore Tricarico is? He organized the skilled workers and now he's getting to be a big shot. If we aren't careful, pretty soon he'll be local councilor. They say he is a man who doesn't argue, he just gets rid of anything in his way.

MIMI: Do you think I don't know all this? I know the family. In Turin his cousin shot four people . . . I saw the whole thing.

PIPPINO: You were an eyewitness? Did you turn him in?

MIMI: I mind my own business. And anyway, that the hell do you want from me? You're always criticizing, telling me what I should be doing. Who the hell are you to say these things? You're a nothing, that's what you are. You've been working all these years and you still have patches on your ass. You and your left-wing ideas, your stupid little cart! A failure is what you are. Leave me alone, leave me! I don't want to know you, go away!

(Pippino is really offended. Mimi walks away, and walks by the killer, who is forever hopeful.)

KILLER: Do you need me now?

MIMI: Fuck off!

SCENE 69

(Street of Catania—exterior—daytime. Amalia Finocchiaro is with her five children. As is quite often the case with the wives of Italian customs officials, Amalia Finocchiaro is shaped like an enormous pear. A tiny head and an enormous bulbous body. She has a Neapolitan temperament and is annoyed by her noisy and troublesome brood. She is big, strong, and domineering. Amalia turns to each of her five children and slaps them hard across the face.)

AMALIA: Enough is enough! Blow your noses, and I want you all home by seven, now move! And if you dare get into any trouble I'll kill you all!

(The three oldest children run off like young ponies. With a sigh she tugs at the remaining children and, ungracefully undulating her mastodontic hips, moves away. A woman who walks with a sense of purpose. Mimi's intense, pale face can be seen in the semidarkness of a doorway as Amalia walks by. He is stalking his prey with the typical look of the Mediterranean lover.)

MIMI: Beautiful! Hey, beautiful!

(Amalia is slightly surprised but decides to do nothing about it. She continues walking, stepping up her pace, just a little. Mimi walks out of the doorway and starts following her close behind. She feels followed but tries to ignore it. Mimi's presence and intense stare are like a dagger in the small of her back. Her curiosity is overwhelming. With the excuse of turning to drag one of her children along, she manages a glimpse of her suitor. She goes around a corner and Mimi gets even closer.)

MIMI: You're so beautiful!

(She no longer has any doubts, but Amalia is a serious lady and she quickens her pace. Mimi is still gaining on her. He whispers sensuous words into her fleshy, rosy ears, first in the right one, then the left.)

MIMI: You drive me crazy . . . I long for you, your fiery eyes. When can I see you alone?

(Amalia is blushing.)

AMALIA: Aren't you ashamed to say those things in front of these innocent creatures?
MIMI: Beautiful, beautiful, I've been following you for months. I've been worshipping you silently. I can't keep quiet any longer. I want to have a meeting with you . . . when?
AMALIA: Go away or I'll call for help.
MIMI: I just can't resist anymore, I've got to kiss you, I've got to caress you, rub myself against you!
AMALIA: What do you take me for, huh? I'm a good housewife and a good mother. Are you trying to compromise my good name? Piss off, you shit!

MIMI: I want to meet you!
AMALIA: Never!
MIMI: You won't escape me!

(*Amalia starts walking away.*)

SCENE 70

(*Streets, squares, and marketplaces in Catania—exterior—day-time. It has almost turned into a race. She tries to shake him off by abruptly changing direction, stopping, starting, and running. Mimi won't let up. Like a pointer after its prey, he won't let her get away. They run through the markets and squares of the city. Amalia has finally reached the end of her run. She stops in front of a doorway and pushes her children inside. Mimi places himself nonchalantly in front of the closed door.*)

SCENE 71

(*Seamstresses' workshop—interior—daytime. We are in Amalia's workshop. It is an enormous room where sheets are sewn together to be used to protect the orange groves from bad weather. Mimi walks in and moves up to a little woman bent over her sewing machine. He is wearing a raincoat, a hat, and a pair of sunglasses.*)

WOMAN: Who are you looking for?
MIMI: Mrs. Finocchiaro, I'm a relative . . .
WOMAN: End of the room, on your right.
MIMI: Many thanks.

SCENE 72

(*Amalia's room in the workshop—interior—daytime. Amalia sits alone in the large room, at her sewing machine. She is singing.*)

AMALIA (*singing*): "Do whatever you want to me . . ."

(*Mimi sneaks up on her and takes her hand.*)

MIMI: You're driving me crazy!

(*Amalia jumps.*)

AMALIA: Jesus, Joseph and the blessed Virgin Mary! You're really crazy, aren't you? Are you trying to get me into trouble?

MIMI: I crave your body!

AMALIA: Let go of my hand! Go away, leave me alone!

(*Mimi lets go of her hand.*)

AMALIA: Go away, you madman! How dare you?

(*Mimi takes off his glasses and lets out his killer look.*)

MIMI: I've told you already, my blood boils when I think of you! I've got to talk to you! Where and when?

AMALIA: Shut up or you'll get me into a lot of trouble. Go away or they'll fire me. I'm trying to work.

MIMI: I'm not going to budge from here until we've set a meeting place.

AMALIA: I'll get into trouble.

MIMI: Where and when?

AMALIA: Can't you see how much trouble I'm going to get into?

MIMI: Where and when?

AMALIA: What are you looking for? I told you, this is an impossible love . . .

MIMI: Where and when?

AMALIA: Okay, as long as you go away . . . let's meet tomorrow at four at the Church of St. Nicholas.

MIMI: Till tomorrow at four at the church.

(*He throws her a kiss and walks away.*)

SCENE 73

(*Church of St. Nicholas—interior–exterior—daytime. Amalia is carefully made up and hiding behind a black lace veil and a large pair of sunglasses. Mimi is next to her. Amalia is as happy as a lark. She shows that romantic temperament she had to conceal during her many years of marriage. Together they walk down the aisle.*)

AMALIA: Holy Jesus, you mean it's been three months since you started courting me and I never even noticed? What a fool I've been. I can understand your feelings, love truly is blind. But I must tell you that I am a very serious woman and I have to say no to your proposition. But let me say that it's not because of that pig husband of mine, he deserves a lot worse. You know what he did? He took me in the flower of my youth, took my virginity and took stinking advantage of my age. I was eighteen years old, he was from Torre Annunziata and he was a customs guard.

(*They walked toward the cloister as Amalia continues talking while Mimi is devouring her with his eyes.*)

AMALIA: He dishonored me, he took advantage of the fact that I was such a warm-blooded lass—you see I'm from Naples. Well, if my father—may he rest in peace—hadn't come with his revolver and forced that son of a bitch to marry me, he never would have. Even though I was only eighteen and pregnant. That son of a whore! After he ruined me and dragged my honor through the mud this fucker forced me to bear five children, one after the other. I don't quite know why, but I have a feeling he's fed up with me, he doesn't want me anymore. Never a kind word, never a gift . . . and I really care for those things. I'm a very romantic woman, and that's why I can understand the way you feel right now. Did you really dream of me every night?
MIMI: Yes, of course.
AMALIA: This is mere infatuation. You're young and handsome and I've got a big ass and lately I've put on some weight.
MIMI: That's exactly what I like about you, Amalia. You know, when I dream of you I dream you are naked, round, and have enormous tits.

(*Overcome by passion, Mimi kisses her on the cheek. Amalia moves away.*)

AMALIA: No! Now you're getting a bit too fresh! Keep your hands to yourself! I think I made myself clear, didn't I? This was supposed to be a platonic meeting, so I could explain the situation to you.
MIMI: I apologize, Amalia, it was a moment of weakness. I promise it won't happen again, I swear it.

SCENE 74

(*Exterior—daytime. A white shack at the seashore. A deserted beach. This is Cianfrotta's house, an old, whoring sea lion in front of the house. By the small pergola, we see a table. On it are a plate of figs and two glasses of wine. An old record plays a scratchy, languid melody. Mimi and Amalia are dancing cheek to cheek. Cianfrotta watches the whole scene from his hiding place behind the house. He slips the two thousand lire into his*) *wallet, picks up his spade, winks at Mimi, and heads for his gar-den. Amalia whispers to Mimi, her eyes closed. Mimi is blowing in her ear, clearly bored by the whole thing. He tries leading her into the steps of a passionate tango.)*

AMALIA: Mine can't be called a life! It's a pile of shit, that's what it is! And that's the only reason that I agreed to meet you here. I gave in to this dream, with you, the music, the waves . . . I gave myself to you, to your arms, to this dance. Don't ask more of me, though. I want to treasure this moment for the rest of my days!

MIMI: Amalia!

AMALIA: When the music ends I want you to take me home . . . it will be farewell forever!

(Mimi bites one of her ears.)

MIMI: You'll drive me crazy!

AMALIA: You'll drive *me* crazy!

MIMI: Look at me, Amalia!

AMALIA: Are you thinking about me, Mimi?

MIMI: Darling be quiet, close your eyes, let yourself go.

(Mimi has a very determined look. With a daring dance step he directs Amalia toward the house. Amalia lets herself go with her eyes still tightly shut. She then realizes that Mimi is trying to lead her to the house.)

AMALIA: No, leave me go!

(Amalia catches a glimpse of the bed.)

AMALIA: No, I don't want to go in there! Leave me, you bastard, I don't want to go in there!

(The dance has become a regular wrestling match and Amalia is fighting very hard to retain her virtue. She grabs hold of the doorpost and hangs on for dear life. Mimi is having a very hard time because of her girth.)

SCENE 75

(Cianfrotta's bedroom—interior—daytime. Mimi is pushing Amalia, trying to embrace her, attempting to sweep her off her feet.)

AMALIA: You bastard, I don't want to, leave me alone!

(Amalia is resisting him with all her strength. Mimi decides to attack with even greater determination. His hands go straight up her skirt and into her blouse. As she tries to defend herself, Amalia falls. Mimi quickly shuts the door. They are on the ground. The room is simple, the bed is large, high off the ground, and ancient. The wrestling gets wilder and wilder.)

AMALIA: No, stop it, go away, not on the bed! Stop, I have five children, don't do this to me!

(Mimi manages to pick her up and drag her to the bed. He throws himself on top of her.)

AMALIA: No, not the bed! Why are you doing this to me? What do you want from me? Why, why, what do you want?

(Amalia is by now almost naked, her skirt halfway down her thighs. We catch a climpse of her underwear, her enormous meaty breasts straining against her shirt. In the meantime Mimi is taking off all his clothes as well.)

AMALIA: You really want me to this extent?

(Amalia is excited and perturbed and is turning pink.)

MIMI: What more proof do you need?
AMALIA: You really find me beautiful?
MIMI: More than any other woman. This is it, either you give in to me or I'll kill you!
AMALIA: Well, I give in to violence, do your worst!

(Amalia sits up in the bed. She is disheveled and blushing. Looking at Mimi with sensuous determination, she starts to

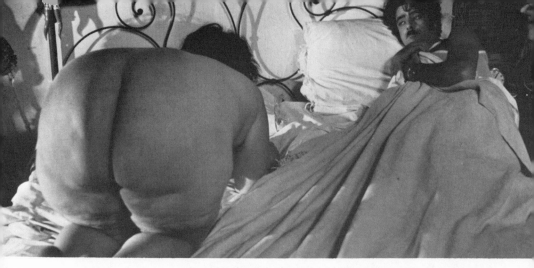

undress completely. They start to perform a striptease to the music of a tango. Amalia covers her most intimate parts with the clothes she is removing. She moves to the bed and slides in under the sheets. Mimi is naked. He has a last-minute hesitation, almost as if he felt he might not quite make it, then, gathering all his courage, he swan-dives onto the bed. Amalia welcomes him with an erotic scream. Mimi starts pawing her. She whispers to him.)

AMALIA: I'm not used to these things. What should I do?
MIMI: Do what you think is best.

(Amalia is overcome by sexual rapture. She turns with a sexy move and buries Mimi under her enormous, pink, flaccid body. Mimi is stunned by the impact of her body on his. It's done. Mimi is completely worn out from his supreme act of courage. Amalia is a languid, passionate figure overcome by the act.)

AMALIA *(singing)*: "Don't whisper words of love in my ears . . . "Just tell me how much you love me."
MIMI: Okay, okay, but shut up now.
AMALIA: Why the hell should I shut up? I'm happy, my love, my love . . . "You took my life away . . ." You're so beautiful, I really like you a lot. And what about you, how much do you love me? "I love you more than you could imagine . . ."

(Mimi doesn't reply. It is clear that he can't take her anymore.)

AMALIA: Come on, tell me how much you like me, go on! Do you love me? I want you to say "I love you."

(Amalia is upset.)

AMALIA: You don't want to say it anymore?

MIMI: No, I don't love you.

AMALIA: What are you saying? Have you gone crazy? Now that I've given in to you . . . you're joking, aren't you?

MIMI: No, I'm not fooling. Now that we're here I might as well tell you. I wasn't honest with you.

AMALIA: No, it's not true! But why the game?

MIMI: Your husband made my wife pregnant and I had to get my revenge.

(*After a moment's hesitation Amalia comes to grips with the terrible truth. She turns on Mimi and lets him have a series of powerful slaps.*)

AMALIA: Pig, bastard fucking filthy pig shit, what have you done to me?

(*Mimi tries to protect himself from her anger. Escape is impossible because her enormous body is in the way. Luckily the slaps end and Amalia breaks down into a flood of tears.*)

AMALIA: You coward! And I was the fool to have believed you, to have believed that love had finally knocked on my door as well. It's all his fault, my husband's fault! This time I'll kill him, he's going to pay for it all! I'm going to kill him right now!

(*With an agile leap she darts for the door, completely nude. She realizes that she has to put her underwear on. Mimi takes advantage of the moment to slip on his clothes.*)

MIMI: Yeah, you kill him so you end in jail and your five children go straight to the nearest orphanage.

AMALIA: Shut up, you shit. I don't want advice from a traitor.

(*As she buttons up her shirt she starts to walk out. Obviously Mimi's words have sunk in and she stops.*)

AMALIA: Why me, you bastard fucker? What do you have to gain from having done this to me? Moral satisfaction?

(*Mimi has a flash in his eyes.*)

MIMI: No, dear Amalia. I'm a metallurgist, I'm civilized now. My mind works very well right now.

SCENE 76

> *(Refinery courtyard—exterior—daytime. In the courtyard a group of skilled workers are discussing a strike action. It's one of their breaks and the workers are in small groups. A few union leaders are explaining things and are conducting discussions with the various groups. Farther away, Mimi is arguing with Fiore. He is angrily eating his lunch.)*

FIORE: So you're the one who wants to take revenge on your wife for having cuckolded you. You're dying to commit a massacre, so why don't you take a gun and shoot her? At least it will be over and done with.

MIMI: No, Mimi Mardocheco, metallurgist and group head, won't shoot.

> *(Mimi's group walks over to him. One of the workers turns to Mimi angrily.)*

WORKER: Mardocheco, we've decided on a slowdown . . . we wanted to know what you thought about it.

> *(Mimi leaps to his feet.)*

MIMI: No sir, no more strikes!

> *(The workmen look at him as if he were a madman. His eyes are falling from their sockets.)*

WORKMAN: What are you saying?

MIMI: I've had enough strikes. Strikes, disorder and changes, I've had more than my share. All these hassles have gone to our heads. No one knows what the fuck's going on anymore. This progress is getting us all confused. It was a lot better in the old days when one just pulled out a gun and shot and that was that!

WORKMAN: Shot who?

MIMI: That's my own business. You mind your own. My group isn't going to strike. We have to keep things under control. If they're not, how do you expect this factory to survive?

> *(The workmen watch the whole scene without understanding what is going on.)*

MIMI: How can a poor devil carry on if things aren't under control?

(*He turns his back to the group and walks away, shouting at the sun.*)

MIMI: . . . I'll make sure things are kept under control, God is my witness. No strikes, order! Things must be better organized around here. I'll get everything under control!

SCENE 77

(*Beach—exterior—daytime. From behind a curtain in Cian-frotta's shack Amalia nervously points out something to Mimi.*)

AMALIA (off camera): There he is, he's always there. I noticed him last month as well.

(*On the beach we see the killer. He is still following Mimi.*)

SCENE 78

(Cianfrotta's bedroom—interior—daytime. Amalia is nervous. Both she and Mimi are wearing dark glasses.)

AMALIA: I don't want to think it was my husband who sent him to spy on us.

(Mimi yawns and reassures her.)

MIMI: No, he's just a ball-breaker who's there to do my bidding.
AMALIA: Well, regardless, I don't want any eyewitnesses. Have you been getting yourself ready?
MIMI: As the doctor said, eight days of abstinence.

(Amalia pulls out a series of papers and diagrams from her shopping bag.)

AMALIA: Here we are! This is the diagram of the basic temperature. . . . I've followed the hormone treatments to a T. The days are fertile, ovulation is high. So then, get to it. . . .

(She begins undressing with clinical precision. Mimi starts undressing as well.)

MIMI: Amalia Finocchiaro's basic temperature . . . you know, when you show up every month with all your charts you really get on my nerves. I told you, you must have faith in me.
AMALIA: No sir. This must be clear, it isn't for pleasure, this is a duty we are performing.
MIMI: Yeah, it's easy for you, you just lie there and . . .
AMALIA: It isn't my fault, it's one of the crosses I have to bear.
MIMI: You think it's easy for me?
AMALIA: Come on, Mimi, don't care. Let's get to it—I haven't got all day.
MIMI: Well, there is a slight problem. You see, in certain cases a man has to be helped . . .
AMALIA: Helped? You make me sick. I am sacrificing myself only to spite my husband. He makes me sicker than you do. I just can't be part of this. The most I can do is let you have a look.

(Amalia barely lifts the sheets. This doesn't really help Mimi.)

MIMI: No, don't worry, there isn't any need for you to trouble yourself.

(He gets into bed as well.)

MIMI: What must be done, must be done!

SCENE 79

> *(Square—exterior—morning. Mimi stands with his legs spread wide in the village square. He sees Pippino walking at a distance from him.)*

MIMI: Pippi' . . . Pippino! Weren't you asked to come here this morning? It's a very important morning. Why are you going away?
PIPPINO: I'm just a peasant after all. A poor bastard with patches on his ass. A nothingness, as you so kindly called me. I've got better things to do, and besides didn't you tell me that you wanted me to leave you alone?
MIMI: All right, as you wish, but you're going to miss a fine spectacle.
PIPPINO: Who with, huh? With him?

> *(Pippino points to the ever-present killer, who is walking close-by.)*

MIMI: Him? He's okay. It's just as well that he's here, in that way he can go back to whoever sent him and tell him the way a civilized man behaves.
PIPPINO: So you would be the civilized man? Why—just because you have a car?

> *(Mimi's expression becomes hard.)*

MIMI: There he is, Brigadier Amilcare Finocchiaro! Today we'll have fun with him!

> *(The Brigadier walks toward the church with a seven-month-pregnant Amalia on his arm.)*

PIPPINO: What do you want to do? Watch it, Mimi, he's armed.
MIMI: Don't worry, it's all been planned, down to the smallest detail.

SCENE 80

> *(Preparations sequence—interior)*

MIMI'S VOICE (off camera): The whole plan has been carefully thought out.

(Amalia makes a mysterious phone call. Then she removes her husband's pistol from its holder and unloads it. Then she puts it back.)

SCENE 81

(Square—exterior—daytime. Pippino is rather worried by this whole scene.)

PIPPINO: Don't be an asshole.
MIMI: Everything is going according to plan.

(Mimi looks at the time.)

MIMI: The show is about to begin.

(Pushing a baby buggy, Rosalia appears at the other end of the square. Mimi moves with purpose. He walks up to her.)

MIMI: My humble respects, Mrs. Mardocheco.
ROSALIA: What do you want?
MIMI: You. Now, I want you to come into church with me.
ROSALIA: You're a pig. I don't want to talk with you! Talk to the lawyer.
MIMI: This is no longer a time for lawyers. This innocent creature bears my name, doesn't it? So then, everyone must see us. We're a nice family and the whole world must see us.
ROSALIA: No, I won't go into church with you.
MIMI: If you don't come in with me quietly, I'll kick you all the way in!

(People start appearing in the square. Mimi walks with the baby in his arms. People start turning around to look at them. Pippino and the others turn pale. Fiore is there as well, obviously having been asked to come. She is clutching her baby in her arms. She turns pale.)

FIORE: Hey, wha . . . what are you planning to do? Are you mad?

(Rosalia is being pushed by Mimi, an iron grip on her arm. She is crying.)

ROSALIA: I'll eat that whore's heart out!
MIMI: Shut up, she's got nothing to do with it!

(The clock tower strikes nine. Mimi and Rosalia are crossing the square. In front of the main door to the church we see the figures of Amalia and her husband, Brigadier Amilcare Finocchiaro. They hurry away toward the door to the church. Mimi calls him from below.)

MIMI: Brigadier Amilcare Finocchiaro! May I have a word with you?

(The atmosphere is tense. Amalia and the brigadier stop. Amilcare has a distrusting look and gives Rosalia an embarrassed look. The people following the sequence of events from the café are tense and nervous. The passers-by turn around curiously.)

AMILCARE: Are you talking to me?

(Still dragging Rosalia behind him, Mimi walks up the first two steps toward the church.)

MIMI: Yes sir, I was talking to you, Brigadier Finocchiaro—if you don't mind, of course!
FINOCCHIARO: Well, I was just going into church.

MIMI: I'll only take a moment of your time, just to straighten a few things out. Right here, in the light of day, in front of our friends. As everyone knows, my wife's child belongs to you and the one that your wife is about to give birth to in a few days belongs to me. If you agree, when your wife's baby is born we could exchange them. To each his own, as it were. We'll straighten out this ridiculous situation once and for all. And as the saying goes, to each his own little bastard! Do I make myself clear?

> (*The people in the square have gathered around, their ears perked up. Mimi's last words have shocked the whole square. Everyone's eyes are on the Brigadier. Amilcare Finocchiaro is as pale as the marble he is standing on. Then he suddenly becomes as red as a beet.*)

AMILCARE: What are you saying? What is this bastard saying?

> (*Amalia smilingly moves away from him.*)

AMALIA: My pretty husband, it's the truth! You cuckolded me, so I went and cuckolded you. You're a cuckold, my dear brigadier! We're even now! Don't get too angry, as a father you're as much a shit as he is, which makes you a pair of turds. So, what the hell!

> (*She begins to laugh uncontrollably. Amalia is reveling in her triumph. Hatred pours out of Amilcare's nostrils. A deep terrible shout comes from the very hollow of his chest. The man's honor has been shattered.*)

AMILCARE: Look what she did to me! I'll shoot, so help me God, I'll shoot!

> (*At this point, as the people are shouting and running away, Mimi comes forward, letting Rosalia and the child move away.*)

MIMI: Ladies and gentlemen, please be careful, because the brigadier is going to shoot!
AMILCARE: I'll kill you. I'll shoot!

> (*Like a matador, Amilcare comes forward provokingly.*)

MIMI: Shoot, shoot, come on, Brigadier, shoot!

> (*Mimi has walked hardly two steps when the brigadier pulls his pistol from its holder and, pointing the pistol, shoots straight at Mimi's heart. The pistol fires blankly. At almost the same mo-*

ment, we hear two bangs. The brigadier is shot in the forehead and with the last famous words—

AMILCARE: But how?

—he falls down the steps quite dead.)

AMALIA: They killed him, my handsome husband, they killed him!

(Mimi's smile has frozen on his lips. He turns around to look behind him. The killer moves quickly through the crowd and hands him the still-smoking pistol.)

KILLER: It was a murder of honor, you were provoked. Don't worry.

(The man disappears as quickly as he had appeared. Amalia's shout calling for her Amilcare breaks the tense atmosphere filled with terror. Now everyone is shouting and screaming. In all this confusion Mimi comes to. Mimi starts running like a madman through the people who are moving in to take a look at the dead brigadier's body.)

MIMI: I didn't shoot, it was him, I was just joking, I didn't shoot!

(Pippino makes a quick decision.)

PIPPINO: Mimi, Mimi, we have to stop him or else no one will believe you.

> (*Bravely he rushes forward shouting. This gesture shatters centuries of the Sicilian code of silence.*)

MIMI: Murderer, murderer, stop him, stop that man!

> (*Pippino runs after the killer. Amalia is crying and shouting over her husband's body.*)

AMALIA: He killed him, killed him!

> (*In all this confusion Rosalia and Fiore have happened to be close to each other. In fact, Fiore has helped Rosalia, who had almost fainted.*)

FIORE: No, he didn't damn it, it wasn't him who shot! Everyone saw that it was that other guy . . . everyone saw it!

> (*We hear the police sirens. The confusion is undescribable. The women of the Mardocheco family hold up Uncle Cicciu under Vito's watchful eyes.*)

MIMI: I didn't shoot!
FIORE: It was the other guy!
AMALIA: Murderer!
MIMI: Holy Virgin Mary!

(On the overpass a large black Mercedes that has stopped. A few prelates have stepped out of the car to look down on the scene. They look as if they are giving their blessing. The cardinal who has just stepped out of the car has on his cheek the same three birthmarks we have seen before. Once again Mimi can hear the tune of the Italian national anthem, "Brothers of Italy." It's too much for him. He pulls his fingers through his hair in desperation.)

MIMI: Holy Mary, mother of God!

(We hear Fiore's voice reading a letter to Mimi, who is in prison.)

FIORE'S VOICE (off camera): Today little Mimi asked me what the word "honor" meant. I told him it was a very stupid thing.

SCENE 82

(Prison cell—interior—daytime. Mimi is in prison, without his mustache and without his black curls. A tiny scarf around his neck. He is reading Fiore's letter.)

FIORE'S VOICE (off camera): Just like when he plays war with his friends and then forgets that it's all make-believe and ends up hurting himself. That's why his daddy is in jail. As far as I'm concerned, things in this world go wrong because there is such a great confusion in people's heads. Think of that, darling Mimi, and you'll see that you'll have grown up by the time you get out of that dreadful place. What I mean is that you'll have become simple, like a child who understands real things. . . .

(The peephole in the door opens. Mimi looks curiously at the door. Framed in the peephole we see Tricarico, smiling and well-dressed as always.)

TRICARICO: Hey, boy . . .

(Mimi turns pale as he sees Tricarico staring at him in that paternal and hypocritical way.)

MIMI: You've come to make fun of me here as well . . . what are you doing here?

TRICARICO: I've come here on official business. You're so ungrateful, I let you have the minimum penalty. You've got your respect back, you've defended your honor. The amnesty will soon get you out. What more do you want?

MIMI: A murder doesn't cleanse my honor, it soils it! You've ruined my life!

TRICARICO: Your life is just beginning. The time is ripe, the moment has arrived to take over and I need young men who are respected, and now you are respected. When you come out of jail we'll talk about it. I'll be waiting for you.

(*Mimi turns pale as he listens.*)

MIMI: I won't come!

TRICARICO: You'll come, oh you'll come. You see, in your situation, one needs money, and you have no idea how much you'll need.

SCENE 83

(*Prison entrance—exterior—daytime. The entrance to the prison flies open and Mimi walks out, gazing skyward in the classical way. After a few moments he smiles. He sees her. Fiore and Mimi II are waiting for him. Mimi also sees something which doesn't make him smile quite as much. Rosalia and Amilcare II are also waiting. A third thing makes Mimi almost faint. Amalia with her brood. Six of them now are waiting for him. Mimi is really quite pale. The three mothers let their children go. The children race toward their father screaming.*)

CHILDREN: Daddy! Daddy! Daddy!

(*Mimi looks at the charge of infants with fear. Mimi II is the first to arrive and jumps on his father's neck. The child has hardly time to kiss him before the rest of the children reach them. Behind them the mothers come forward. The children surround Mimi, all shouting out his name. Mimi bangs on the prison door, pointlessly trying to seek refuge from the onslaught of women and children.*)

SCENE 84

> *(Streets of Sicily—exterior—daytime. The same black car we saw at the beginning of our story. The same sequence of events. The only difference is that the face on the pamphlets is Salvatore Tricarico's and the man with the megaphone is Mimi.)*

MIMI: Workers, vote for Salvatore Tricarico . . . for a pleasant future without purse-snatchings and strikes! A future of order and well-being. Vote for Salvatore Tricarico!

> *(Shouting his message through the megaphone, Mimi suddenly freezes. Among the blue and green plastic containers on the cart we see Pippino, Mimi II and Fiore, who are looking at him. Mimi feels himself melting into a pool of shame. The faces of his friends and family, so disappointed in him, are worse than a blow to the gut. Behind him another voice through another megaphone is shouting its message.)*

VOICE (through loud megaphone): Workers, vote for Salvatore Tricarico! Tricarico is your candidate for the future! It means loyalty and honesty! For a future of well-being, vote Tricarico!

> *(Fiore nods at Mimi. Mimi is sweating, he has a stomach ache, but he manages to gather enough courage to walk up to the cart. Fiore nods again. With a sigh, Pippino puts the cart into gear and takes off. Mimi tries to stop them.)*

MIMI: Wait! I can explain everything! I didn't want to, I can explain, Fiore!

(He runs after the cart, almost as if his life depended on whether or not he catches up with it. The cart, with its blue and green plastic containers and the sad pale faces, gets farther and farther away.)

MIMI: Fiore, Fiore, don't leave me! I didn't want to! I believed in a better world! I believed in a different world as well! They're all cousins. You don't know this but, they're all cousins! Wait for me! It wasn't my fault, don't leave me Fiore!

(Mimi can't catch up with them. He continues to run after them anyhow, through the white valley which in some way could very well be the Valley of Jehoshaphat. Music from La Traviata.*)*

FINALE: "And everything ended."

2

LOVE AND ANARCHY

LOVE AND ANARCHY

CAST

Tunin	Giancarlo Gianinni
Salomé	Mariangela Melato
Tripolina	Lina Polito
Spatoletti	Eros Pagni
Madame Aida	Pina Cei
Donna Carmela	Elena Fiore

CREDITS

Written and Directed by	Lina Wertmüller
Photography	Giuseppe Rotunno
Sets and Costumes	Enrico Job
Editor	Franco Fraticelli
Sound	Mario Bramonti
Music	Nino Rota
American Editor and Creative Supervisor	Fima Noveck

Running time: 108 minutes

The first American showing of LOVE AND ANARCHY was on April 14, 1974 at the Little Carnegie Cinema in New York City.

SCENE 1

*(Rice fields and surrounding countryside—exterior—day. Pan-
oramic shot showing a cross-section of the open country in Lom-
bardy. The land is radiant in spite of the light fog which envelops it.)*

SONG:
"Oh where are you going, my darling Tunin? . . .
"One morning, Tunin went off to war,
"But there was no war to be found.
"The people cried out,
" 'But that young boy is crazy!'
"Oh no, Tunin isn't crazy at all."

*(Along the path bordered by tall grass a figure is seen running.
When it gets closer, we see the face of Michele Sgarravento, an
old, strong, and noble peasant. A wonderful open face, smiling
and full of life. He thumbs his nose.)*

SONG (cont.):
"When the clouds chase one another
"The years go gently by,
"Then fly and fly, across the open sky. . . ."

*(Michele continues on his merry way in the midst of the beauti-
ful foggy and ancient countryside.)*

SONG (cont.):
"On Sundays the whole world dances, maybe
"It is useless
"To go and fight wars like Tunin."

(The title Love and Anarchy *appears on the screen, the open
countryside is used as backdrop.)*

SCENE 2

*(Trees and bushes in a rice field—exterior—daytime. Michele
Sgarravento is seen stuck between the branches of a tree. Like a
grotesque puppet, limp and quite dead. The morning is cold and
gray. The countryside is still enveloped by the fog. There is a
feeling of indifference and tragedy in the air. A few youths,
some hunters, some policemen, and amongst them we see Tunin,*

who can't take his eyes off Michele's face. There is a mysterious look in the dead man's half-open pale-blue eyes and his mouth is frozen in a teasing grin.)

SCENE 3

(A farmhouse—interior—nighttime. One evening the young child Tunin smiles at his mother.)

TUNIN (as a young child): Mommy, what is an anarchist?
TUNIN'S MOTHER: Oh, he is one of those terrible men who kills kings and queens, throws bombs and is then hung for doing it. Now shut your mouth.

(On a different evening, as young Tunin is sitting on his chamber pot, he listens carefully to the grownups talking. In the adjoining room his father is discussing politics with Michele Sgarravento in front of an open fire.)

TUNIN'S FATHER: What we need is socialism! Screw anarchism—that only leads to the gallows.
MICHELE: Yes, people will have to die on the gallows but we must reach our ultimate goal. There we will be at peace with one another, sharing, in harmony. We were created as equals, and we must therefore live as equals.

SCENE 4

(Farmhouse courtyard—exterior—daytime. Tunin is by now a grown man. He is seen feeding chickens inside their coop. He turns, smiles, and thumbs his nose, which has now become his welcoming sign. We see old Michele in the spacious courtyard cluttered by bales of hay. Michele gives Tunin a valise, which he in turn hides under one of the bales. The two of them sit down, and this is a scene of happiness and great friendship. Michele laughs.)

MICHELE: I've returned to knock off Mussolini.

(There is no hint of hate or violence in his soft voice. It almost sounds as if this is one of Michele's usual pranks. Then, as if to confirm that it is a prank, he makes his playful thumbing gesture. In the middle of the courtyard Michele starts improvising

*dance steps and wild leaps among the geese and other animals.
Still laughing, Michele walks away.)*

SCENE 5

*(Trees and bushes in the rice field—exterior—daytime. Now,
merry Michele is hanging like a motionless puppet from the
branches.)*

SONG: "The years go by . . . they fly away . . ."

(Lowering his head, Tunin walks on the grassy path.)

SCENE 6

*(Rome—exterior—daytime. A series of shots of Rome; a power-
ful, imperial, and Fascist Rome. A band plays in the back-
ground extremely loud. The band plays a Fascist march, "All
Hail, Country of Heroes." Shot of the Victor Emanuel monument enormous and impressive with all its shiny columns.
Statues of heroes and of martyrs, of angels bearing wreaths.
These are the symbols of everlasting glory. We move now to one
of the more bourgeois sections of Rome.)*

SCENE 7

*(Via dei Fiori—a street—exterior—daytime. Via dei Fiori is a
tiny street in the old section of Rome, at the end of which there
is a gigantic statue of flowers, which gives the street its name.
Tunin is walking down the street with his suitcase.)*

SCENE 8

*(Brothel doorway—interior—daytime. A light filters through the
decorative design on the colorful, multifaceted glass door. It's a
warm, sunny day. Summer is in the air. Tunin sweats profusely
as he stands in the doorway in his high-rimmed hat and gray
suit. Close by, Zoraide is polishing the colorful tiles in the marble hallway. Beside her is a miniature white poodle inside a
small box. Zoraide stands up and moves farther along the hall.)*

ZORAIDE (sings): "Oh darling, darling . . ."

(Passing by Tunin, she turns to him brusquely.)

ZORAIDE: Young man, we're closed . . . this is a first-class joint, you know? We open at eleven and that's all there is to it. . . . (She sings) ". . . bring me a bunch of roses . . . oh, bring me a lot more . . . be sure to pick the thorniest ones . . ."

(Tunin hasn't quite followed what she's been saying and he remains still.)

SCENE 8B

(Brothel sitting room—interior—daytime. In the sitting room Odette, in full livery, is dusting the furniture. Zoraide turns to her rudely.)

ZORAIDE: Hey you, go get the rooms done up. . . . (She sings) "I'll hold them to my bosom . . ."

(Zoraide walks into the grand waiting room. All around the room are benches where the customers can sit and wait for the whore of their choice.)

ZORAIDE: You've got to be deaf . . . I said we're closed until eleven. No use you insisting. Shit, are you ugly! Where the hell did you come from, anyway? Have you got any money? This is a first-class place and it's expensive, you know, a fuck'll cost you seven lire.

(Zoraide laughs as she looks at this poor, helpless, silent peasant.)

ZORAIDE: Are you scared? Did your cock shrivel up?
LOREDANA (off frame): Odette! Odette!

(She appears at the top of the stairs and then races down half-naked.)

LOREDANA: Odette!
ODETTE: I'm here.
LOREDANA: Odette! Where the hell's the clean linen? I've been looking for it for the past hour! Where the hell are you when I need you . . . damn it!

(Loredana vanishes.)

ODETTE: Holy Mother of God . . . they never find a damn thing in this place.

(She also walks off, leaving Tunin alone with Zoraide.)

ZORAIDE: Look, if you want to get your rocks off so badly, why don't you go to La Pace or the Pellegrino where you can get fucked for a lot less. Let me give you some advice—instead of getting laid, why don't you just jerk off right here? You'll enjoy it and you'll save some money.

(Zoraide laughs heartily. Tunin probably hasn't understood a word of Zoraide's broad Roman slang.)

TUNIN: Actually, I'm looking for Miss Salomé.
ZORAIDE: Ah, shit!
TUNIN: I'm a relative of hers.

SCENE 9

(Staircase and brothel waiting room—interior—day. Like a whirlwind, Salomé glides down the staircase enveloped by veils, wearing an embroidered dressing gown, slippers, and nightdress. Her blond hair is up in rollers, her make-up is a mess.)

SALOMÉ: Where the hell is he, then? . . . Damn it, Zoraide, you're a real jerk to wax these stairs, one of these days someone's going to fall and bust his ass . . . where is he, then?

(*Salomé enters the waiting room running.*)

SALOMÉ: Can this be my cousin? Oh my Lord how you've grown! And what a handsome lad you've become! It's about time you came to see me, you know!

(*Tunin blushes with embarrassment. Salomé is really overpowering. She envelops him in her perfumed veils and hugs him.*)

SALOMÉ: Sorry, I can't give you a kiss but I'm covered with all this beauty cream . . . don't I have a handsome cousin, Zoraide? And how is Aunty? She's well? Do her varicose veins still give her trouble? Come upstairs so we can chat comfortably, and Zoraide, please tell madame that I can't work this morning, I have relatives visiting.

(*Tunin is pushed up the stairs where so many others have walked before him. The maid looks at the two with an angered expression. Tunin is still blushing. For him the* Thousand and One Arabian Nights *have become a reality. They are no longer a fantasy.*)

SALOMÉ: My room is a den full of mirrors; the finest in the "house." Really, it's like a scene from the *Thousand and One Nights.* People refer to me as "the great lay in Madera." . . .Oh, I don't know if I'm that good . . . anyhow, follow me.

SCENE 10

(*Brothel, upstairs corridor—interior—daytime. Salomé continues to talk as she leads Tunin, her voice echoing down the corridor. Tunin looks around at the great opulence of the marble tiles, statues, and paintings.*)

SALOMÉ: Look, look at those beauties. You know something, this is the fanciest whorehouse in town.

(*Tunin has been unable to react for a while. Suddenly an aggressive voice blocks their path.*)

CARMELA: Who the fuck's this piece of shit?
SALOMÉ: Shut up, he's a relative. Tunin, let me introduce Carmela, the house watchdog.

TUNIN: Morning.

(Salomé proceeds down the long hall as Carmela continues to shout after her.)

CARMELA: Good morning my ass! My *dear* madame, who the fuck do you think you are? Who the hell is going to do the morning shift?
SALOMÉ (out of scene): Oh, shut up! I'll ask Yvonne to do it.
CARMELA: Bullshit!
SALOMÉ: Look, for God's sake, my cousin arrived this morning. Give us some time to be alone, won't you?
CARMELA: Cousin? Cousin my ass! That creep's just come here for a free fuck.

(Tunin and Salomé continue down the hallway.)

SALOMÉ: Hold on a minute, I'm going to ask my friend for a favor.

(She knocks on a door.)

SALOMÉ: Yvonne! Yvonne! Bah, listen to her, she's snoring like a trooper. Yvonne!

(The door next to Yvonne's opens and we see a tiny head belonging to a petite brunette with enormous black eyes and close-cropped hair. She is pale and sleepy and has a strong Sicilian accent.)

JACQUELINE: What the hell are you shouting for, you cunt!

(Salomé turns around slowly and replies sweetly.)

SALOMÉ: I apologize, dear baroness, but you know, I just have no control over my voice. Christ, it's so hoarse!
JACQUELINE: Damn it! Sleep is sacred; you should never disturb someone when they're asleep.
SALOMÉ: All right, all right, I'm sorry, now hold your horses, let me introduce my cousin to you.

(Tunin looks away quite embarrassed. Jacqueline gives him a polite smile.)

JACQUELINE: *Enchanté* . . .

(Finally Yvonne's door opens and she appears half-naked.)

YVONNE: What the hell do you want?
SALOMÉ: Look, I'm terribly sorry to disturb you, but my cousin has

just arrived from the country and I was hoping you would take over the morning shift for me. . . . Now, let me introduce my cousin, this is Mrs. Yvonne.

TUNIN: Good morning.

YVONNE: Good morning to you too. Okay, so your cousin has arrived. All that means is that I get screwed by having to take over your shift. Damn!

SALOMÉ: Oh, come on, stop being such a pain!

YVONNE: Yeah, it's all very well for you to talk.

> (*Salomé is well on her way down the corridor. Yvonne walks off in the opposite direction singing "La Petite Tonkinoise" to herself. Tunin is unable to resist the urge to look back at those rounded buttocks as they sway down the corridor. He's totally absorbed by the sight and is unable to move.*)

SALOMÉ (off camera): You going to stand there all day?

SCENE 11

> (*Salomé's bedroom—interior—daytime. Salomé walks into her room, which is covered in oval mirrors.*)

SALOMÉ: Come on in, then, make yourself at home.

> (*Tunin is standing in the doorway. He is nearly trampled by one of the "girls," who is seen pirouetting down the hallway.*)

MARIANNA (singing): "It's the witching hour and Marianna is off with her fireman . . ." Ooops! Sorry. (She gives him a playful wink.)

SALOMÉ: Leave him be, you cheap slut! . . . Ah, shit, look at all this junk lying on the bed. Come in, come on in. Remember, this is like home for you. Relax . . . be comfortable.

> (*Tunin enters the room cautiously, his suitcase in hand. The room is a mess.*)

SALOMÉ: Sorry if I introduced you as my cousin, but that way they'll leave us alone.

> (*Anita can be heard singing at the top of her lungs.*)

SALOMÉ: Shut the door.

> (*Tunin obeys without saying a word.*)

SALOMÉ: Those dumb bitches are always walking up and down the hallway.

(*Salomé's expression has changed. Her vulgar, whorelike look has given way to one of warmth and gentleness.*)

SALOMÉ: So then, you're Antonio Soffiantini, better known as Tunin? I'm Salomé—and I'm so glad to meet you.

(*Salomé stretches out her hand, which Tunin shakes without uttering a sound.*)

SALOMÉ: Did you have a nice trip?

(*Tunin nods.*)

SALOMÉ: Marvelous! Now, why don't you just make yourself comfy.

(*Salomé leads him over to the couch. His apparent disinterest in Salomé's enthusiasm is in fact nothing but sheer embarrassment at the whole situation.*)

SALOMÉ: Look at this, we live like tramps! The help hasn't even cleaned up my room yet.

(*Salomé tidies up the couch as best she can, then notices the portable bidet is in full view. She moves it away.*)

SALOMÉ: Now you can sit down comfortably.
SALOMÉ: How about a nice cup of coffee?

(*She opens the door and Anita can still be heard singing. Salomé shouts.*)

SALOMÉ: Odette! Two coffees in room nine! Immediately!

(*She shuts the door and goes to sit down in front of Tunin. She now appears to have a simple air about her, so different from the hard mask she must wear in her business.*)

SALOMÉ: So, then, the information has been confirmed. Everything is ready . . . Wednesday, July eighth, it's the definite date. On Sunday we'll go take a good look at the place.

(*Salomé pulls out her curlers.*)

SALOMÉ: Now listen carefully. In my letter to our comrades I gave a description of the windows that face directly onto the square. I'm telling you this in case you would prefer to use a gun.

(Tunin just barely shakes his head.)

TUNIN: No, no, that's all right. I'm not used to guns and I don't trust a pistol.

SCENE 12

(Upstairs corridor in the brothel—interior—daytime. Odette, whose real name is Filumena and who was born near Cosenza, in the deepest southern part of Italy, is the chambermaid. According to Madame Aida, the proprietor, a name, like the white apron and bonnet, is of the utmost importance to add class to a brothel. Madame is very particular in her desires to add class and distinction to her "house," especially in the upper floors. Odette is seen carrying Salomé's coffee down the corridor. Her path crosses with Yvonne and Lisa, who are on their way downstairs for the morning shift. It is apparent that the two don't like one another.)

LISA (singing):
   "The more you touch it,
   "The more you stroke it,
   "The harder it gets,
   "And the longer it grows . . ."

YVONNE (annoyed): Sing! You can't sing, you have no idea how to sing, you stupid ugly slut. Leave me alone! Who the fuck do you think you are?

(The two start pushing one another down the hall, passing by Odette, who gives them a filthy look.)

LISA: Oh, go to hell!

YVONNE: Good God, if someone doesn't give her a good stiff cock she's going to crack up one of these days.

LISA: Ah, shit, who would ever touch that ugly bitch?

(Jacqueline, looking pale and sleepy, appears in the doorway.)

JACQUELINE: Shut up, you noisy bitches. (Turning to Odette) Coffee!

(Disgusted, Odette ignores her and moves on.)

ODETTE: You are a disgrace to our land. I won't serve you a thing, you cheap slut!

SCENE 13

(Salomé's room—interior—daytime. Tunin is sitting on the couch in front of Salomé. He still has an embarrassed look but she is more and more relaxed and friendly.)

SALOMÉ: Come in, Odette. Ah, at last the coffee is here. My mouth feels like the bottom of a latrine. That's what happens if I don't have my early morning coffee. . . . Have you seen Madame Aida?
ODETTE: No, but Madame Carmela is already seated on her throne down in the sitting room. Want me to tell her something?
SALOMÉ: No, let sleeping dogs lie. But if she asks, tell her I have people in my room. In other words, tell her not to bother me.

(Odette gives Tunin a suspicious look. Salomé notices it.)

SALOMÉ: Well, what are you staring at? He's my cousin. I could be his aunt. Jesus Christ, these spying bitches are always thinking bad things. Fuck off, you dumb broad—and shut the door!

(Odette slams the door as Salomé is sugaring the coffee.)

SALOMÉ: One or two lumps?
TUNIN: Two, thanks.

(Salomé hands him the cup.)

SALOMÉ: Well, we've told one another more or less everything there is to be said. The information should be accurate . . . my trade consists mainly of officers, fascist officials and the like. All a bunch of vain pigs who love to talk about their parades and gatherings. May they burn in hell. If only you knew what pigs they were. . . . Mmm! Good luck!

(Salomé toasts Tunin with her cup.)

SALOMÉ: To the eighth of July.

(Tunin gives her a furtive look. They toast each other.)

TUNIN: The eighth of July!
SALOMÉ: Well, then, did you really come from Paris? Mmm, if it's a secret you'd better not tell me.
TUNIN: In these cases, the less said the better.
SALOMÉ: Let's hope to God we can go back there one day. Shit, I don't know why I do these things. You people are all insane. . . . Per-

sonally I hate those people who say those nice things but then turn this world into the pile of shit that it is now. What about you? Isn't it all the same to you? You're so young; what makes you do this?

> (*Tunin looks at her breasts, which are protruding from her nightgown. Her legs are like alabaster.*)

TUNIN: Tyrants make me sick.

> (*His cup shakes violently. He is unable to take his eyes off those legs, which are now almost totally uncovered. Salomé follows his look. She's known men's weaknesses for too long not to know what's going through his mind. That look, the blushing, the shaking cup and saucer. It's all so familiar to her. She wants to laugh, then lights up two cigarettes.*)

SALOMÉ: Tell me the truth, Tunin, it isn't tyrants you are thinking about right now . . . what are you looking at?
TUNIN: Oh nothing, well . . . shit!
SALOMÉ: It's my thighs, that's what you're looking at like a hungry child. I can't stand to look at those starving eyes . . . haven't you ever been in a brothel?

> (*Tunin smokes nervously.*)

TUNIN: When I was in Cuneo during my military service there were some girls under the bridges, but never in a proper brothel! Never, not even in Paris—there I had more to do.
SALOMÉ: Poor boy! You could have told me before, instead of sitting there like a hungry kitten . . . just think!

> (*Salomé gives him a warm smile and unfastens her dressing gown. The dressing gown and nightdress float by his eyes and Tunin is glued to his seat.*)

SALOMÉ (Continued, off camera): What we really need is a good fuck. It's a great honor for me to introduce you to these pleasures; it might even bring us luck. Come on then, move your ass, let's get down to it, or do I have to beg you?

> (*She is lying sensually on the bed; we see her reflection in the oval mirrors.*)

SALOMÉ: If you'd rather not, it's all the same to me.

> (*Tunin is very embarrassed.*)

TUNIN: Well, it's just that I must settle into a hotel and find a room. Perhaps later, if it's not any trouble. Thanks again.

(Tunin gets up to go. Salomé lies on the bed, fanning herself provocatively.)

SALOMÉ: Oh, of course. We can always find a moment. You be sure to tell me when you're ready. Okay?

(Tunin thanks her again.)

SALOMÉ: By the way, the Margherita Hotel is around the corner. I booked a room for you.
TUNIN: That was very kind of you.

(He puts his hat on, picks up his case, and heads for the door.)

SALOMÉ (off camera): Manziana Street, it's the first on the right as you go out the front door. And once again, if you need anything, you'll let me know, won't you?
TUNIN: Thanks, thanks again.
SALOMÉ: Once you're settled down, you can come back for lunch.

(Tunin opens the door.)

TUNIN: Thanks.
SALOMÉ: I'll be waiting for you.
TUNIN: On second thought . . .
SALOMÉ: Pardon?

(He approaches the bed.)

TUNIN: I can always settle in later on, as long as it's still the same for you?

(She continues to fan herself.)

SALOMÉ: But of course! I told you, one needs a little pleasure in life. With all these girls running around you've got to do something to take your mind off them.
TUNIN (nodding): You're quite right, thanks.

(He puts down his suitcase and hangs up his hat.)

SALOMÉ: Come on, then . . .

(Throwing back the sheets, she makes room for him.)

SCENE 14

(Salomé's room—interior—daytime. Panoramic shot of the bedroom. We hear Salomé talking to Tunin. Pillows, bottles, dolls, and pin cushions are strewn around the room. There are fake flowers and colored glass as well.)

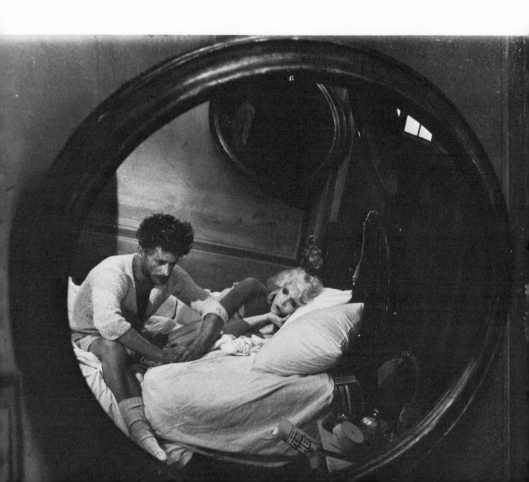

SALOMÉ (off camera): I'm talking about Anteo Zamboni, the fellow accused of the attempted murder of Mussolini in Bologna.

TUNIN (off camera): You were there as well?

SALOMÉ: Yes, we were together but we had nothing to do with it. There we were in Via Rizzoli, it couldn't have been later than five-thirty, as Mussolini's car drove by during the parade. He was standing up, surrounded by all those "black shirts."

> (*The camera now pans onto Salomé's and Tunin's reflections in the oval mirrors. They are lying in bed staring blankly into space.*)

SALOMÉ: Suddenly there was this loud gunshot, so loud I can still hear it. A man in his thirties, the guy who had actually fired the shot, threw a pistol at Anteo's feet and started shouting, "Murderer, he did it, he's the one!" then he disappeared into thin air. Cowardly bastard! If I live to be a hundred I won't forget his face. Anteo just stood there, hair in his eyes, a few pimples still covering his boyish face, Christ he was like a child—he *was* a child, he was only fifteen! Without the strength to cry out, to ask for help, to say he hadn't done it, he just stared at me with imploring eyes. In the meantime those wild beasts were all over him, beating him up, fists flying in all directions.

> (*Salomé's eyes fill with tears.*)

SALOMÉ: I don't want to go on! Those bastards tore him apart! The beatings were so vicious that even Balbo, yes, Balbo, that cold son of a bitch, threw up when he saw what they had done to him. Then, just to make sure he was to end up on the gallows, they made up more and more lies about things he had never done, then they wiped out his entire family.

TUNIN: Why? What did they do to them?

SALOMÉ: Mamolo Zamboni, Anteo's father, and his sister, Virginia Tabaroni, were ex-anarchists . . . and now they'll rot in jail for the next thirty years. No one will ever know if they are dead or alive. Anteo's mother died last year in an insane asylum, and you can believe me, she's still a lot better off like that. As for me—well—I was Anteo's girl . . . but I had to leave. . . . I changed my name and now here I am.

> (*Tunin remains still. Salomé gets up, throws a sheet around her naked body, and goes behind the screen.*)

SALOMÉ: Yes, here to play the role of Salomé, but mainly to feed you, to prepare you for the eighth of July. You see, I swore to myself

and to those imploring eyes that someone was going to pay. That pig must die!

> (*Salomé starts crying. She starts washing herself behind the screen.*)

SALOMÉ: Words are quite pointless. (She sings angrily.)
"I'm singing for myself, I sing to the moon and the stars,
"I'm singing with anger, I'm angry with you. . . ."

> (*Tunin is dazed.*)

SCENE 15

> (*Brothel dining room—interior—daytime. The girls are all gathered around the table for lunch. There are about fifteen of them, all in their dressing gowns. Madame Aida sits at one end of the table with Carmela on her right and Maurizia on her left. At the opposite end is Tunin, Salomé on his right and Isa on his left. Salomé is acting overprotectively toward Tunin, as if to shield him from the other girls' clutches.*)

SALOMÉ: Eat up, Tunin, a strong young man like you who has just come from the country needs to eat well! . . . And oh, Madame Aida, thank you *so* much for letting him stay for lunch. It would have been a shame to have him eat alone in a restaurant.

> (*Madame Aida gives a condescending smile. The scene is cheerful and the girls add color and life with their laughter and outrageous outfits.*)

SALOMÉ: Madame, thank you so much.
JACQUELINE: Madame, this egg isn't fresh!

> (*Madame Aida raises her eyebrows.*)

MADAME AIDA: My eggs come straight from a farm the very day they're laid!
JACQUELINE: The very day, my ass! The chick is nearly hatched!

> (*Madame Aida is rather irritated by the girls' laughter.*)

MADAME AIDA: I didn't understand what she said.

> (*A buxom brunette with catlike features tries to interpret Jacqueline's accent for Madame.*)

THE CAT: She said that the chick will hatch any minute now . . . meaning that . . .

MADAME AIDA: Veeeery funny. . . . . *She's* the one who's got chicks hatching in her head.

> (*Madame Aida taps herself on the head, then turns to Tunin and asks for his opinion.*)

MADAME AIDA: In this house, nothing but the very finest foods are served.

LOLA: Oh, crap! When you think that in Florence, at Madame Saffo's "house," Miss Valeria had a cook specially brought in from Paris to make her girls happy.

MADAME AIDA: Valeria? Mmmm. Sounds fishy to me. . . . By the way, the cook's name wouldn't be René by any chance?

LOLA: Yes, why? Do you know him?

MADAME AIDA: Work in the kitchen? Shit! He works in the bedroom, Valeria's bedroom! She makes sure she gets good service for the money she pays him. That woman is no fool.

YVONNE: In Turin, there's a "house" in Fratelli Calandra Street where the food is out of this world.

> (*Madame Aida interrupts once again and turns to Tunin.*)

MADAME AIDA: No, no, no, this is the house where you eat best of all! Don't you agree, young man?

> (*Tunin doesn't know what to say. He's had no past experience in such matters. With his mouth full he tries to sound knowledgeable.*)

TUNIN: As a matter of fact, I find the food delicious and it certainly is plentiful.

SALOMÉ: Bah! It has the same culinary standards as an army mess!

> (*Very loud laughter. Madame Aida and Carmela are not amused.*)

MADAME AIDA: You've got the sense of humor of a retarded pygmy!

CARMELA: Our ladies are just so delicate, poor dears!

> (*The laughter continues, but Madame Aida continues talking as if oblivious to what is going on around her.*)

MADAME AIDA: Just think how ungrateful these women are, young man. On Sundays I even let them go out and buy a sherbert at Faraglia's store!

SALOMÉ: If you listen to what Madame says you'll end up believing the food here is better than that at the Danieli in Venice.

YVONNE: Oh, don't bring back memories of the Danieli. I used to hold court there—the Danieli was my kingdom.

SALOMÉ: Yeh, I'll bet you were the queen of the dishwashers!

YVONNE: I hope you get breast cancer, you cunt!

SALOMÉ: Here's hoping it'll strike *you!*

YVONNE: Monsieur Tunin, I have absolutely nothing in common with these cheap sluts! I am a real artist. You want to know what they called me back in my cabaret days? They called me the Josephine Baker of Italy, can you imagine?

(*More laughter from the girls. It's clear that the Josephine Baker story has been heard time and time again. The girls tease Yvonne.*)

YVONNE: Silence, you whores! what do you know of my past life! When I walked on the stage in my silver lamé gown and feather boa, royalty would stand up for me. I was a great singer, Monsieur Tunin.

LOLA: Oh, no, she's going to start singing now!

YVONNE: Why not? Listen, monsieur, my voice is still very good.

(*In a pathetic, scratchy voice, Yvonne starts singing a song in Josephine Baker's repertoire.*)

YVONNE: "C'est l'heure de mon champagne . . ."

(*The girls roll over with laughter and make terrible noises. They tease her and call her names. Yvonne takes the whole thing terribly seriously and is offended.*)

YVONNE: You shits!

SALOMÉ: She just hasn't been the same since she got a dose of the clap!

(*More laughter. There's no stopping Yvonne.*)

YVONNE: (singing): "C'est l'heure de mon champagne . . ."

SALOMÉ: You stupid bitch, don't you think we can sing just as well as you can?

(*She starts singing and the girls all join in.*)

CHORUS OF GIRLS:
"We are like little fireflies,
We live in total darkness . . ."

(Yvonne stops singing and shouts to Salomé.)

YVONNE: Shit-face!
SALOMÉ: Dumb ass!
CHORUS:
". . . slaves of a cruel world,
"We are the flowers of evil . . ."
CARMELA: Oh, screw the whole bunch of you!
JACQUELINE: How they shout! Oh, they're so loud! I'm going to end up with a migraine!

(Madame Aida gives the girls a filthy look. Tunin sits very embarrassed in the middle of these wild females.)

TRIPOLINA: Come, come, Yvonne, you'll give the Baroness a migraine!
LOLA: Baroness! Oh, Baroness, you're the Baroness de La Cunt!

(The girls love Lola's last remark and they stop singing. Madame Aida stands up and addresses them in an angry voice.)

MADAME AIDA: Let's cut it out! Where the hell do you think you are?
SALOMÉ: I believe we're in a whorehouse, Madame.

(Even the sour-faced Carmela breaks down and laughs. Madame, however, doesn't find it amusing in the least.)

MADAME AIDA: No, my dear girls, this is not a whorehouse, this is an exclusive brothel. Whoever doesn't see the distinction between the two can just pack her bags and go.

(Madame leaves the room with her head held high. Maurizia gets up to follow her.)

MAURIZIA: She's right—you know?

(Silence reigns in the dining room. At last Salomé stands up and slaps her ass offensively, pointing it in Madame's direction.)

SALOMÉ: Up yours!

(*Carmela is second in command in the house and she reacts angrily.*)

CARMELA: Ooohhh!

(*Salomé isn't in the least bit worried.*)

SALOMÉ: You can go right ahead and tell her, I don't give a shit.
CARMELA: You're really beginning to break my balls! I *am* going to tell her!

(*The girls start leaving the table.*)

SALOMÉ: Oh, go tell her, you virgin whore! (Turning to Tunin) Eat, eat and don't look at this scum of the earth.

(*As the help begins to clear the table the girls start roaming around the dining area and the adjoining room. Tunin keeps on eating in silence. Isa starts strumming a guitar and singing. Yvonne spitefully hands Salomé a magazine.*)

YVONNE: So this is where Miss Jean Harlow over here copied her hairdo!

(Salomé ignores her and throws the magazine across the room.)

YVONNE: Go get stuffed, and I hope it bleeds!

(Isa sings an old Neapolitan song.)

ISA:
"I went and planted a small tree.
"I looked after it so lovingly,
"But one day a harsh wind came and blew it down
"And now all the leaves have changed color . . ."

(Isa continues to sing with passion. Yvonne, nearby, openly disapproves of her singing.)

YVONNE: Lord, now she's going to start with this sentimental crap . . . shit, these Southerners are such a pain in the balls.
ISA (continues song):
". . . All the fruit fell off their branches and those sweet
"Fruits have now turned sour.
"And to you, my young lovers, I say:
"Love is a difficult thing to attain, the path is long and bitter . . ."
YVONNE: These peasants all fancy themselves great singers. If only they could hear themselves!
ISA (continues song):
"Even though it's long and bitter,
"I love you just the same, oh yes, I do . . ."

(Tripolina sits on a chair, which she leans against the tiled wall.)

TRIPOLINA: What a pretty song, I love it!

(Salomé approves of the performance as well.)

SALOMÉ: Go on, sing us another, we've got plenty of time.

(Tunin is still seated at the table, which by now has been totally cleared. He is eating his fruit. Isa hands the guitar over to Loredana, who is sitting beside her.)

ISA: You know what you should sing? "Maremma."
TRIPOLINA: Yes, that's so lovely, it's so romantic.
SALOMÉ: Go on, then, sing!
ISA: Pick up the guitar, Loredana, let's start.

LOREDANA:

"How I am suffering, suffering, suffering,

"My heart is breaking . . .

"Oh, I am going to kill myself because you are dead and gone,

"And I know not what I'm going to do . . .

"How I am suffering . . ."

(The other girls keep on talking and wandering around. The magazine has ended up in Lola's hands.)

LOLA: Douglas Fairbanks!

YVONNE: Heavens! As far as I'm concerned there's nowhere like Paris! These Neapolitan songs really bother me, they're so provincial.

LOREDANA (singing):

"I'm nothing but a lost sheep

"That has strayed away from its fold.

"The watchdog is starving to death, and one of these days

"He's going to turn on me. . . . Oh, I'm so desperate,

"My heart is breaking . . ."

(Throughout the whole song Tripolina has been staring at Tunin. He notices it and eats his pear rather nervously. A firm rapport is established between the two by the series of intense, meaningful glances. Salomé notices these looks and doesn't appear to be too happy.)

LOREDANA:

". . . I am so desperate, oh, how I'm so desperate

"And my heart is breaking . . ."

(Zoraide walks into the sitting room.)

ZORAIDE: Miss Salomé! You're wanted on the phone!

(Salomé gets up hurriedly and turns to Tunin.)

SALOMÉ: Come on, then, it's probably your father.

(The girls continue to sing. One of them gets up and performs a few classical dance steps.)

SCENE 16

(Corridor and sitting room on the ground floor—interior—daytime. Salomé is on the phone, speaking seductively.)

SALOMÉ: Oh, you dirty old man, cut it out, we're on the phone . . . mmm, yes. . . . Look, cutie, I just don't know, because Sunday is my only day off. . . . What? No! I said day of rest. . . . Now, stop that dirty talk . . . O.K. . . . but only if you promise to behave. Oh, by the way, my cousin is in town and he's acting as if he were Alice in Wonderland, so there's no way that I'm going to leave him here.

> (*Tunin waits beneath an enormous painting of a naked woman while Salomé is talking. The girls start trickling downstairs for the afternoon shift.*)

SALOMÉ: No, I just can't! Well, I'll just have to ask Tripolina along. Yes, fine, it's settled. . . . Pardon? Ugh, you pig!

> (*She hangs up and goes over to Tunin. Her voice has changed.*)

SALOMÉ: Jesus, I've done it! You know who that was? Spatoletti himself. We're going to have a look at the place tomorrow.

> (*Tunin has an annoyed expression.*)

TUNIN: Well, who the hell is Spatoletti?
SALOMÉ: You're joking, aren't you? He's the person who places the

secret service agents around the square for Mussolini's protection. I've been working on this pig for three months. He was one of the original members of the Fascist Party.

SCENE 17

(*A country road cutting across open fields—exterior—daytime. A square-jawed, helmeted Spatoletti drives his powerful motorcycle through the countryside. He is wearing enormous goggles. The music is an excerpt from Rossini's* The Silk Staircase. *Tunin is sitting uncomfortably behind Spatoletti, hanging on to his hat. Salomé and Tripolina are in the sidecar. Salomé is wearing a fox-collared coat and a beret that covers one eye. Tripolina has on her Sunday-best and wears a charming, gay, straw hat. It's a beautiful, warm spring day. The motorcycle races across the countryside. As they pass an expensive-looking sports car, probably belonging to a Fascist official, Spatoletti raises his right fist in the fascist salute.*)

SCENE 18

(*A modern building complex incorporating a church—exterior— daytime. An oversized church built in the 1930s style stands in the sun-drenched square. The frescoes and mosaics are all contemporary and depict scenes of Mussolini sowing the fields along with the farmers. The powerful marble statues of warriors and*

gymnasts stand proudly beneath the blue sky. In the surrounding countryside there is a feeling of negligence and antiquity contrasting with the modernity of the buildings. This contrast creates a surrealistic atmosphere which was perhaps the very same that inspired the artists De Chirico and Savinio in creating their works of art. As the other three wait on the motorcycle, Spatoletti gives orders to the secret agents.)

SCENE 19

(A country road and an inn—exterior—daytime. Spatoletti is seen driving his motorcycle, ranting and raving in a pronounced Tuscan accent which establishes a connection between him and the dreaded Tamburini Regiment, the original fascist group. Salomé listens with apparent interest, occasionally giving Tunin a long-suffering look.)

SALOMÉ: You left us baking in the sun, what do you think we are! . . . Anyway, listen—there are going to be so many people in that square that we won't be able to see a fucking thing. It's a shame because I would have *loved* to have caught a glimpse of Mussolini.
SPATOLETTI: Be still, be good my tasty dish, Spatoletti will find you a place in the royal box.
SALOMÉ: That doesn't matter, I want to be next to you or at least beside one of those secret agents. If they really are secret they could use a lady next to them to make their cover look more convincing. Are you certain these agents are really there?
SPATOLETTI: Of course they're there, all thirty-five of them, just think . . .
SALOMÉ: So many?
SPATOLETTI: That's right, there're thirty-five men. Mussolini's safety is in my hands. As long as Spatoletti is here, Italy can sleep comfortably. Just let those bastards try anything—I'll bite their heads off. . . . Watch your asses!

(The motorcycle hits a bump.)

SPATOLETTI: Just let them dare to touch the Duce!

(Tunin and Salomé give each other a knowing look. At last they reach the restaurant, which has an outside terrace and tables.)

SCENE 20

> (*The Three Muskets Inn—exterior—daytime. A group of children can be seen chasing the motorcycle as it goes around the yard scaring away gaggles of geese and chickens. Very few customers can be seen in the restaurant.*)

SPATOLETTI (singing):
"Oh, restaurant of the Three Muskets,
"Tra la la la la la la,
"Spatoletti has arrived!
"Tra la la la la la la,
"If you don't give us something to eat
"We're going to be forced to cut off your feet.
"Oh, give me your cunt, you sexy blonde,
"Oh give it to me, please give it to me."

> (*The motorcycle comes to a halt. We see the innkeeper rushing forward bowing respectfully. Two urchins come running up to the group. Spatoletti gets off his motorcycle.*)

SALOMÉ: You drive like a maniac, I swear I'll never set foot on your motorcycle again . . . never!

> (*Spatoletti lifts Salomé out of the sidecar and heads toward the restaurant. The man exudes strength from every pore. Tunin follows close behind with Tripolina by his side. The innkeeper rushes on ahead in order to straighten up the table. He has the look of a professional ass-licker.*)

SPATOLETTI: Romoletto, look at these gorgeous broads I brought you today!

> (*Spatoletti pushes Salomé forward. His hands don't stop groping her.*)

SPATOLETTI: Move, you succulent cunt!
SALOMÉ: Oh, go get stuffed! Keep your hands to yourself!
SPATOLETTI: Come on, then, come on, move it. I'm so hungry I could eat a horse. (Points to Tunin) You sit down there. . . . Hey, Romoletto! What have you got cooking in the pot?

> (*They're all seated beneath the pergola while Romoletto tells them what he has on his menu.*)

ROMOLETTO: Captain, we have bucatini with a bacon and tomato sauce, homemade fettucini, chicken . . .

SPATOLETTI: Bucatini will be just fine. You have a terrific menu, dear Romoletto, you're a good man, a good man!

(Two young girls are setting the tables as quickly as possible. Spatoletti notices them.)

SPATOLETTI: Who are these young things? Are they your daughters?

(Spatoletti grabs them by their asses and gives them a couple of hearty whacks.)

SPATOLETTI: Ah, firm and rounded! Lucky for them that in 1922 they weren't ripe yet!

(The girls slip away from his clutches and Spatoletti pours the wine.)

SPATOLETTI: There were two thousand of us in Tamburini's ranks. This is where we camped before marching on Rome. Romoletto, do you remember?

(Romoletto gives him a filthy look, then quickly checks himself.)

ROMOLETTO: How could I ever forget . . .

(He lifts up his hands, showing everyone that he is missing his index and his ring finger.)

ROMOLETTO: Ever since that day they've been calling me "Mr. Five and Three is Eight."

(Spatoletti bursts into fits of laughter.)

SPATOLETTI: "Five and Three is Eight!" That's right, who did it to you? Cusini, or was it Govoni? We were famished, drunk as skunks on that cheap wine of yours and we were getting very rowdy. . . . He was very slow in serving us and at one point he said, "Captain, you must be patient." Suddenly a knife flashed out of nowhere and his two fingers went flying in the air. Hell, what can you do, we're fascists! Boy, we were really pissed off!

(Spatoletti laughs heartily. Romoletto and the two girls are also laughing. Only Tunin remains serious.)

SPATOLETTI: After all, it was a revolution and Mussolini's Italy was just being formed, so if you lost two fingers you should feel honored in the same way as if they had given you a medal for bravery in action.

ROMOLETTO: I am honored, but there's a slight political problem. Whenever I raise my arm in a fascist salute, it looks as if I'm giving the cuckold sign.

> (*Everyone bursts into laughter as Romoletto lifts his mutilated hand.*)

ROMOLETTO: I'd hate Mussolini to get offended.

SPATOLETTI: Ah, you're a born comedian, my dear Romoletto.

SCENE 21

> (*The Three Muskets' Inn—exterior—daytime. A child is flying his kite in the green meadow behind the restaurant. Tunin walks by himself. A gaggle of geese lead the way. Tripolina is leaning against the cow paddock, staring dreamily at the surrounding fields, her enormous eyes savoring the beauty of the fields, her nose picking up the earthy scents in the air. Nearby, Salomé is lying on a wooden cart. Spatoletti heads toward her with lascivious intent.*)

SPATOLETTI: Stop lying in that seductive way, my tasty morsel. If you don't stop I'm going to jump on you and tear you to pieces, you sexy bitch! You like it when I talk dirty, don't you? I turn you on; your mouth starts watering when you're with me, admit it!

> (*Salomé tries to sound convincing and casual, but her expression is a desperate one.*)

SALOMÉ: I've always gotten off on macho brutes like you! After all, you're rude, strong, vulgar and you have such a dirty mind—how *could* I resist you?

> (*Spatoletti becomes more and more excited and starts shouting.*)

SPATOLETTI: Romolettoooooooooo!

SALOMÉ: Why are you shouting like that?

> (*Spatoletti starts running back to the inn.*)

SPATOLETTI: Romoletto! Hurry up and come here, or, so help me God, I'll have you locked up!

(*As Spatoletti goes off with Romoletto to choose a room, Salomé beckons to Tunin. Tunin goes up to Salomé, looking quite miserable.*)

SALOMÉ: Look, I'll keep him busy for the next few hours.
TUNIN: You're going off with that piece of shit?
SALOMÉ: I'm going to get him to explain the security measures he's taken for the ceremony. In the meantime you can go and have a good look around.

(*Spatoletti returns, terribly excited.*)

SPATOLETTI: Tralalalalalala . . . come on, you gorgeous blonde, are we going or not?

(*Spatoletti embraces her.*)

SPATOLETTI: If it's really true that I turn you on, this is the time you can prove it to me. Come on, let's go!
SALOMÉ: Yes, my dear, but hold on just one moment.
SPATOLETTI: Well, what's the matter? If you really do like me, you could put out for free.
SALOMÉ: When I was sixteen my lover got me pregnant and I swore from that day that I would never do it for free, not even for the Pope— I'd rather close down shop!
SPATOLETTI: You could always make an exception to the rule.
SALOMÉ: There's no way, Captain. I've told you quite clearly, I wouldn't even do it for Pius XI. . . . Oh, by the way, today is Sunday, which makes the price go up to twelve lire.

(*Tunin looks on with a tortured expression.*)

SPATOLETTI: Just this once, please let me have the satisfaction.
SALOMÉ: Twelve lire or nothing.
SPATOLETTI: O.K., I'll give you twelve lire.
SALOMÉ: Aren't you generous, twelve whole lire!
SPATOLETTI: I still insist that you could have done it for free just this once.

(*Spatoletti and Salomé head back for the inn. Tripolina, still standing by the cow paddock, looks at the couple walking off together.*)

SALOMÉ: Oh, just imagine doing it with a bawdy Tuscan like you for free!

SPATOLETTI: Yes, but you could have done it out of love!
SALOMÉ: *What* love?

(*Spatoletti feels her up.*)

SPATOLETTI: Oh, you cynical bitch!
SALOMÉ: Come on, I've had enough, I've busted my ass for you all
day long.
SPATOLETTI: You love me! I know you love me, so I'm going to
shove it up your ass right here and now!

(*Tunin and Tripolina heave a sigh of relief as the two voices get
farther and farther away.*)

TRIPOLINA: Phew! They finally made it, the captain was giving me a
splitting headache with that loud voice of his.

(*Tunin is very silent. His natural shyness and deep thoughts
seem to inhibit him.*)

TUNIN: Yes, ma'am.

(*Tripolina smiles at his formal address.*)

TRIPOLINA: Ma'am? My name is Tripolina.

(*Tunin smiles.*)

TUNIN: Ah, Tripoli, land of love . . .
TRIPOLINA: You see, I was looking for an exotic name, and Tripolina
just popped into my head. Perhaps it was because I always loved
Africa, palm trees, and Rudolph Valentino playing the part of the
sheik.

(*Tripolina laughs at herself.*)

TRIPOLINA: Aren't I silly?

(*Tunin smiles sweetly.*)

TUNIN: You should have called yourself "Curly-locks."
TRIPOLINA: Oh, yes, that's cute . . . Curly-locks!

(*Tripolina breathes in the clean country air.*)

TRIPOLINA: Oh, how I love the countryside, the fresh air, the green
fields. . . . The sun is so hot, it's the swimming season now—do you
like going to the seashore?

(*Tunin stares at her as she basks in the sun.*)

TUNIN: No, I've never seen it.
TRIPOLINA: What! You've never seen the sea?
TUNIN: You see, I've always lived in the country.
TRIPOLINA: Aah, that's the reason why you have such an honest face.

SCENE 22

> (*In the Pergola behind the restaurant—exterior—daytime. People are dancing to the music of a gramophone. Tunin and Tripolina are in the midst of a group of couples. He holds her awkwardly for fear of rubbing against her dress. He dances just like a peasant, awkwardly, but very seriously.*)

TRIPOLINA: You're a terrific dancer, you know.
TUNIN: Well, not really.

> (*Tunin stares right through her, he is totally absorbed in his thoughts. But she seems unable to avoid the intensity of his stare.*)

TRIPOLINA: What are you staring at like that? Why do you stare at me so sadly? It really depresses me.
TUNIN: Oh, sorry, I wasn't staring at you, I was just thinking.
TRIPOLINA: Ah, so you stare right at me but don't see me.

> (*She acts offended and, releasing herself from his awkward clutches, heads for the gramophone.*)

TRIPOLINA: Hey, can't we put on something a little livelier? A fox trot? Or even a one-step?

> (*She starts thumbing through the records. A young man comes up to help her.*)

YOUNG MAN: Miss, if you'll allow me, I'll change the record for you.

> (*Tripolina hardly deigns him a look.*)

TRIPOLINA: Good idea, you change it while I go back to my fiancé!

> (*She leaves him standing there like a fool, but Tunin by now has disappeared.*)

SCENE 23

(*Modern building complex incorporating an enormous church—exterior—daytime. The shiny, white forms of the statues and buildings loom up toward the sky. [Guitar music—"Rockabybaby on the Treetop."] Tunin gazes at the shapes. The stage has almost been finished. It is framed by banners and flags which wave in the warm spring breeze. Tunin is frightened by the task he has set himself.*)

SCENE 24

(*A field—exterior—daytime. Walking across the green field, Tunin heads back to the inn. (The guitar continues to play). He's taken off his jacket and perspires profusely in his uncomfortable Sunday outfit. He stretches out on the grass with his hands behind his neck, pre-establishing a contact with Mother Earth.*)

SCENE 25

(*Stable—interior—daytime. We see Tripolina's silhouette against the door of the stable, her hair is untidy, her figure seems to be framed by the sun's rays.*)

TRIPOLINA: Oh!
TUNIN: Hey, there.

(*A cow turns its head, then lifts its nose to have a good sniff. Tunin is in the stable staring at the cow. With his shirt sleeves rolled up, his jacket thrown casually over his shoulders, his hat lopsided, he takes on the appearance of the peasant lad he really is. He pulls out his handkerchief to wipe the sweat off his neck.*)

TRIPOLINA: Hey, so you're here. That wasn't very nice of you to leave me like that.
TUNIN: What do you mean?
TRIPOLINA: Were you angry with me?
TUNIN: Oh, no, of course not.
TRIPOLINA: Is it something I did?
TUNIN: No, no, no, of course not.
TRIPOLINA: Well, then, what the hell was it? . . . Boy, is it hot today, shit!

(Tripolina goes over to sit on the hay.)

TRIPOLINA: Look, you've got to explain to me what happened, why did you behave like that?
TUNIN: Well, I just went off for a walk. . . . Oh, shit, now you're angry, sorry.
TRIPOLINA: Well, just a little.

> *(Tunin goes over and sits down beside her. She lies back in the hay and lets the skirt fall back, showing off her dark garter belt and lily-white thighs.)*

TUNIN: Look, I'm honestly sorry.
TRIPOLINA: God, you're so handsome! Hey, did I tell you there's some guy that was making a pass at me?

> *(Tripolina laughs.)*

TRIPOLINA: You know what I said to him? I told him that you were my fiancé.

> *(Tunin smiles shyly.)*

TRIPOLINA: Do you mind me saying that?

> *(Tunin shakes his head, then looks ,at her.)*

TUNIN: I wish I were.

> *(Tripolina is still laughing.)*

TRIPOLINA: You're not serious, are you?

> *(Tunin's wide-eyed look is almost animalistic, but sad.)*

TRIPOLINA: Just look at that face, why is it you always have that sad expression?
TUNIN: Oh, no reason, really . . . well, it could be that it's spring.
TRIPOLINA: Ah, the beauty of spring.
TUNIN: They're beautiful cows, don't you think?

> *(Tripolina inhales deeply from the lemon she is holding.)*

TRIPOLINA: Mmmmm! Isn't the smell of lemons fabulous. How I love it.

> *(She offers the lemon to Tunin so he, too, can smell.)*

TRIPOLINA: Do you like it!?

(Tunin smiles affectionately.)

TRIPOLINA: You know something? I was thinking this morning how I wish you weren't Salomé's cousin.
TUNIN: Well, what difference would it make if I wasn't?
TRIPOLINA: To begin with, we could have an affair! But you two are related so we can't.

(Tunin is taken aback by her words. When he comes out of shock he lets her have it.)

TUNIN: Why the hell shouldn't we have an affair? If two people want to make it they are entitled to it! This just goes to prove that you aren't really all that interested in me.

(Tripolina takes him by the arm and looks him straight in the eyes.)

TRIPOLINA: You fool, that's just the problem, you'd be good for me. That's the reason we shouldn't get involved . . . it would hurt me too much.

(He lets her words sink in. He grabs her and embraces her. Their eyes and lips meet. She looks frightened.)

TRIPOLINA: Noooo, Tunin, please don't.
TUNIN: What do you mean "don't"? Yes, I will, I will.

(Tunin crushes his lips against hers; he is awkward in his movements. She sighs beneath his weight; they roll freely on the hay. A sudden noise makes Tunin leap to his feet. Romoletto has walked into the stable. He smiles at them.)

ROMOLETTO: You'll excuse me . . . sorry to just walk in like that, but I thought perhaps you might want a bedroom?

(Tunin looks at him with a guilty and embarrassed look.)

TUNIN: There's really no need to bother, thanks.
ROMOLETTO: Please, it's no trouble. As a matter of fact, you would be doing me a favor. You see, I have those two innocent creatures who are walking around, you understand . . . it would be terrible if they happened to come in and see you. We don't always give out rooms, but for a friend of Captain Spatoletti we'll make an allowance.

(Tunin stands still. Tripolina walks up to him, gives him an encouraging look, and follows Romoletto into the sunshine. Tunin

removes his hat and lets her walk out first, then he closes the
door behind him.)

SCENE 26

(Hallway   and   Romoletto's   bedroom—interior—daytime.
Through the half-open door we see an old woman rocking a
baby in her arms.)

OLD LADY (singing):
"Rock-a-bye baby on the tree top . . ."

(Romoletto smiles mischievously. Tunin and Tripolina are alone
in the center of the huge rustic bedroom. The bed is an enor-
mous eighteenth-century piece. The closets, bureau, and hope
chest seem dwarfed by the size of the room. On the wall hangs
an effigy of the Virgin Mary looking down on them. Tripolina
takes out a cigarette. In a corner we see a chair on which there
is a sewing basket. Tunin picks up a sock with the darning egg
still inside it.)

TUNIN: This place really reminds me of home. My mother spends her
days sitting in a chair in a corner darning socks. Stitch upon stitch until
there is no more sock left. . . . It becomes one great stitch.

(Tripolina starts crying silently. The unlit cigarette is still in her
mouth. Tunin notices her tears and goes up to her.)

TUNIN: Please don't cry, come on, stop it.

(She turns to him and grabs him by the lapels.)

TRIPOLINA: Come on, take your pants off, let's fuck, what's all this
sentimentality for . . . you forgotten who you're with? Tripolina, that's
who! So take them off and let's get to work.

(She begins to undress rapidly. Tunin looks at her lovingly.)

TUNIN: Hey, what the hell's gotten into you? . . . Behave yourself!

(She pays no attention and tears her clothes off even faster.)

TRIPOLINA: What are you doing standing there like a fool? . . . People wait in line for a poke at Tripolina! . . . Move that ass! I'll show
you the greatest time, you'll never forget this fuck, that's for sure . . .
now get undressed.

(Tripolina is now in her black slip, kneeling on the bed trying to undo Tunin's trousers. As she undresses him she keeps on crying.)

TRIPOLINA: A fuck will make you stop staring at me with sweet eyes, so let's get to it, no more sweet talk, let's fuck!

(Tunin stands in front of her, half-naked. She cries uncontrollably. Tunin grabs her by the shoulders and shakes her violently.)

TUNIN: For Christ's sake, stop it!

(He presses her head against his chest. Then sits down and puts her on his knee, just as you would a child. Feelings he can't fully comprehend are at work within him. His down-to-earth instincts tell him how to act at a time like this even though he has never been in a similar situation. He rocks her in the same way a mother would rock her child, then whispers into her curly locks.)

TUNIN: Listen to me . . . you mustn't act like this because this way

the whole thing becomes really ugly . . . it musn't be ugly . . . do you understand?

(Tripolina slides gently onto the bed, and turns away from him. Tunin delicately turns her toward him.)

TRIPOLINA: Don't hurt me.
TUNIN: Hurt you? . . . Never . . . I'm going to be so gentle with you, my curly locks.

SCENE 27

(The Pergola at the Three Muskets Inn—exterior—afternoon. Hours have gone by and the midday light has given way to slanting afternoon sun. Salomé looks at the half-open blinds in her room. Close by, Spatoletti and Romoletto are talking to each other.)

ROMOLETTO: They've been in my brother-in-law's bedroom for the past three hours.

(Spatoletti laughs and moves closer to Salomé.)

SPATOLETTI: Ah, your cousin sure fooled us! He's been pumping away for the past three hours! You'd have never believed he had it in him!

(Salomé has an odd expression on her face as she stares at the blinds.)

SALOMÉ: Shut up, you swine! . . . He's a country lad and isn't used to these pastimes, leave him be.

(Spatoletti begins to get ready to go.)

SPATOLETTI: It's one thing to get your rocks off a couple of times in a row, but I can't believe that he's been shooting his load all afternoon. He must have dried up eventually . . . I'm sure he's fast asleep. . . . Hey there, cousin! If you're asleep, wake up! If you're still at it, put your pants on because we're leaving!

(Salomé looks toward the blinds apprehensively, then turns to Spatoletti and smiles gently.)

SCENE 28

> *(Romoletto's room—interior—afternoon. Tunin and Tripolina are still in bed. We can hear Spatoletti's loud voice.)*

SPATOLETTI (off camera): Let's snap to it . . . move our asses . . . on with our panties . . . let's go!

> *(Tunin stares into space.)*

TUNIN: One day I'm going to beat the shit out of him!

SCENE 29

> *(Via dei Fiori—exterior—nighttime. The motorcycle noisily comes to a halt. The night is still. It is very late and only a cat or two are roaming the streets. The brothel entrance is locked. As usual, Spatoletti gropes Salomé as he lifts her out of the sidecar.)*

SALOMÉ: Cut it out! It's so late . . . now we'll have to listen to Zoraide's bitching. Goddamn you, you put a run in my stockings! . . . Are you going to buy me a new pair of silk stockings?
SPATOLETTI: Yes, I'll buy you your damn stockings . . . and panties . . . and anything else your little heart desires.

> *(Spatoletti lifts her high into the air. She tries hitting him with her handbag.)*

SALOMÉ: Hey, what are you doing? Put me down . . . down . . . !
SPATOLETTI: Aaah! My golden thighs . . . just feel this ass, so firm. . . . Salomé, you know something? Fucking is really good for you!

> *(Salomé is put down in front of the door. She rings the doorbell and straightens up her skirt.)*

SALOMÉ: Leave me alone . . . I'm tired!

> *(Tunin and Tripolina walk toward the door whispering to one another.)*

TRIPOLINA: So, you're going to come here tomorrow? . . . Come in the evening around eleven, we'll be closed by that time. I'll be waiting for you.

> *(Tunin nods. In the meantime Spatoletti continues to annoy Salomé.)*

SPATOLETTI (off camera): You're my milking cow, that's what you are! . . . You'd better be off, if I suddenly feel like it, I'll screw you up against this wall!

(Salomé breaks away from his grip.)

SALOMÉ: Cut it out! I've told you over and over that I'm tired.

(Spatoletti pushes her away.)

SPATOLETTI: Oh, fuck you!
SALOMÉ: Just listen to him!

(Tunin is getting annoyed at Spatoletti's attitude toward Salomé. Having pushed Spatoletti away, Salomé falls back into Tunin's arms. Tunin holds her tightly. Spatoletti is now faced by the three of them. Tunin is between the two girls, his arms protectively around them.)

SPATOLETTI: Aaaah! They're getting that piece of shit to protect them, that freckle-faced punk! That puny weakling!

(Spatoletti snickers.)

SPATOLETTI: Hey, shithead, if you try and act fresh with me I'll rip your heart out!

(Spatoletti stops laughing and is now advancing menacingly. Salomé gets in his way and tries to divert his attention by making some light remarks.)

SALOMÉ: Hey, there . . . come here, then . . .

(Salomé embraces him, but Spatoletti still tries to get at Tunin.)

SALOMÉ: Be good, relax . . . calm down . . .

(Luckily Zoraide has finally opened the door and is standing in the doorway half-asleep, swearing in her strong accent.)

ZORAIDE: These fucking people just won't let you sleep in peace!
SALOMÉ: Come on, Zoraide has opened the door!

(Spatoletti won't stop. He's drunk and sways back and forth.)

SPATOLETTI: Hey, Salomé, I'm going to beat your cousin to a pulp!
SALOMÉ: Tripolina, are you coming or not? . . . As for you, go home to bed!

SPATOLETTI: I don't feel like it, I don't want to go, stay . . . please stay!

(Spatoletti's hands continue to wander all over Salomé's body.)

SALOMÉ: Enough is enough!
SPATOLETTI: One last thing, what are you doing tomorrow?

(Salomé hits him right in the gut with her elbow. He bends over in agony.)

SPATOLETTI: Ahhhh!
SALOMÉ: Oh, go to hell, you've been groping me all day long, I can't take it any longer.

(Finally Tripolina and Salomé have managed to go inside and have left Zoraide to fend for herself. Zoraide stands in Spatoletti's way.)

SPATOLETTI: Get the fuck out of the way, damn you, you ugly shrew. This isn't a nunnery, it's a brothel and those young ladies, thank God, aren't nuns but sluts, so let me in.

(Spatoletti gives Zoraide a hearty whack on her ass.)

ZORAIDE: And don't you forget, you fagot, that we have our schedules to keep.

(She slams the door in his face. Spatoletti laughs at Zoraide's insults, then gives the door a good swift kick.)

SPATOLETTI: Who are you calling a fag? Go call your son a fag, not me!

(Spatoletti turns to Tunin. They are alone now.)

SPATOLETTI: Did you hear her? She called me a fag!

(Spatoletti keeps on laughing. He whacks Tunin on the shoulders.)

SPATOLETTI: Well, it was only Zoraide after all, and I've known her for so long that she can say what she wants to me.

(He goes to have a drink from the water fountain.)

SPATOLETTI: Boy, did we drink! What a fine day. . . . We laughed, we drank and we ate, we farted, fucked and we burped . . . and we crapped . . . what more can you want from a Sunday? Know what we're going to do right now? We're going for a nice ride.

(*By this time Tunin hates him passionately but tries to contain himself.*)

TUNIN: Isn't it a bit late?
SPATOLETTI: Don't be such a ballbreaker . . . don't you feel the fresh air?

(*Spatoletti merrily lifts Tunin onto the motorcycle.*)

SPATOLETTI: This is the time of night when I get the urge to relive the good old days when we would go through the streets clubbing anarchists over the head. Then we'd arrest them and force castor oil down their throats . . . aaah yes, those certainly were the days.

(*The motorcycle disappears into the darkness as we hear Spatoletti singing a Fascist tune.*)

SCENE 30

(*The capitol—exterior—nighttime. The statue of Marcus Aurelius on horseback dominates the square. Spatoletti brings the motorcycle to an abrupt halt at the base of the statue. Spatoletti stands up on his motorcycle and salutes the statue with the usual fascist salute.*)

SPATOLETTI: Hail Emperor Marcus Aurelius! Do you see the light burning in HIS study from your vantage point? HE is in there, working for all of us, for you too, oh great emperor! Duce, you are the light! Hey, emperor! aren't you a bit worried that one of these days we're going to come up to your horse, take you off it and put a statue of HIM in your place? . . . (He turns to Tunin.) What a man . . . what a man. . . . Have you ever seen HIM up close?

(*Tunin shakes his head.*)

SPATOLETTI: You haven't? In that case, you have no idea what I'm talking about. . . . Whenever I set eyes on HIM I start shaking . . . HIS eyes are enormous, like tennis balls . . . I bet HE has big balls as well, HE could fertilize the entire world! . . . I tell you, only one in a million could ever be like HIM.

(*Spatoletti takes out the bottle of wine from the sidecar.*)

SPATOLETTI: I'm talking about men with real balls . . . eh, there aren't too many like that . . . the rest of the people . . . they're the dregs of the world! They're the masses!

(*Spatoletti drinks.*)

SPATOLETTI: They're nothing but a bunch of primitive beings, ready to shit in their pants at the first sign of danger . . . they would sell their sisters and themselves for a piece of bread . . . those are the masses! Those bastard Socialists used to feed their faces with what they could get from them.

TUNIN: Captain, it's fear that makes people behave in that way . . . you see, bravery is a thing for the wealthy . . . take me for example . . . I come from a humble home. My mother, my friends, the priests all taught me that it's better to swallow your pride and live rather than to be brave, rebel and then be killed.

> (*Tunin is very drunk as well. He gets out of the sidecar with the bottle of wine in his hand and walks toward Spatoletti, who is peeing against a streetlamp.*)

SPATOLETTI: That's the philosophy of cowards . . . that's why we need a fist of steel, we need order! If someone doesn't understand that, then we'll beat it into their heads. . . . Give me the bottle.

TUNIN: Well, you're right . . . but it's dangerous because one could also end up like the innkeeper.

SPATOLETTI: What are you talking about?

TUNIN: Back home, there was an innkeeper who had an old mangy dog . . . this innkeeper was constantly kicking the shit out of the poor animal, but the animal never rebelled—the more he was kicked around the more he went back to lick the innkeeper's hand, because he knew that if he didn't go back he would starve to death . . . finally one day the innkeeper hit the dog one time too many and the animal turned on him and bit him.

SPATOLETTI: And then what?

TUNIN: He wouldn't let go. . . . He bit and bit until the innkeeper was on the ground, dying, with foam coming out of the side of his mouth.

> (*They walk beneath the marble archway. In the darkness Spatoletti lights up a cigarette.*)

TUNIN (Continues): You see, what I'm trying to say, Captain, is that perhaps one evening . . . a poor soul . . . say, someone like me who

just can't take it anymore . . . You come along with your fists of steel
and the poor soul sinks his knife into your throat.
SPATOLETTI: The man isn't born yet who could kill Spatoletti!

(Spatoletti laughs. Tunin looks at him.)

TUNIN: One just never knows nowadays . . . there are so many
wretches in this world who just don't think they could do something
like that . . . then suddenly, one bright day, they discover they can
. . . they're desperate people, and as you know desperate people are
insane, and they'll do anything.
SPATOLETTI: I don't give a shit. (singing)
   "We are electricity, a very powerful voltage!
   "Whoever dares touch a Fascist risks losing his life . . . !
   "Bim, bum, bam, we don't give a shit about dying!"

SCENE 31

(The capitol—exterior—nighttime. Spatoletti has climbed into
the arms of a statue of Neptune, God of the Seas. Tunin listens
to him in silence.)

SPATOLETTI: It's so good to be sitting here in the arms of the God of
the Tiber. . . . You feel marvelous; master of Rome. . . . There is
nowhere in the world greater than Rome. Hey, from here you can see
all of Rome . . . Rome! . . . Someone should set a match to you like
the great Nero did once before! Rome! You're the greatest prostitute of
all! How many secrets do you hide in your dark corners? Rome, you're
the capital, saturated with cowards and the scum of the land . . . if
only HE would listen to me . . . all I need is the word and I'll get rid
of the anarchists, subversives, traitors, the whole damn lot of them!
. . . I would love doing it, it would be like a wonderful party for me.
. . . I've killed so many of them with these bare hands. . . . Now we
have to be good; we have to be gentle. . . . HE says that violence isn't
a good policy. . . . You know what I feel like doing now? I'd like to go
wake Salomé up . . . what a great piece of ass. . . . You see, we Fascists don't normally pay for our women, we just fuck them, but with
Salomé it's different. She's someone that really gets you hard . . . you
ought to see the queues back at the brothel to get a poke at her. . . .
What a whore! Now, I don't know whether or not, being her cousin,
you can understand these things. . . . As for your Tripolina, she's really got no spunk. . . . I'm an expert with whores and I tell you, your
Tripolina doesn't make the grade.

(Tunin has reached the end of his rope. He climbs up the statue and starts tugging at Spatoletti's arm, trying to pull him down.)

TUNIN: Enough! No more . . . you've been breaking my fucking balls all night. . . . I'm going to tear you to pieces!
SPATOLETTI: Hey, calm down! What's wrong, are you crazy?

(Spatoletti manages to break away from him.)

SPATOLETTI: Hey, cut the shit!
TUNIN: Don't you dare mention those two names again, do you hear?
SPATOLETTI: You're angry because of what I said about Tripolina?
TUNIN: You're the shit of this world, the cream of the crud!
SPATOLETTI: I get it, he's in love . . . the young pup is in love . . . can you believe it?

(Tunin is very lucky that Spatoletti has taken the whole thing jokingly. Tunin doesn't accept this, he's finally cracked.)

TUNIN: I warned you, goddamnit, we poor wretches are mad. . . . I'll bite your balls off, I'll bite them off, I swear!
SPATOLETTI: They're nothing but whores!

(Spatoletti jumps down from the statue. Tunin starts running away.)

SPATOLETTI: Hey there, where are you off to?

(Tunin starts running down the capitol's steps. Spatoletti chases him drunkenly.)

SPATOLETTI: You're right . . . I feel sorry for you . . . drunk as you are. . . . You're much better off running away, you fag. . . . If I catch you I'll throw you in the fountain, that'll sober you up fast enough.

(Spatoletti jumps on his motorcycle and starts chasing him down the steps.)

SPATOLETTI (singing): "Oh darling, darling, why are you such a whore . . . ?"

SCENE 32

(Via dei Fiori—exterior—nighttime. Tunin runs in the night. He reaches the door of the brothel totally breathless. He starts shouting for all he's worth.)

TUNIN: Tripoli . . . Salomé . . . Tripolina . . . !

(He rings the doorbell like a madman.)

TUNIN: Tripolina . . . Salomé . . .

(The entrance opens slightly and Zoraide appears in the door-way carrying her poodle.)

ZORAIDE: You're still here? Fucking hell, stop shouting!

(Carmela has been awakened by the shouts and she too comes downstairs wearing her dressing gown and hair net.)

CARMELA: God, Jesus, Joseph and the Virgin Mary! This son of a bitch is still here? Won't you let us sleep in peace?
TUNIN: Tripoliiiii . . . !
CARMELA: Oh, fuck Tripolina, go away, goddamnit, go!
ZORAIDE: It won't take a minute to call the police.

(Madame Aida, the face-cream goddess, arrives. She is not amused.)

MADAME AIDA: Who is it? A drunk? If it's a drunk get rid of him or else he'll vomit all over my carpet. . . . Call the police—get rid of him!

(Tunin tries to get past the human barrier.)

MADAME AIDA: Slam the door!

(As Zoraide tries to shut the door, Tunin pushes with all his might. Finally he manages to get his foot inside the door.)

MADAME AIDA: Slam it! Slam it in his face!
ZORAIDE: I can't, his foot is in the way.
CARMELA: You rat, get your foot out of the way!
TUNIN: Not on your life! Tripolina!

(Tunin manages to get his head inside the door as well. Madame Aida notices that it is Tunin.)

MADAME AIDA: But isn't that Salomé's cousin?

(Tunin is hopeful that she might let him in.)

TUNIN: Yes, madame, it's me . . . won't you please let me in?
MADAME AIDA: Let you in at this time of night? You've got to be joking!

TUNIN: Madame, have a heart, *please* . . .
MADAME AIDA: Out, get him out of here!

> (*Madame looks down at Tunin's foot in the door. She lifts her cane and gives it a hard whack. Tunin removes his foot and lets out a blood-curdling yell. At the same moment Zoraide slams the door on him.*)

TUNIN: Fuck, she got me right on the toe! Shit!

> (*The door opens and Madame Aida appears in the doorway.*)

MADAME AIDA: Well!
TUNIN: You really hurt me, goddamnit.
MADAME AIDA: I didn't intend it to give you pleasure!
TUNIN: You witch! That's no way to treat people.
MADAME AIDA: What are you complaining about? You can still walk. So go home, off to bed where you belong. . . . Tomorrow, if you like, you can come back and see your Salomé and you can have lunch with us, too.

> (*Madame Aida slams the door. Tunin walks away limping into the night.*)

TUNIN: Damn bitch! She broke my foot . . . goddamn her!

> (*He sits down on a step and starts massaging his ailing toe.*)

TUNIN: She had to hit me right on my corn, goddamn her! Ahhh! Now my nail is going to drop off.

> (*A black and white kitten comes up to Tunin and starts licking his shoe. Tunin chases him away.*)

TUNIN: Piss off, you stupid cat! What do you want from me? Piss off . . . go on . . . go!

> (*Tunin starts climbing the steps toward the fountain, but the kitten doesn't let up.*)

TUNIN: So you're a stubborn one. . . . Why are you following me, you little shit? I'm not a she-cat, you know? . . . Anyhow, you're too young to have those interests.

> (*Tunin reaches the fountain, takes off his jacket, and has a drink. The kitten keeps on rubbing itself against his trousers.*)

TUNIN: What happened to you, did your girl friends kick you out of the house too?

(Tunin throws the jacket over his shoulders.)

TUNIN: You're lonely, aren't you, little thing!

(He picks up the kitten.)

TUNIN: It's a hard life, isn't it!

(He looks up at the sky.)

TUNIN: It's probably because of the eerie light the streetlamps give off, but I find the nighttime in the city is a lot scarier than in the country. . . . Hey, what are you purring at?

> *(Tunin walks off into the darkness, talking to his newly found friend. His heavy peasant shoes make a loud noise which echoes in the night. At the end of the street a column rises threateningly.)*

TUNIN: Listen to me, kitten . . . you should go looking for someone else . . . you're a lot better off without me, I assure you. . . . Shit . . . what a city! Look at all this. . . . Eh, do you have somewhere to stay? I'm staying in a hotel, you could come stay with me if you like. . . . You're not getting a fair deal, though. . . . I tell you, little one, today I'm here but tomorrow I'll be gone.

SCENE 33

> *(Hotel room—interior—nighttime. In his barren room, under the kitten's watchful eye, Tunin practices in front of a mirror how he's going to pull his gun out of his shirt.)*

SCENE 34

> *(The Gianicolo—one of the seven hills of Rome—exterior—daytime. From this marvelous vantage point you can see the rooftops of Rome. Tunin is shooting multicolored balloons in a shooting gallery. The owner looks at him with gratitude and admiration.)*

YOUNG WOMAN: Congratulations, sir! You're quite a marksman! Where did you learn to shoot like that, in the army?

(Tunin is noncommittal.)

TUNIN: No! Another round, please.

YOUNG WOMAN: God bless you, you've been at it all morning.
TUNIN: I do it to relax!
YOUNG WOMAN: What you need is a girl friend to be with, you shouldn't be spending the whole day shooting!

(*Tunin's eyes seem to get rounder and rounder.*)

TUNIN: Yes, I suppose you're right.
YOUNG WOMAN: Shall I read your palm? I'll tell your fortune.
TUNIN: No, I'd rather you didn't, but thanks for the nice thought.
YOUNG WOMAN: Do you have a girl friend or don't you?
TUNIN: Well, more or less . . .
YOUNG WOMAN: Well, why aren't you together?
TUNIN: Because she works.
YOUNG WOMAN: And what does she do?
TUNIN: She's in business for herself.

SCENE 35

(*Inside the whorehouse—interior—daytime. The girls are all gathered in one of the rooms waiting to be called out by Carmela.*)

CARMELA: Come on my lovelies, another day of work is about to start. Let's go!

(The girls come running down the stairs and split up in the waiting room. Music: "La Tonkinoise" is being played on the gramophone. The camera studies each girl individually. They smile seductively, they uncover themselves provocatively. The clients look, wink at the girls, make their choices. Carmela and Maurizia urge on the buyers and advertise their merchandise. At the top of the stairs is Salomé, languidly leaning against a statue: she's the pride of the household. She takes long drags from her cigarette.)

A BEARDED CLIENT: Good morning, hookers!
ISA: Up yours!
THE CAT: Oh, go to hell!

(The girls laugh. Yvonne makes some rude gestures.)

YVONNE: Sucker!

(Carmela protests jokingly.)

CARMELA: How rude! Hey, come on! What the hell's the matter, no one getting it up this morning? Are you all fags today? Come on move it, let's get to the bedrooms.

(Isa grabs a little bald-headed man and smothers him in an embrace.)

ISA: Come on, darling, the first fuck of the day is always the best. If we wait any longer you'll never get it up again.

(The other girls follow Isa's example and try to force the clients into the rooms.)

TAIDE: Come on. Let's hump, let's go, let's go!
JACQUELINE: You going to stand there all day? Come on, move it. I haven't got all day!
AMAPOLA: Why are there so many people here this morning? What's the occasion?
THE CAT: There's a Fascist gathering this morning.
YVONNE: I could never understand why business is so good when there is supposed to be a gathering. Instead of being there they come looking for a fuck.

(*Madame Aida and Maurizia look at the scene from a private room. Carmela rushes over to assure them that business is good.*)

CARMELA: Have you seen how much business we're doing this morning?

THE CAT (singing): "Oh, play me a tune on your violin . . ."

(*Yvonne shows off her legs as she sits provocatively on a pillow. A group of elegant young men walk into the house.*)

MAN'S VOICE: May God bless you!

(*Carmela goes to greet the newcomers. The girls start doing their best to be noticed.*)

CARMELA: What is all this? Come on, do you think you're back at the barracks? Hands off!

YOUNG MAN: Hey, Carmela, you great piece of ass, don't you recognize me?

(*The young man has a good look at Yvonne, who is still lounging on the pillow.*)

YOUNG MAN: Wow! What a piece of ass!

(*Lola comes forward, wiggling her ass.*)

LOLA: Well, then, who's going to pop my cherry this morning? I'm in bloom again.

OTHER YOUNG MAN: What a beauty . . .

(*Salomé walks down the stairs and shows herself off to the clients.*)

SALOMÉ: Here she is folks, straight from Bologna! Come and get it!

(*The young men look at her with great interest.*)

ANOTHER YOUNG MAN: Is she stacked!

SALOMÉ: Come, come, young men, I have just about a quarter of an hour to kill, so let's get down to some serious action.

(*Lola doesn't stand a chance against Salomé and leaves her two prospective clients.*)

LOLA: My dears, if any one of you likes me, just follow . . .

SALOMÉ: Come now, my love, I'll show you a heavenly time . . .

CARMELA: Let's go, you beautiful youths, make up your minds. . . .
Boy, what a day.

TRIPOLINA (singing):

"Tripoli, land of love . . .
"Here she is, folks, Tripolina has arrived!"

(Tripolina walks downstairs. On her head she is wearing a fringed turban. She falls directly into the arms of a portly gentleman who was being approached by Isa.)

ISA: Come on, love, are you deaf? Are you going to make up your mind or not?

TRIPOLINA: Dear professor, what a beautiful beard you have . . .

CLIENT: Yes, well . . .

(Carmela verbally attacks a young boy who has been standing around for the whole morning looking.)

CARMELA: Look, kid, you just can't stand here all day! Go away—you're only a student.

THE BOY: Please be kind, just for five minutes—I have exams tomorrow.

(Carmela is without mercy. She starts pushing him toward the door.)

CARMELA: Go on, get the hell out of here, you have no money . . . out! Off to the bedrooms, young men, let's go. . . . What beautiful erotic things can we come up with this morning?

MADAME AIDA: Carmela . . .

(Yvonne has come back downstairs, less fresh and cheerful than she was earlier. She goes and sits down and tries to pull herself together. At that very moment Tunin walks in the door.)

ANITA: Hey people, I'm from Modena, each flick of my tongue will make you faint!

YVONNE: Monsieur Tunin, what are you doing here, did you come for breakfast?

TUNIN: No.

(Yvonne poses provocatively against the door.)

YVONNE: You're not going to tell me you came here as a client? I give relatives a special treatment, you know? I'm at your disposal. Not dur-

YOUNG OFFICER: Hey, what's your problem?

(*Tunin and Tripolina exchange intense gazes. Then he grabs her and starts climbing up the stairs. Carmela stands in their way.*)

CARMELA: Where do you think you're going, you son of a bitch?

(*Tunin takes out some money and gives it to Carmela.*)

TUNIN: Here, goddammit, here's your fucking seven lire. I have just as much right as everyone else.

(*Carmela can't argue with that. She turns to Tripolina.*)

CARMELA: Hurry up, then, this is the rush hour!

(*Tunin and Tripolina disappear up the stairs.*)

SCENE 36

(*Upstairs—corridor—interior—daytime. Tunin can be seen dashing along, dragging Tripolina behind him. In his hurry he walks right into the wrong room.*)

TRIPOLINA: No, Tunin, that's the wrong room, it's the toilet.

(*They come across Salomé, who looks at them sternly.*)

SALOMÉ: So, what's the meaning of all this?

(*Tunin isn't prepared to start explaining.*)

TUNIN: Look, I just can't explain right now, let us alone.

(*He continues his escape. Tripolina throws up her arms in a helpless gesture.*)

TRIPOLINA: What can I do about it?

(*Salomé runs after them.*)

SALOMÉ: What the hell do you mean—hold on a minute. . . . Tunin!

(*Tunin and Tripolina disappear into a room and slam the door in Salomé's face.*)

SALOMÉ: Tunin! Come on! For fuck's sake, open the damn door!

(*Isa walks out of her bedroom.*)

ISA: So, the cousin is off with Tripolina, he really got hooked on that one! Salomé, you're not jealous, perhaps?

(*Salomé is too angry to think up a clever retort.*)

SALOMÉ: Stop breaking my balls, you old hag! If you don't leave me alone I'll punch your face in.

(*Salomé begins to be really concerned.*)

SCENE 37

(*Tripolina's bedroom—interior—daytime. Tunin has his back to Tripolina. He stares angrily and sullenly out of the window.*)

TRIPOLINA: Hey, why are you acting like this, what's bugging you now?
TUNIN: I just can't stand seeing you in this place! Look—I want you to stay with me for two whole days.
TRIPOLINA: What are you talking about?
TUNIN: For two days, that's all.
TRIPOLINA: Two days, then what?

(*Tunin is embarrassed, he doesn't want to have to talk or explain.*)

TUNIN: After that? Well . . . I'm going to have to leave. Oh look, just don't ask any questions. Are you going to stay with me for two days or not?

(*Tripolina goes up to him. She looks at him sweetly but is firm.*)

TRIPOLINA: Look, I've lost my head over you and I'll do whatever you want me to do—but you've got to tell me the truth.

(*Tunin leaves her standing by the window and without even looking at her goes to sit on the bed.*)

TUNIN: I have nothing to tell you . . . absolutely nothing.
TRIPOLINA: Bullshit, do you think I'm that stupid? From the very moment I set eyes on you I could see you were hiding some dark secret. There are times when you have a crazed expression on your face . . . come, tell me the truth.
TUNIN: For Christ's sake, leave me alone. I can't tell you a thing, all I want to know is if you're going to stay with me for the next two days.

TRIPOLINA: You just don't trust me at all. . . . I like you a lot, you know?

(Tunin begins to relax.)

TUNIN: Look, it isn't that I don't trust you, it's just that the less one knows about these things the better off they are.

(At last Tunin has decided to tell her the truth. He stands up and slowly unwraps a small parcel he has in his vest pocket. He pulls out a bullet, which he shows her. On the bullet are scratched the initials B.M.)

TUNIN: You see this bullet? Look carefully at it. You wanted to know the reason for my secretness? I have come to shoot this bullet right between Mr. Benito Mussolini's eyes.

(Tripolina is dazed.)

TRIPOLINA: Holy Virgin Mary, you're an anarchist?

(Tunin nods affirmatively.)

TUNIN: Now, my love, my life rests in your hands.

(Tunin carefully wraps the bullet once again. Tripolina moves away from him in tears.)

TUNIN: Stop it please, where are you going?
TRIPOLINA: Leave me alone!
TUNIN: Wait! Wait! Don't go!

(Tripolina is far too distraught.)

TRIPOLINA: If you want to get yourself killed by the Fascists, please be my guest. Just leave, leave right now. I'll go back downstairs. . . . I'll go and let them fuck me, up against a wall if they wish, at least it will take my mind off you.

(Tunin tries to calm her down, to hold her back.)

TUNIN: Listen darling, don't go, don't turn down two days of real love like this. Not everyone gets a chance to have two full days of love, don't give it up.
TRIPOLINA: You're the one who's giving up the chance, not me! Why? For politics! What the hell is politics to us? What the fuck do we care?

(Tunin embraces her lovingly.)

TUNIN: Why? You ask me why?

(He makes her sit next to him on the bed. They look like two frightened schoolchildren.)

TUNIN: There comes a time when one says "enough" . . . the day comes when we feel we have to do something positive. . . . I am going to go through with what I have set out to do!

(Tripolina is still crying.)

TRIPOLINA: The way I see it, I was born unlucky, and I'll die unlucky.

(Tunin gently takes her hand.)

TUNIN: Calm down, calm down, my lovely curly locks.

SCENE 38

(Madame Aida's sitting room—interior—daytime. Madame Aida is furious.)

MADAME AIDA: Are you mad? Two days of leave at the height of the season? Only a madwoman could dare to ask something like that!

(Standing before her we see Tripolina, pale and nervous, but with her mind firmly made up.)

TRIPOLINA: Well, Madame, if you're not giving me permission, I am just going to take the two days off anyhow.

(Madame Aida can't believe her ears.)

MADAME AIDA: So you're going to go anyhow? Listen—if you dare do this to me I will ruin your career. If you leave the top brothel circuit you're done for! Anyhow, who are you doing this for? For that freckle-faced country bumpkin? You're insane, you just don't know what men are like, they come, they screw and they leave.

(With her lips firmly sealed, Tripolina is the very picture of stubbornness.)

MADAME AIDA: And don't you forget, we have a contract. You'd better weigh your odds, my dear, and then tell me if it's worth it or not!

TRIPOLINA: I've never had anything free in my life.
MADAME AIDA: I've seen so many girls end up on the sidewalks out of love. You won't be the first.
TRIPOLINA: I don't care.

(*Madame Aida offers Tripolina a cigarette and then lights one for herself.*)

MADAME AIDA: You dumb-ass whore. . . . You still believe in knights in shining armor. . . . After all these years in a whorehouse you still aren't convinced they don't exist.

(*Suddenly the door opens and Loredana comes in. She's in a panic.*)

LOREDANA: Madame! Madame! One of the guests has passed out, he suddenly fainted on me. Now he's as pale as a ghost and shaking all over!

SCENE 39

(*Loredana's room—interior—daytime. The client is lying with his mouth wide open. His eyes are half-closed and his coloring verges on green. He's obviously very ill and is making terrible wheezing sounds. Maurizia and Carmela listen to the old man's heartbeat. With the help of the other girls they manage to lift him up off the floor and onto the bed.*)

CARMELA: Hurry up, let's get him on the bed.
LOREDANA: Hey! . . . Up we go!
MAURIZIA: Be gentle . . .
LOREDANA: Shit, is he heavy!
CARMELA: Fuck, he looked so thin to me.

(*The old client is delirious.*)

OLD CLIENT: Giuliana, will you ever forgive me?

(*Madame Aida watches the whole scene from a corner of the room. She then calls, in a firm but low voice.*)

MADAME AIDA: Maurizia! Go call Zoraide, but be sure not to say a word to anyone else about this!

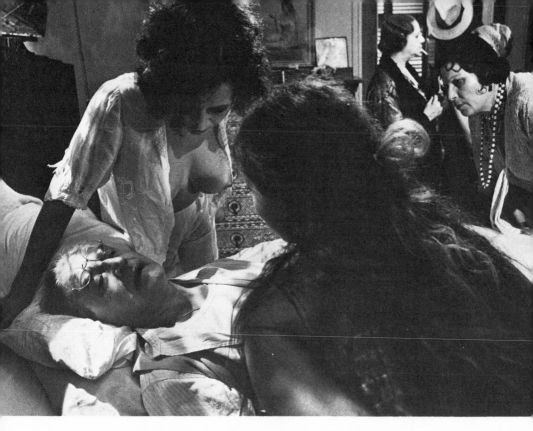

(Loredana and Gea, helped by Carmela, are trying as best they can to give the old gentleman a massage. It is hard for them to make themselves useful as they are only partially dressed.)

CARMELA: Who the hell is this Giuliana he's calling for?
GEA: How the hell do I know?
LOREDANA: Well, who do you think it is? It was his wife, that's who. She died a little while back, poor thing.

(Madame Aida sends Maurizia away. Maurizia leaves the room and Madame Aida hovers near the bed so she can beckon to Carmela without the other girls noticing it.)

MADAME AIDA: You, my dears, keep on massaging him with vinegar.
LOREDANA: It makes me queasy.
MADAME AIDA: Queasy? What do you mean, it makes you queasy? If you were any good at your job these things wouldn't happen. . . . Come along, then, it's not a big deal, just an old man feeling sick.

(Carmela hands Madame the old man's wallet. She looks through it thoroughly, and leaves all the documents but takes

the money. The girls continue to massage the old man. They are terrified.)

GEA: Poor dear, is it really true his wife died only last year?

LOREDANA: Yes, it's true, it was a short time ago. . . . He was so fond of us all. He used to say he came here because the smell of us young things made him feel twenty years younger.

GEA: He's turning to ice!

(From a distance Madame Aida looks at the old man.)

MADAME AIDA: He's really at death's door. We've got to get him out of here.

CARMELA: Wouldn't it be better to tell someone? Someone important like the inspector's nephew, or perhaps the general? They're all habitual clients.

MADAME AIDA: Neither of those guys would ever put his ass on the line to help us, you can be sure of that! No, we've got to get rid of him right now. He can die anywhere he wants, but not here.

(She glances nervously at the man as he continues to breathe loudly. Loredana continues to massage him.)

CARMELA: It isn't a simple thing to do, you know?

MADAME AIDA: Regardless of how difficult it is, we've just got to do it!

(The bedroom door opens and Zoraide walks in holding her poodle.)

ZORAIDE: Here I am, madame—you sent for me?

CARMELA: Come here, Madame Aida wants to ask you something.

(Only now does Zoraide notice the old man on the bed.)

ZORAIDE: Holy Mary! Is he dead?

(Madame Aida doesn't answer but takes her by the arm and pulls her aside.)

MADAME AIDA: Listen Zo, does your brother still own that horse and buggy?

ZORAIDE: Of course he does, he parks it right around the corner from here. If you need something, I'll go call him.

MADAME AIDA: Okay, tell him to come here right away.

(Zoraide walks out. Madame Aida gives the old man an optimistic look.)

LOREDANA: Boy, is he sweating!
MADAME AIDA: Poor dear, I think he's beginning to look better, but I think he'd be better off in his own home.

SCENE 40

(Madame Aida's sitting room—interior—daytime. Sitting in front of Madame Aida, Tunin nervously sips a liqueur.)

TUNIN: I really don't know Rome that well. Where is it you want me to take him?

(Madame adopts a blasé tone of voice.)

MADAME AIDA: Right around the corner from here is the Forum. At this time of day it's so hot that only the cats are roaming the streets . . . as for the old man, he doesn't care where he is. But what about us, can you imagine the scandal? You could help me avoid a lot of trouble, and by the way, if you do me this favor I'll let Tripolina take the two days off. The girl is so valuable to the house I wouldn't do it even for Benito Mussolini, but in this case I'll make an allowance.

(Suddenly the door to the sitting room opens and Salomé enters like a whirlwind, slamming the door behind her. Tunin, Madame Aida, and Carmela jump to their feet.)

SALOMÉ: Now look here, you . . . I was sure he was mad, but you . . . I never expected it from you, Madame. . . . There I am working and you go and get my cousin into trouble.
MADAME AIDA: I had given orders that no one else should hear about this.
CARMELA: I never opened my mouth about this, I don't know who did!
SALOMÉ: Ah! Keep things quiet in this place? Everyone has a big mouth here! Anyhow, my Tunin mustn't do this, do you hear?
MADAME AIDA: I didn't know you were acting as his nanny, anyhow, he's come of age, he's quite responsible. And what's more, if he does me this favor I will do him one in exchange.
SALOMÉ: Yes, I'm sure; you'll bring him sweets in jail! Anyway, I don't know why we're wasting our breath because my cousin isn't going to go through with this!

(Salomé looks at him seriously. Tunin doesn't answer as one would expect. He smiles.)

TUNIN: Oh, come on, with this heat there isn't a soul around. . . .

SALOMÉ: That's what Madame Aida says, isn't it?

TUNIN: Not true, and anyhow, what if there is?

SALOMÉ: What if a policeman should see you with this stiff? I said I don't want you to do it. It's too dangerous, do you understand?

(Salomé is firm, but Tunin's character finally emerges from behind his meek façade.)

TUNIN: Enough is enough! I said I'm going to do it and I am! Let's go!

SALOMÉ: No, Tunin, wait a minute! Don't go!

(Salomé grabs him by one arm, while at the same time Carmela grabs him by the other and starts directing him toward a back door.)

CARMELA: Come, come, let's move it, we've got work to do.

(Salomé runs after them as Madame Aida tries to stop her.)

MADAME AIDA: Stop breaking our balls!

SALOMÉ: If he goes I go too!

MADAME AIDA: Are you mad? Carmela will go with him! Shit, what am I going to tell those young men when they ask for their Salomé?

SALOMÉ: You can tell the young men that Salomé's fallopian tubes have shut down for the day!

(Salomé follows the other two out the door.)

SCENE 41

(Entrance to the brothel on Via dei Fiori—interior–exterior—daytime. The horse and buggy are parked in front of the brothel. Maurizia gives the "all clear" signal.)

MADAME AIDA: Now! The coast is clear!

MAURIZIA: Hurry! Hurry!

(Tunin and Carmela are carrying the old man like a drunkard down the length of the hall. Salomé gives them a helping hand as Madame Aida looks on. To a passer-by the scene would appear to be that of a group of drunks after a heavy lunch. The old man's hat hides his pale green face. This is the hottest time of day and everyone is still at home eating lunch. Maurizia tries

to help them put the man on the buggy, but Salomé pushes her aside.)

SALOMÉ: I'll do it, don't bother.

(Madame Aida hands Carmela a hat. Salomé pushes Tunin into the driver's seat. Tunin is obviously used to dealing with nags and he easily gets the horse moving. Madame Aida heaves a sigh of relief.)

SCENE 42

(Shots of the streets of Rome around the Forum—exterior—daytime. The horse and buggy meander through the hot, deserted streets. On the buggy Carmela and Salomé try to prop up the old man, who keeps on swaying from side to side. Tunin is in the driver's seat guiding the horse across the tram lines and cobblestones, but he isn't used to them and the horse slips a few times.)

SCENE 43

(The Roman Forum—exterior—daytime. A narrow Roman street leading to the Forum. The heat has driven even the bravest into the shelter of their homes, away from the streets and the ruins. Tunin stops the buggy, ties up the reins, and looks around. The two women look around as well. The dying man's presence is making them nervous. Tunin jumps down, rolls up his sleeves, and looks at Salomé.)

TUNIN: You stay right here—if someone comes you whistle.

(Salomé doesn't agree to be the lookout.)

SALOMÉ: No, I'll come with you, he's heavy and Carmela has varicose veins and wouldn't be much use.

(Carmela is overjoyed at being able to stay on the buggy.)

CARMELA: Yes, I'd much rather stay here, I'm not feeling too well.

(Tunin and Salomé prop the old man up between them and start walking away. The Forum is totally deserted, the sun beats down without mercy, it's a nightmarish scene. They are having a hard time keeping the old man up. They discover that the only

*way to enter the Forum is by climbing over a fence. They are
really having a difficult time.)*

SALOMÉ: Come on, lift him up.
TUNIN: Be careful!
SALOMÉ: Hurry up!

*(They walk along the ancient streets, making their way among
the ruins. Salomé is obviously moody. Even though Tunin's
mind is on what he is doing, he's unable to put up with her long
face for much longer.)*

SALOMÉ: Let's carry him over to the column, it's more secluded.
TUNIN: Look, if you're pissed off with me you'd better tell me right
away, because I'm getting sick of that face.
SALOMÉ: Look here, a joke is a joke and I'm the first to enjoy a good
one. Life is so shitty that if one doesn't have a good laugh every now
and then it just isn't worth living. But you, you've set yourself a task,
and here you are pissing around like this . . . what's wrong with you?

*(Salomé and Tunin walk along the "Holy Way." Between them
we see the hat and the old man's waxlike profile.)*

TUNIN: I'm well aware of how I must behave.
SALOMÉ: No, you've no idea at all. I pictured you as being a dedi-
cated person whose only thought was to carry out his task, to vindicate
all those who had already died for the cause. . . .
TUNIN: I suffer like they did, but I just don't want to die! I don't want
to die, to hell with that!
SALOMÉ: Well, then, don't do it! You've fallen in love, now take your
Tripolina and go back to France and don't think about it ever again.

*(Tunin is shocked by her words, by her tone of voice. They are
both so rapt in their own thoughts that they don't notice that
the old man has opened his eyes and is slowing coming to.)*

OLD MAN: Giuliana . . . Giuliana . . . Sorry, I'm so sorry, Giuliana.

*(The old man turns to Tunin, thinking he's his wife. Salomé and
Tunin look at each other in horror. Salomé is the first to pull
herself together and speeds up her pace, heading toward the columns.)*

SALOMÉ: Relax, old man, relax.
OLD MAN: Giuliana . . .

TUNIN: Oh, God, he's regaining consciousness! Come on now, don't get excited, relax.

(Even though he's delirious, the old man seems to realize that something is not quite right. A look of terror appears on his face.)

OLD MAN: Giuliana, I'm sorry.

(He throws his arms around Tunin, who staggers under the weight of the man. They get closer to the columns; Tunin is embarrassed by the old man's waxen face so close to his own.)

TUNIN: Let's leave him right there, lean him up against the column.

(Salomé and Tunin lean the old man against a column in a sitting position. The old man keels over, horror in his eyes, his hands gripping for Tunin's jacket.)

TUNIN: Don't worry, sir, there's nothing wrong, it's just this heat. It's all over now, sir . . . be brave, you'll see it's all over now.

(The old man is suddenly very still. Salomé becomes as white as a ghost.)

SALOMÉ: He's dead.

(Tunin opens his eyes wide. Dramatic strumming of guitar.)

SALOMÉ: Come on, let's move it. Let's get out of here!

(Tunin and Salomé run off. The old man's body remains there, leaning against a column, as Salomé and Tunin run away through the ruins.)

SCENE 44

(Upstairs corridor—interior—daytime. Salomé goes running down the hall angrily, taking her hat off. Tunin is close behind her. Tripolina is waiting for them in the corridor.)

TRIPOLINA: How'd it go?

(Salomé continues toward her room, answering rudely.)

SALOMÉ: Beautifully! A very pleasant sightseeing tour.

(Tripolina throws herself around Tunin's neck.)

TRIPOLINA: I was so frightened!

(Yvonne is walking down the hall with a client.)

YVONNE: Hey, Tripolina, are we getting sentimental?

(Tunin breaks away from Tripolina's embrace and tries to catch up with Salomé.)

TUNIN: I must speak with Salomé . . . hey, wait up!

(Tripolina is offended.)

TRIPOLINA: Tunin, wait a minute!

(Tunin pushes through the whores and clients who have begun to converge in the hall. He heads for Salomé's door, leaving poor Tripolina behind.)

SCENE 45

(Salomé's room—interior—daytime. Salomé enters her room. She slams the door behind her and starts to undress in a hurry. Tunin storms in right after her. She turns and faces him aggressively.)

SALOMÉ: What the hell are you doing in here? Go make love to your Tripolina, you'll see what's going to happen to your aim after a few days of exercise . . . you won't even have the strength to pull the trigger! Get out, I never want to speak to you again!

(Tunin stares at her with his enormous eyes. Suddenly he locks the door and leans his forehead against her face, as if he was suddenly overcome by great fatigue.)

TUNIN: Listen, listen to me. I'm probably going to be dead in two days' time. I need to stay here. Please . . .

(Salomé is stunned.)

SALOMÉ: Hey, what the fuck's wrong with you?
TUNIN: I just can't stay in that hotel room by myself anymore, look at how my hand is shaking; I think about it too much, I'm becoming too nervous. . . . I am always thinking of that instant when I'm going to have to pull the trigger. I get sick. . . . I feel like shitting in my pants. . . . I'm really scared, that's why I wanted to take that poor man to the Forum, to see if I could overcome this fear.

(Salomé tries to encourage him but she is apprehensive about his behavior.)

SALOMÉ: Well, you overcame it, didn't you? Look, stop thinking about it. Fear is only human. Look at the Fascists, they aren't scared, and so they kill people—but you, you're an anarchist.

TUNIN: Like hell I'm an anarchist, I'm not Michele Sgarravento! I'm Antonio Soffiantini, and that's all.

(Tunin is bitter, trying to understand himself, trying to find his identity, a reason for his actions, for the desperate sentiments that are confusing but which he feels are just.)

SALOMÉ: What do you mean? You're a comrade, aren't you?

TUNIN: Yes, but I've only been involved with these things for a short time. I've been a part of these things since the day I saw Michele Sgarravento shot in the back by the police. . . . Before that I couldn't have cared less. . . . Antonio Soffiantini *was*, I repeat *was*, a farmer. . . . In other words, one of the masses. Michele—well, he was different. Shit, compared to him I'm nothing. You should have seen him, even when he was dead, his mouth full of dirt . . . he still looked like a king.

(Salomé sees that the situation isn't improving.)

SALOMÉ: For shit's sake, why the hell did the comrades send you? Let's get this straight, are you one of Brighenti's group or have you been on your own up to now?

TUNIN (modestly): I'm really nothing, only a friend of his, I was like a brother to Michele. When he came back I was the only one he confided with. He said to me, "I've returned to kill Mussolini"—that's exactly how he put it. Then he told me his whole plan. He left me his briefcase, then said that if anything were to happen to him I was to go to the comrades and tell them what had happened. It was as if he knew he was going to die.

SALOMÉ: So, then, where do you come into the picture?

TUNIN: I'm part of this because when I saw his body, I sold my cow, took the briefcase, and went to Paris to meet with Brighenti. I told him I was going to kill Mussolini, so they taught me how to shoot.

(Salomé is now very concerned because the whole situation is cast under a different light.)

SALOMÉ: Have you thought about it carefully, Tunin? Michele was a born anarchist, he had dedicated his life to this one goal. But you, maybe at the moment you saw his body, all you could think about was revenge, but now . . . you see, you mustn't go through with it if you don't feel like it. This is a desperate plan, there's no way out once you've done it.

(Salomé is filled with concern. Tunin is shaking with fright.)

TUNIN: You think I'm going to end up like Anteo?

SALOMÉ: Forget about Anteo . . . if they catch you they'll put you before a firing squad, or, what's even worse, they'll throw you into the San Antonio jail.

TUNIN: San Antonio?

SALOMÉ: They'll club you to death and no one will ever hear from you again, just like they did to Bresci.

(Tunin is really frightened. He looks her straight in the eyes—a sincere but angry look.)

TUNIN: Are you trying to scare me? Believe me, there's no need. You can't even start to imagine how scared I am.

(Tunin glances toward the washbasin, looks at himself in the mirror, and starts speaking to himself.)

TUNIN: I've got to do this. I've got no choice but to go ahead with it, even though I'm really not an anarchist . . . perhaps they'll make me one later on. You see, I swore it to myself, I've just got to do it! . . . I swore I would stop living the way I was, like a slave. I just can't take it anymore, not even rats live the way we do. I want to start living like a human being, to stop groveling like a snake in the mud. This one gesture will make me feel like a man again, at last. Oh, but now you probably don't trust me anymore.

(He comes across strongly and honestly in his speech, but then he looks at Salomé; perhaps he has said too much. Salomé shakes her head.)

SALOMÉ: No, it isn't that I don't trust you, it's just that I ask myself, why should you sacrifice your young life for an ideal you don't even know the first thing about when there are so many of us who could do it?

TUNIN: Well, after I kill Mussolini, then I will be part of the group, won't I?

(Salomé decides she's going to trust him.)

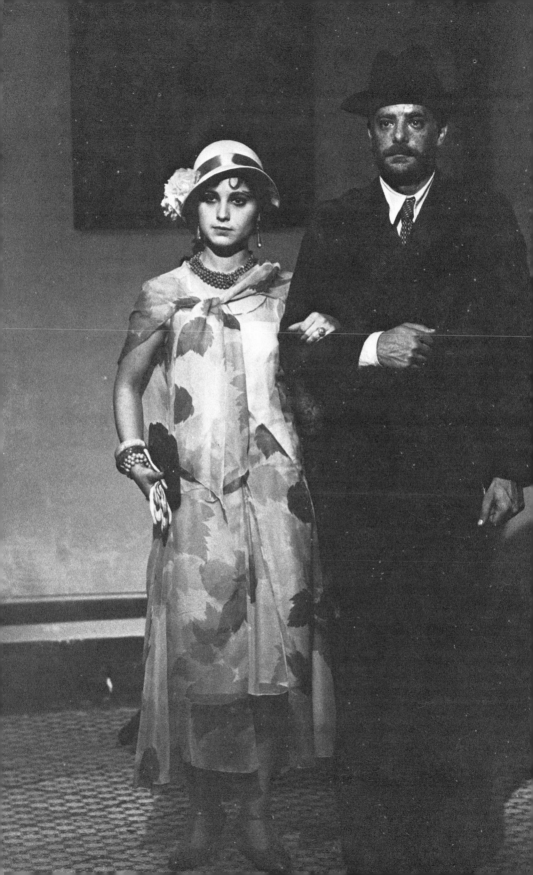

SALOMÉ: Okay, yes, I'll trust you. Now go on to your little lady, she's so much in love she hears bells ringing every time you kiss her. Poor Tripolina, she's put up with so much in her lifetime. Go, run along, go to her—she's waiting for you.

SCENE 46

(*Tripolina's room—interior—daytime. Helped by Tunin, Tripolina is trying on some clothes to wear on their unexpected outing. Music: "A Walk Around Rome." They laugh and play like lovers.*)

SCENE 47

(*Brothel entrance—interior—daytime. Tunin is seated in the empty hall. He looks like a client waiting for his whore. Music continues.*)

SCENE 48

(*Tripolina's room—interior—daytime. Tripolina lets her dress twirl around her. She looks like a ballerina. Finally she's chosen her outfit. It is her "in love" outfit. Music continues.*)

SCENE 49

(*The streets of Rome—exterior—daytime. Tunin and Tripolina are walking arm in arm around the sunny streets of Rome mingling with the crowds of passers-by. Music continues.*)

SCENE 50

(*A terrace overlooking Rome—open-air café with a live band— exterior—daytime. An elegantly dressed lady is walking her collie. We're now at the Casina Valadier, a charming open-air café, with a terrace overlooking the roofs and domes of Rome. The music continues until it dissolves into "Frou Frou del Tabarin," played by an all-woman band that is entertaining the guests*

seated at the small tables on the veranda. Tunin and Tripolina sit eating their ice creams at one of the small tables. Tunin is happy. Suddenly a voice visibly shakes them.)

SPATOLETTI: Good morning!

(Tripolina and Tunin, somewhat embarrassed, look at him.)

SPATOLETTI: I knew it! I knew our little cousin had fallen head over heels for you! Do you know that the other night this bastard almost split my skull open with a wine bottle? I didn't rip him to pieces because I felt sorry for him . . . he was as drunk as a skunk! . . . Well, Tripolina, who knows if this isn't the right one for you at last! Good luck!

(Spatoletti returns to his table, where he is sitting with a "Black Shirt" and some "respectable" ladies.)

SPATOLETTI: Pardon me . . .

(Spatoletti whispers something to the ladies, who turn toward the other table with a malicious look. It is clear that he is explaining who Tunin and Tripolina are. Tripolina feels uncomfortable under their stares. She is an inexperienced young whore who is humiliated by the name with which society brands her. Tunin wants to protect her. He pays the check and takes her away. They walk arm in arm, like two "respectable" lovers. The table of "respectable" people follow the couple with stares and mocking laughs.)

SCENE 51

(Tripolina's room—interior—nighttime. Tunin has taken his pistol apart and is greasing it carefully. Salomé sits on the edge of the bed in her bathrobe giving him some last-minute instructions.)

SALOMÉ: So then these are the false passports our comrades got us. It's much safer this way. It will be easier to cross the border as normal emigrants rather than refugees. If everything goes well and Mussolini is really killed, there will be one hell of a mess at the borders, so we must be ready.
TUNIN: Ah, yes, if all goes well; then we'll see.

(Tripolina has tears in her eyes as she listens to this conversation to which she really can't contribute as she has no part in the plan.)

SALOMÉ: I'll wake you up at six. . . . I'm certain everything will be just fine, now put those things away and don't let your kitten wait any longer.

(Salomé gives Tunin a long kiss on the mouth and smiles.)

SALOME (jokingly): Isn't love strange, look at the odd places it hides in.

(Tunin clears the bed. "Rock-a-bye Baby" is played on the guitar. Tunin and Tripolina start making love in the dark.)

SCENE 52

(Via dei Fiori—exterior—nighttime. Everything is silent in the little street.)

SCENE 53

(Shots of imperial Rome—exterior—nighttime. Even Rome, with its monuments to war, marble eagles, and massive statues, is asleep on this clear evening.)

SCENE 54

(Tripolina's room—interior—nighttime. With the first light of dawn, Tunin and Tripolina are coming to the end of their night of passionate love-making. After climaxing, Tunin is tired and stretches out on the enormous bed. He gives her one last loving look.)

TUNIN: Sorry, angel, but I must get some sleep or else . . .

(Tripolina starts crying.)

TRIPOLINA: My darling, my love!
TUNIN: You're a real crybaby! Now come over here, you musn't act like this or it will make matters worse.

(Tunin holds her in a delicate embrace, drunk with fatigue. They look at one another, a deep, passionate look. Tunin smiles childishly.)

TUNIN: Look, my curly locks, you've got to admit it's really been nice, just the two of us, alone like honeymooners, even if it was only for two days.

(*Tripolina is disheveled and her face is tear-stained, but she tries to smile feebly.*)

TRIPOLINA: Time really flew, didn't it?

TUNIN: Now we've got to sleep, enough tears, and oh, there is one last thing I want to tell you . . . you're the finest thing that has happened in my whole life, and I want you to know that.

(*Tripolina is coming apart. She kisses him with passion. It is a kiss she wishes would linger on forever. At last she pulls away and notices that Tunin has fallen asleep. His regular breathing seems to soothe her. She gently slides out of bed, goes over to her trunk, and places a small statue of the Virgin Mary on it. She prays. Recurring shots: her white skin, her curly locks, those deep eyes. She's a woman torn apart by love, she's like the wife of a sailor, a miner, or a soldier who suffers like them yet knows that she is so different from them. She looks around the room. She sees the squalid bidet, the bottle of lysoform next to it, the Arabian dressing gown, her feathers, make-up, and face powder. The windows have locks on them. She looks back at Tunin's sleeping face, his childlike neck. She looks like a child too, but an experienced one. She picks up a sweet and starts sucking on it as she curls up at the foot of the bed to look at him, waiting for morning to arrive. She sucks the sweet as a child would, her dark eyes gazing at Tunin.*)

SCENE 55

(*Shots of Rome—exterior—daybreak. Dawn plays gently across the roofs and domes of Rome, over the pine trees and palms, across the churches and marble buildings, over the monument to the unknown soldier. Rome wakes up to the pealing of a thousand church bells.*)

SCENE 56

(*Salomé's room—interior—morning. Salomé hasn't slept a wink. Beside her is an ashtray heaped with butts, newspapers are spread all over the bed. She is still engrossed in her paper when the alarm clock rings. She gets up, takes a sip of water, and heads for the door.)*

SCENE 57

(Upstairs hall—interior—morning. Everything is quiet in the hallway. Salomé heads for Tripolina's room. She looks around to see if everything is quiet, then rapidly walks down the hall. Tripolina is waiting for her in the hall.)

SALOMÉ: What are you doing awake? Is he awake yet?

(Tripolina shakes her head.)

TRIPOLINA: No . . .
SALOMÉ: We've got to wake him up.

(Tripolina puts out her arm to stop Salomé.)

TRIPOLINA: No, you're not going to wake him.

(Salomé doesn't understand what is happening. She tries to get away but Tripolina holds her back.)

TRIPOLINA: Come with me, I've got to talk to you!
SALOMÉ: Come on, Tripolina, we haven't got time to waste, it's already very late.

(Tripolina whispers to her.)

TRIPOLINA: I'm warning you, if you wake him up I'm going to cause such a scene that the two of you will end up in jail. Come on, let's go to the bathroom and talk.

(Taken by surprise, Salomé follows Tripolina into the main bathroom.)

SCENE 58

(Bathroom—interior—morning. Tripolina pushes Salomé into the bathroom and locks the door. It is one of those old-fashioned, ornate bathrooms with antique tiles. The two disheveled girls stand on the cold tiles, trembling in their dressing gowns. Salomé studies Tripolina carefully. She reaches for a cigarette in her pocket. Tripolina looks totally distraught.)

SALOMÉ: O.K., let's have it.

TRIPOLINA: You aren't going to wake him up, that's all there is to it. He's fast asleep, and when he wakes up on his own it will be too late.

(Salomé turns red with anger.)

SALOMÉ: Look, you little tart, get the hell out of here! This isn't a romantic love story, you know! You've got nothing to do with all this, now just give me the key and let's forget it!

(Tripolina is not listening.)

TRIPOLINA: I'm well aware of all these ideals, all this justice you seek, but you're not going to wake him! Is there any justice in this poor young man going to get himself killed like a dog? He is going to get killed, and you know it!

SALOMÉ: Of course he's going to die like a dog, in the same way others before him were killed. They were younger than he is, I saw them die with these very eyes. They were more innocent than he, I saw them—with my own eyes—dead! It's all the same to him, he'll die, he knows it, but he'd rather die like a dog than live like one for the rest of his days. One must die for these ideals, and he's going to die, in the same way we're all prepared to die. Now move out of the way, you can't understand these things, give me the key!

(Salomé tries to grab the key away from Tripolina but she defends herself like a tiger. They start fighting.)

TRIPOLINA: Leave me, leave . . .

SALOMÉ: Give me that fucking key, goddamit! What the hell are you trying to do?

(Salomé and Tripolina roll onto the floor, clawing at one another.)

SALOMÉ: If you don't watch out, I'll bust your . . .

(Though Salomé is the more powerful of the two, Tripolina is so filled with anger that she manages to overcome her. At one point, as her fingers grow more taut around Salomé's throat, Salomé has the distinct feeling that she's going to be strangled. Tripolina hears her making a terrible rattling noise.)

TRIPOLINA: You watch it! I'll kill you!

(Salomé barely manages to break away from her grip and shoves

her with her elbow. Tripolina stands up, more menacing than ever, as Salomé tries to catch her breath again.)

SALOMÉ: You're really insane!

(*Tripolina is desperate.*)

TRIPOLINA: I'll kill you, I'll kill you with these hands! Then I'll jump out the window! . . . . I just don't give a shit anymore . . . you've got a heart of stone and you don't give a damn about that poor boy . . . he's just like a child . . . he's got this fine ideal in his mind . . . a beautiful, ah, such a beautiful ideal. Maybe one day it will come true, the goal you strive for will actually happen, but in the meantime he has to die this morning. . . . . No! If you try to wake him, I'll kill you!

(*Salomé is on her feet again, fully in control.*)

SALOMÉ: Ssssssh, don't shout! Do you think, you idiot, that you're doing him a favor? He made up his own mind. If we don't wake him he'll hate you forever!

(*Tripolina picks up the shawl and throws it over her shoulders. She knows in her heart that Salomé is right.*)

TRIPOLINA: I know that. He'll wake up and he'll be full of hatred and he'll walk off, but at least he'll walk off in one piece, and that's how I want it to be!

SALOMÉ: I don't want it like that! Someone must kill that bastard! I swore it on a young boy's body, and he trusted me. The comrades trust me, Tunin trusts me, I can't sit here and listen to your reasons!

(*Tripolina senses that Salomé is beginning to see it her way.*)

TRIPOLINA: You're going to listen to me! You're going to listen to me . . . and you know why? Because you're jealous, you love him too! Please help me, I don't want him to die. . . .

SALOMÉ: Of course I love him . . . poor boy, he's fallen in the middle of this political mess . . . just like Anteo, so young, oh . . . my heart breaks when I think of how young they are. . . . If only I knew how to shoot I would do it myself. . . . Enough! Sentiments are a luxury we can't afford at a time like this . . . this is war! What the hell would happen if at a time of war all the mothers and girl friends stood in the way of soldiers?

(*Tripolina sees the truth in this paradox.*)

TRIPOLINA: Well, my father died on the battlefield, it would be a great thing if all mothers *did* do it! Why not? War isn't the answer. It hasn't solved anything, there will always be hatred. Where are our men now, they're all buried. I say, stop this senseless dying!

> *(Tripolina has touched on the right note. Salomé remembers Anteo.)*

SALOMÉ: Goddamn you, goddamn myself, we're just a pair of sentimental sluts! Goddamnit, open this door! I can't stand this bullshit anymore, I make myself sick!

> *(Tripolina goes up to Salomé and kisses her. Salomé, disgusted, pushes her away.)*

SALOMÉ: It's true what they say, you can't trust a whore!

> *(Salomé walks out of the bathroom.)*

SCENE 59

> *(Tripolina's room—interior—daytime. We hear the first few notes of "Tripoli, Land of Love." The late morning sun filters through the half-open blinds. Tunin is still fast asleep, just as we left him. Tripolina sits at the foot of the bed looking at him sweetly. Tunin shakes his head, yawns, scratches his skull, and in a haze sees Tripolina smiling at him. He smiles back. Then, realizing the time, he leaps out of bed and grabs his watch from his vest pocket. Seeing what the time is, he turns pale, then red as a beet. He shuts his eyes, hatred and pain exploding within him.)*

TUNIN: Why didn't you wake me?

> (*He gives her a powerful slap across the face, then beats her without mercy.*)

TUNIN: Damn, damn bitch! Slut! Why didn't you wake me up?

> (*Tripolina doesn't react to the slaps and smiles apologetically. The door opens and Salomé walks in, her face bearing the marks of a sleepless night. Tunin turns to her in a rage.*)

TUNIN: And you, you traitor! You cheap whore! Why didn't you call me, why?
SALOMÉ: Because by now you would be lying with your chest torn apart by a gunshot.
TUNIN: I'm worse off now than if I were dead. I'm nothing but a crawling worm! There I was, sleeping in a whore's bed . . . that's all you two are to me . . . whores!

> (*Tripolina and Salomé hold on to one another and listen to his abuses with their heads held high. Tunin continues to pour his venom into them.*)

TUNIN: Now what am I going to do. . . . I'm going to kill myself, that's all I can do!

> (*Tunin pours the contents of the drawer onto the floor as he looks for his pistol.*)

TUNIN: My pistol! What have you done with it?

> (*He acts like a wild beast. The women try to hold him back, but there's no holding him.*)

SALOMÉ: Tunin, wait! Don't go on like this!
TUNIN: Well, that bullet is going to end up right between my eyes . . . right between my eyes, you ugly bitches!

> (*Salomé grabs him by the arm, but he violently pushes her away, knocking over the screen and pieces of furniture.*)

TUNIN: Away! Away, you whores! My pistol, where is it, I'm going to shoot myself, I don't give a damn now, I'm going to shoot myself!
SALOMÉ (to Tripolina): Stop crying, we've got to stop him!

> (*Tripolina can't stop the flow of tears.*)

TUNIN: Christ, give me that bloody gun! I can't wait any longer, I

have to shoot myself! Right away, shoot myself . . . can't live like
this. . . .
TRIPOLINA: Nooooooo! Tunin, calm down, calm down!

> (*We hear the alarmed voices of the other whores, who have been
> disturbed by all this racket.*)

CARMELA'S VOICE: Hey, what the hell's going on?

> (*Salomé is holding on to Tunin, begging him to stop.*)

SALOMÉ: Shhhh! Don't shout like that. . . .

> (*Knocks on the door.*)

CARMELA'S VOICE: Tripolina, Salomé, open up, what's wrong?
TUNIN: Oh, mother . . . holy mother!
SALOMÉ: Tunin, shut up now . . . please shut up or you'll ruin the
whole thing.

> (*Salomé raises her voice. She is in full control.*)

SALOMÉ: I'm coming, shit . . . what the hell's the matter, anyhow?

> (*The knocking gets louder and louder. Tripolina is terrified and
> embraces Tunin. Salomé goes to open the door, quite sure of
> herself.*)

SCENE 60

> (*Upstairs—corridor—interior—daytime. A group of girls, Ma-
> dame Aida, and Carmela are gathered around the door.*)

CARMELA: Salomé!

> (*Salomé answers aggressively.*)

SALOMÉ: Well, can't one have a nice family argument? What the
fuck! Look at all you ugly whores huddled around like a bunch of
chickens. Mind your own business!

> (*Madame Aida is really very angry.*)

MADAME AIDA: Curiosity's got nothing to do with it, Salomé, and
you know it! I won't tolerate all this noise, is that quite clear?
SALOMÉ: What the fuck do I care if . . .
CARMELA: You gave me such a fright! I thought they were slitting
your throat!

SALOMÉ: Oh, shut up!

ANITA: It sounded like you were trying to kill one another.

SALOMÉ: Look who's talking! The other day this one and her Spanish friend started arguing over a pair of panties and they screamed like two bald eagles. . . . Stop breaking my balls!

(Salomé walks back into the room, slamming the door.)

SCENE 61

(Tripolina's room—interior—daytime. Tripolina and Tunin are glancing through the half-open blinds onto the street. They look worried.)

SALOMÉ: What's the matter?

(Salomé rushes over to the window.)

SCENE 62

(Via dei Fiori—exterior—daytime. At first glance it looks like a typical sunny morning, but looking more carefully we see four policemen and a marshal walking up to the brothel entrance.)

SCENE 63

(Tripolina's room—interior—daytime. The three of them are gathered by the window, terrified. The sight of the policemen has put them in a panic. Tunin moves away from the window, a crazed look on his face. His hair is in a mess. He shakes and sweats profusely.)

TUNIN: Oh, good mother of Christ, they're coming for me, they're coming to take me away!

SALOMÉ: What are you saying, relax, relax. . . .

TUNIN: They're coming to get me, someone gave me away, you gave me away!

(Salomé tries to stay calm.)

SALOMÉ: Don't be stupid, no one gave you away . . . shut up!

(Tunin sits on the bed, sweating and trembling.)

TUNIN: Oh God, I can't end up like this, they're coming for me. . . . I knew it, someone gave me away, you did it! Why?

(Tripolina goes up to him.)

TRIPOLINA: Darling, my darling, calm down. . . .

> *(Tunin hardly listens to her. A sudden stomach pain is crippling him. His nervous system has completely broken down from fear.)*

TUNIN: Darling my foot, I'm sick, I'm shitting in my pants. . . . What have you done to me?

SALOMÉ: Now look here, listen, no one gave you away. . . . We kept you here to save your life, we did it out of love.

> *(Tunin stands up and embraces the two of them.)*

TUNIN: I love you both too, but don't leave me, please don't leave me!

> *(Salomé shakes him, trying to knock some sense into him.)*

SALOMÉ: Stop it, Tunin, stop it! I'll go downstairs and try to put them off while you and Tripolina run away. She's got some money and you can also have some of mine. You'll find it in the bottom drawer of my bureau . . . the pistol is in there too.

> *(Salomé points to the trunk. She empties it, then starts to help him with his undershirt.)*

SALOMÉ: Come on, hurry, hurry, you'll see, you'll make it. Go back to Paris, go see Saverio Brighenti, remember that name, Saverio Brighenti. . . .

> *(But Tunin isn't listening. He hugs her passionately.)*

TUNIN: Oh, mother, I beg of you, don't leave me.

> *(Salomé pushes him away firmly.)*

SALOMÉ: Tunin, stop it, stop wasting time . . . don't blame it on yourself. Not everybody has to be a hero, you know.

> *(Salomé walks out, leaving Tunin sitting on the bed. Tripolina opens a drawer and unwraps a parcel.)*

TRIPOLINA: Look, Tunin, here's the money, and here are the passports. We have the gun as well. Hurry up, get dressed.

> *(Tripolina starts dressing him as if he were a child. He doesn't move.)*

TRIPOLINA: My love, I'll help you. Why are you acting like this? Don't worry, everything will be all right. We'll make it, you'll see.

(*Tripolina starts crying. Tunin caresses her hair.*)

TRIPOLINA: I love you so much . . . calm down. . . .
TUNIN: Yes, you'll see, I'll calm down. . . . I'll try.

(*Tunin stands up and starts dressing himself. Then he holds her tight and kisses her. He leaps for the gun.*)

TRIPOLINA: Nooooo . . . what are you doing . . . what do you want to do with that? Let's run away.
TUNIN: No, now I'm going to stay here. I'm not running away.
TRIPOLINA: Noooooooooo, noooooooooooo, Tunin, noooooo!

(*Tunin grabs the gun as Tripolina tries to hold him back.*)

SCENE 64

(*Upstairs corridor—interior—daytime. Tunin opens the door and rushes out. Tripolina tries to grab him by the legs. Totally crazed, he pushes her roughly aside.*)

TRIPOLINA: Tunin, don't shout! For God's sake, don't go!
TUNIN: It's done now, it's all over. I won't run away . . . I can't run.

(*Waving the gun in his hand, he tramples over Tripolina and some of the girls who are getting in his way.*)

TRIPOLINA: Tunin, Tunin . . . noooo!
ISA: Oh, Holy Virgin!

SCENE 65

(*Madame Aida's sitting room—interior—daytime. The four policemen and a marshal are sitting with Madame Aida in her sitting room. Carmela and a few other girls are there as well.*)

MADAME AIDA: The checkup should be on Thursday, my dear Marshal. Anyway, the young girls are all in perfect health, they're upstairs in their rooms. You make yourself at home here, and if you wish to go upstairs you are certainly familiar with the way.
MARSHAL: Yes, Madame, I know the way. Thank you.

(The door to the sitting room opens wide and Tunin appears with a gun in his hand.)

MARSHAL: Hey, who the hell is this?

(Tunin's eyes are filled with tears.)

TUNIN: I want to kill Mussolini!
SALOMÉ: Oh, nooooo!

(Tunin holds the pistol with both hands and starts shooting wildly, hitting the marshal in the chest.)

POLICEMEN: Stop him, stop!

(The police don't even have time to reach for their guns. Tunin shoots them all. The girls start screaming, Tripolina and Salomé try to stop Tunin.)

SALOMÉ: Oh, my God, what are you doing, stop it, stop it!
TRIPOLINA: Stop, stop . . . no . . .

(Madame Aida and Carmela are screaming at the top of their lungs.)

SALOMÉ: Tunin, run, go . . . run away!
TRIPOLINA: Run, my love, Tunin! Run!
TUNIN: Long live anarchy!
SALOMÉ AND TRIPOLINA: Noooo!

(Tunin puts the gun in his mouth and pulls the trigger. There are no more bullets. He angrily throws the gun aside and starts running.)

TRIPOLINA: Tunin!

SCENE 66

(Brothel—interior—daytime. Tunin is running across the waiting rooms and down the corridor. He goes up the stairs and comes running down them. He runs right into one of Zoraide's wash buckets. He falls, and scrambles back onto his feet.)

TUNIN: Fuck!

(He is still being chased by the girls and the surviving policeman. The girls are trying to get in the way of the policeman. Everyone is running after him.)

SCENE 67

(*Via dei Fiori—exterior—daytime. Tunin runs out into the street. We see a colorful market in the small street. It is crowded with shoppers and shopkeepers. The surviving policeman is right behind Tunin. He fires a shot into the air. The women run away, terrorized, but some of the shopkeepers start chasing Tunin like hounds after the fox. They jump on him, and at this point Tunin knows it is all over. He tries in vain to shield himself from their blows. The whores, led by Tripolina, have all come out of the brothel. They are in their nightgowns and slips.*)

TRIPOLINA: Run, Tunin, run!

(*Tunin is being jostled around and ends up falling right into the arms of the whores.*)

SALOMÉ: Don't say a thing, Tunin, it's all over, it's useless to say anything!

(*A police officer comes running up with some other policemen. A car drives by.*)

POLICE OFFICER: Stop that car!

(*The officer is getting things under control. He starts gathering some thugs. They are very good at ganging up on one man. As the police and the citizens begin to form a barrier, the car gets closer. Tunin shouts with his last breath.*)

TUNIN: I wanted to kill Mussolini, I wanted to do it for all of you! Comrades, brothers, all of you, so we could be free like we were meant to be, living in harmony with one another! I want to kill Mussolini!

(*His voice echoes loud and clear, but the people don't understand. His voice rises up, strong and brave. It is the voice of someone demanding justice. But it is soon made to be silent. A violent punch to the throat shuts off the last few syllables, his teeth make a terrible noise as they are ripped away from the bone. . . . Tunin's yell fuses with that of Tripolina, who has seen the whole thing.*)

OFFICER: Make him shut up, for God's sake, keep him quiet!

(*The police start passing him around, punching and kicking him in the mouth.*)

SALOMÉ: No, not like Anteo, you murderers, no! Stop those bastards!

(They kick him all the way to the waiting car. The whores are right behind, still led by Tripolina.)

OFFICER: Make this pig shut up, fucking anarchist! Get those sluts away from here, there are respectable people around here. . . .

(Having shoved Tunin into the car, they speed away. The remaining policemen try to force the whores back into the brothel. Tripolina runs after the car and no one is able to stop her.)

TRIPOLINA: Tunin, my love, my darling, Tunin . . .

(Salomé runs after her, trying to stop her, to save her life.)

SALOMÉ: Stop, stop . . . you musn't . . .

(Tripolina is grabbed by Salomé. She stares after the car where a few minutes before she saw Tunin spitting blood like a water fountain. She doesn't see anyone, she is blind to the world. She shouts and shouts and shouts. The whole group of prostitutes who have been pushed back by the policemen's bayonets are now part of Salomé's and Tripolina's grief. The partially naked girls are pushed around like sheep, leered at by the onlookers, cowards, and police. Salomé screams out.)

SALOMÉ: Someone do something!

(A woman makes the sign of the cross.)

SALOMÉ: It was for you that he was doing this, you bastards! For you who are slaves and don't know it! He was young and he had a heart of gold and he wanted to help you pigs!

SCENE 68

(Spatoletti's office—interior–exterior—daytime. One whole wall of Spatoletti's office is a picture window overlooking a sun-drenched Rome. A group of policemen is beating the living daylights out of Tunin, who is sitting tied to a chair. From a corner a statue of the she-wolf of Rome watches the proceedings with indifference.)

SPATOLETTI: That's enough, he's had enough. Excuse me, Commissioner. Lift him up in his chair, come on. . . .

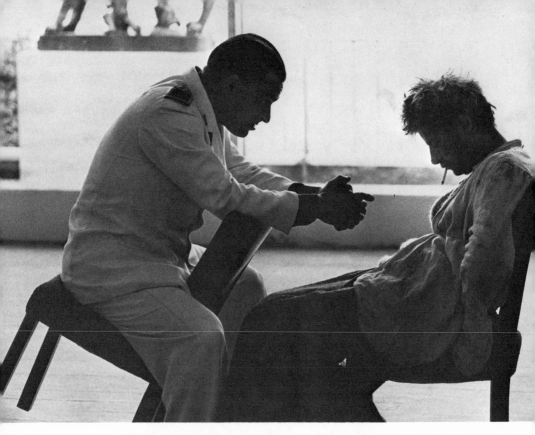

(Spatoletti has almost a sweet tone as he comes over to Tunin, pulls up a chair in front of him, and lights a cigarette, which he places between the poor man's half-open lips.)

SPATOLETTI: Now then sweetheart, have a cigarette. Well, Mr. Soffiantini, let me start by telling you that the prison we have put aside especially for you is approximately ten feet below the sea bed. The little air you will be breathing travels down a thin hose. There is naturally no light. You'll therefore be in total darkness and . . . silence. Sooner or later you will begin to go mad. There was that fellow, what was his name now? Oh yes, Pasanante. We found him down there eating gobs of his own shit . . . he had become completely green, not a hair on his body, he was just like an earthworm. . . . All I ask is for a few names, a few addresses . . . if you co-operate we can always have you plead insanity, and in that way you'll be out in about ten years. I promise I'll look into it myself. . . .

(Tunin barely raises his head.)

SPATOLETTI: Who was it that sent you? Are you part of the Brighenti group? Out with it then, was it Brighenti who sent you? Are you from France? . . . Or from America? You don't think I'm so stupid to believe you came to Rome on your own decision to kill Benito Mussolini, do you?

(*Tunin's voice is barely audible.*)

TUNIN: Long live anarchy!
SPATOLETTI: What was it you said?
TUNIN: I don't know anything about anybody. Just put me in front of a firing squad and let's get it over with.

(*Spatoletti becomes furious and starts beating him to a pulp.*)

SPATOLETTI: You pig! Anarchist shit . . . I'll teach you to say long live anarchy! You son of a bitch!

(*Spatoletti moves away and gives a sign to the thugs to take him away.*)

SPATOLETTI: Take him away! Away! And give him the complete treatment!

(*The policemen untie Tunin and take him away.*)

SPATOLETTI: Be really tough . . . he's got to talk!

SCENE 69

(*Commissioner Pautasso's office—interior—daytime. A very long desk behind which we see an enormous fresco depicting a Fascist motif and a bust of Mussolini. Sitting behind the desk, directly opposite Spatoletti, is Commissioner Pautasso, about to answer the telephone.*)

COMMISSIONER PAUTASSO: Hello? Yes, this is Commissioner Pautasso. . . .

(*The commissioner leaps up to attention, clicking his heels.*)

COMMISSIONER: As you wish, Your Excellency. Of course, Your Excellency, whatever you say, sir, it shall be done. Don't worry, Your Excellency. Good day . . .

(*He hangs up the telephone and turns to Spatoletti, confidentially.*)

COMMISSIONER: They would rather we kept the whole thing silent. . . . He prefers it this way. In the past months these incidents seem to have tripled, and . . .

SPATOLETTI: Commissioner, what are you trying to say? The Italian people love their Duce. . . . It's been two years since there was an attempt . . . and if only he wouldn't stop pardoning them and have them shot instead. . . .

COMMISSIONER: Oh my . . . who did he pardon? Are you joking? Well, maybe those first two, but the rest . . . he may be brave, but he isn't an idiot . . . with certain people it is better to make them disappear without any publicity—that's what they want in this case. It's quicker and more efficient.

SPATOLETTI: Well, I'll be damned!

(The commissioner is back on the phone. In a cynical tone of voice he gives the order.)

COMMISSIONER: Proceed . . .

SCENE 70

(Scene of the murder—interior—daytime. A voice is dictating to an old-fashioned typewriter.)

VOICE OF THE COMMISSIONER: This morning at 10 A.M. in Via dei Fiori comma in the notorious brothel comma an unidentified man comma stricken by a sudden fit of madness comma began shooting on a group of policemen who had rushed over to do their job period. The man was arrested, but shortly after he was to take his life by repeatedly banging his head against the cell wall.

SCENE 71

Tunin's cell—interior—daytime. A handful of plainclothes policemen walk into the cell. Tunin sits in this tiny triangular cell. He is already half dead. The men are straight and to the point and meticulously beat him to death. They put him in a sack, which they continue to kick and punch until the shape is no longer moving. With the empty dark cell as a backdrop there appear the words:

"I would like to stress my horror of the attempted assassinations. These gestures are not only evil, but they hinder the cause they are meant to serve. . . . One must admit, though, that these murderers are heroes as well. . . . When their extreme gesture will be forgotten, we shall celebrate the ideal which spurred them."

Enrico Malatesta

3

SWEPT AWAY

SWEPT AWAY
BY AN UNUSUAL DESTINY
IN THE BLUE SEA OF AUGUST

CAST

Gennarino	Giancarlo Giannini
Raffaella	Mariangela Melato

CREDITS

Written and Directed by	Lina Wertmüller
Producer	Romano Cardarelli
Assistant Director	Giovanni Arduini
Cameramen	Giulio Battiferri
	Giuseppe Fornari
	Stefano Ricciotti
Sound	Mario Bramonti
Music	Piero Piccioni
	(One motif in the film is a free adaptation of a theme by Henry Purcell)
Sets and Costumes	Enrico Job

Running time: 116 minutes

The first American showing of SWEPT AWAY was on September 17, 1975 at Cinema II in New York City.

TITLES:

The Esmeralda II *glides across the clear blue Mediterranean waters:*

On board: Gennarino, a sailor from southern Italy, is tackling the sails.

The woman combing her hair is Raffaella, who has rented the yacht.

SCENE I

(Small island—sea—exterior—daytime. Raffaella's guests are swimming near the most beautiful island in the world. This is the quintessential Mediterranean island.)

RAFFAELLA'S VOICE (off camera): Oh, this is divine! . . . It's paradise! . . . And to think that in a few years it's going to be so polluted . . . they'll fill it up with shit, plastic bottles, and assorted garbage!

(Raffaella's voice continues to be heard talking about the impending ecological disasters.)

RAFFAELLA'S VOICE (off camera): We're really going to wipe ourselves off the face of the earth! . . . Shit, we won't be laughing when there's a hundred million of us . . . that'll be the end of the oceans, it'll all be turned into a gigantic sewer . . . what a pleasant prospect! The world will be transformed into a cement ant hill! Then who's going to call Italy the "Garden of Europe"?

(Her friends would much rather have a good time than listen to her predictions about these forthcoming catastrophes. Toti tries to steer her off the subject.)

TOTI: Very well, Raffaella, but why don't we try and enjoy it while we can? Look at the beauty of this place . . . it's heavenly, so stop breaking our balls with all this ecology crap!

(Raffaella is on an inflatable motorboat. She's wearing an Olympic bathing suit and a black swimming cap. She is covering herself with oil.)

RAFFAELLA: God forbid! What do we care? Let's just enjoy it while we can! You're a fine bunch, you know, I'm really right in saying that all the Italians should be locked up in a "reservation" far from Italy in order to save what little is left . . . especially the more prolific ones. . . .

TOTI: What do you mean? Should there be a law passed for mass sterilization?

RAFFAELLA: Don't be a smart-ass . . . of course that's what ought to be done, it would solve all our problems . . . if you just think, darling . . .

TOTI: Oh Christ, there she goes again . . . I'm drowning!

(Toti disappears underwater.)

RAFFAELLA: It's you Communists that I'm pissed off with. . . . Look, rather than disappoint the clergy you were quite prepared *not* to have the referendum on divorce.

TOTI: What the fuck are you talking about?

RAFFAELLA: Yes, cutie, that's exactly what happened.

TOTI: Well it sure as hell wasn't through Senator La Malfa's help that you got the pro-divorce vote. If it wasn't for the ten million Communist votes, there's no way in hell . . .

(Toti sinks underwater again.)

RAFFAELLA: Okay, Okay!

TOTI (re-emerging): . . . that we would now have divorce in Italy!

RAFFAELLA: Very well, but the abortion issue is never mentioned, is it?

TOTI: You see how stupid you are; you have no idea what the fuck you're talking about! At this very moment there's a Communist-backed bill on the abortion issue. Listen, what do you want, state-subsidized abortions?

RAFFAELLA: Yes, that's exactly what I want, or at least a daily commercial on T.V. explaining the use of contraceptives!

TOTI: Raffaella . . . go fuck yourself!

SCENE 2

(*The* Esmeralda II—*deck—exterior—daytime.*)

RAFFAELLA'S VOICE (off camera): You're completely fucked in the head. Have you forgotten that La Malfa had already predicted it in 1970?

> (*They are all on deck reading their newspapers and sipping apéritifs. Toti and Raffaella are stretched out on deck chairs sunbathing.*)

TOTI: La Malfa is always predicting major catastrophes . . . he's nothing but a jinx!

RAFFAELLA: No, darling, his ideas are far better than those Socialists . not to mention the Communists!

TOTI: What have the Communists got to do with it? What the fuck have you got to say against the Communists?

RAFFAELLA: I'm referring to the Communists as economic organizers. Just look at the example in Russia . . . after fifty years they still wear yellow shoes in Moscow and black ones in Stalingrad . . . and then you dare criticize.

(*Gennarino is busy scrubbing the deck. He scowls at her.*)

TOTI: The Russians just aren't a nation of shopkeepers and petty industrialists. That's why, you see, the Russians are bohemians, they're a nation of artists!

RAFFAELLA: So you see them as artists, huh? And I suppose Stalin was so disorganized. . . . I think he did an excellent job of keeping his camps in Siberia very orderly. . . .

TOTI: Well, I suppose we should admire the wonderful things America did to Hiroshima?

RAFFAELLA: Oh, no, my god, now he's going to start on Hiroshima!

TOTI: Yeah, but what about you and Stalin? Come on, Raffaella! Why don't we come up to date and talk about the present situation? Can't you get it into that thick skull of yours that the Communists have always been the opposition and it's been La Malfa's government that's been licking the Church's ass for all these years?

(*Raffaella, in a sudden fit of anger, throws the paper straight at him, hitting him squarely.*)

RAFFAELLA: The Church! How dare you mention the Church! You're the ones who lick their asses, you're the ones who dream of the day you'll be able to walk down the street linking arms with them. You can get it out of your head, though, because there's no way Fanfani will allow a Communist and Christian Democrat coalition.

TOTI: The truth of the matter is that you're such an anti-Communist that you're terrified that we're going to join forces with the Christian Democrats!

RAFFAELLA: Ohhhh!

TOTI: You know that if that happens, you people are finished!

RAFFAELLA: Oh, sure . . . and that's what you'd like to see!

TOTI: Naturally!

RAFFAELLA: So what you want is a nice confessional and Father Stalin listening to confessions . . . then for your penance you get thirty Hail Marys and thirty years in Siberia!

TOTI: Let's skip Siberia . . . thank God it's so far away . . . with your fear of Communism you've made us suffer through thirty years of

Christian Democracy. (Shouting) You do know that it's been thirty years! You better get it into your head! It's all over for you people! Thirty years have been more than enough, thirty years of breaking our balls!

(Raffaella snorts as Gennarino nods his approval of Toti's speech.)

RAFFAELLA: Change together with you people? Never! From the frying pan into the shit!
TOTI: I suppose you'd prefer it if the colonels came to power?

(On this last remark Gennarino gets up and moves closer to Raffaella, still eying her with hatred. Raffaella notices his look.)

RAFFAELLA: Mmmmm . . . what a stare! Hey, look at him, he's trying to burn a hole through me with his stare! Clearly a member of the Communist Party!

(Gennarino pretends they aren't talking about him.)

TOTI: A member? He's more than that, he's almost a leader of his town's committee.

(Gennarino nods in silence. Raffaella notices it.)

RAFFAELLA: In that case, he must see us as exploiters of the working classes. . . . You don't think that perhaps one of these nights, in a fit of hatred, he's going to slit our throats. Hey, what do you say to that, Gennarino?

(Gennarino manages to contain himself. He picks up his rag and pail and walks away. Toti laughs.)

TOTI: Raffaella, you wouldn't by any chance be scared of the people's revenge . . . you're shitting bricks!

(Raffaella is provoked.)

Me, frightened? Certainly not!

(She shouts at Gennarino.)

RAFFAELLA: Of course it's us who take the bread out of the poor orphans' mouths, it's us who starve the widows and the working masses! I'll take the blame for it all! Oh, and while I'm at it I'll also take the blame for causing silicosis in those poor miners. . . . So now it's straightened out . . . but nevertheless, I want my wine nicely chilled.

(Gennarino crosses the deck, mumbling to himself.)

GENNARINO: Goddamn fucking whore . . . biggest damn slut in the world.

(Gennarino throws the pail and rags on the floor.)

SCENE 3

(The Esmeralda II at sea—exterior—daytime. Raffaella's high-pitched voice can be heard coming from the boat.)

RAFFAELLA'S VOICE (off camera): By the way, Gennarino, don't forget that even Brezhnev likes to drink his wine chilled, and that if you didn't serve it at the correct temperature he'd send you straight to Siberia.

SCENE 4

(Entrance to the galley—Esmeralda II—exterior—daytime. Gennarino is clutching another sailor out of sheer frustration. The sailor is amused and laughs. Raffaella keeps poking fun at Gennarino.)

RAFFAELLA'S VOICE (off camera): Do you understand, dear comrade? It's pretty rough out there, too.

(Gennarino is beet-red with anger.)

GENNARINO: Do you hear her? Slut! You'd think she was paid to get me pissed off!

SCENE 5

(On deck—the Esmeralda II—exterior—daytime. The ladies are sunning themselves on the upper deck. They are almost totally naked. Corrado and Toti are trawling. The clear blue sky is as pretty as a picture postcard. Gennarino is slyly spying on the sunbathers.)

SCENE 6

(Esmeralda II—*upper stern—exterior—daytime. Shots of a series of headlines from the Communist newspaper* L'Unità. *The men are slowly reading the paper. Gennarino walking along the deck carrying the coffee. He puts the tray down on a table in front of Raffaella. Raffaella sniffs the coffee.*)

RAFFAELLA: And what is this?
GENNARINO: What's what?
RAFFAELLA: What is it?
GENNARINO: Madame, it's coffee.
RAFFAELLA (smiling): Reheated, I suppose?
GENNARINO: Well . . . yes . . . yes . . .
RAFFAELLA (still smiling): Thank you very much—but I want you to make a fresh pot. Great way to start . . . what are we, beggars?

(*Gennarino sighs.*)

SCENE 7

(*Galley entrance*—Esmeralda II—*exterior—daytime. With the tray still in his hands, Gennarino moves up to one of the sailors.*)

GENNARINO: Hey, boss . . . come here . . . listen . . . I have a complaint. That blond lady . . .
PIPPO: Who you talking about?
GENNARINO: You know . . . the blonde, the one who rented the yacht . . . Mrs. Pancetti.
PIPPO: You mean Mrs. Pavone Lanzetti . . .
GENNARINO: She called me a southern beggar.
PIPPO: So what?
GENNARINO: Now, listen, boss. She can call her husband a southern beggar if she wants to, but I'm going to pour the coffee all over her head if she isn't careful.
PIPPO: Be patient, it's only a month. They're paying you five hundred thousand lire, aren't they?
GENNARINO: Yes, but that industrial whore must watch herself because if I get pissed off she's really up shit creek.
PIPPO: Hey, Gennarino . . . you expect me to believe that? (Sing. ;)

"If you want to accept their money you must be prepared to play their game."

GENNARINO: Hey boss, you're not making fun of me, are you?

SCENE 8

> (*The deck on the* Esmeralda II—*exterior—daytime. As usual, Raffaella and Toti are arguing. Two other guests are lying on inflatable mattresses reading their papers. Gennarino is watching the whole scene from the lookout box on the main mast. Raffaella is wearing a flowing, tentlike outfit made out of muslin; it is gathered in at the waist by a belt with an oversized buckle.*)

RAFFAELLA: Well, we all know who to blame for the Papal State, don't we!

TOTI (*in a tolerant tone of voice*): Well, of course . . . it was the Communists' fault, who in 1948 . . .

RAFFAELLA: Yes, my dear shithead, it's no use you being smart . . . it *was* the Communists who in 1948 formed a pact with the Vatican instead of raising the anticlerical flag like La Malfa did . . .

TOTI: So now I suppose you and La Malfa are going to teach the Communists what policy to follow?

RAFFAELLA: Certainly!

TOTI: Oh, stop it!

> (*Raffaella hits him with her paper, then throws it at him.*)

RAFFAELLA: La Malfa and I are going to teach you pigs . . .

TOTI: Come along, Raffaella, you aren't being serious. All you see is La Malfa—he's like a God to you!

RAFFAELLA (*trying to provoke him further*): Yes, you're right, I'm wild about the man . . . I love La Malfa physically, I find him terribly sexy . . . I adore him . . .

> (*Only now does Toti seem to notice Raffaella's outfit.*)

TOTI: Shit, Raffaella, what are you wearing? I see it's a very simple yacht outfit . . . all you need is a tiara and you'd look like the Pope.

RAFFAELLA: Well, La Malfa may not be approved of by the party but he's kind of cute. Yeah, well, I suppose you look good in those horrible military shorts!

> (*Toti stands up to show everyone present his shorts. He pirouettes so that everyone can have a good look.*)

TOTI: I would like to point out that these are very elegant Bermuda shorts!

(*They all laugh.*)

RAFFAELLA: Bermuda! Oh my dear!

TOTI: What are you laughing at? What the fuck are you people laughing at? I'd really like to know!

SCENE 9

(Esmeralda II—*deck—nighttime. Gennarino sings, accompanying himself on the guitar as he looks out to sea. It's a beautiful clear night.*)

GENNARINO (*singing*):
"My dearest love,
"How I sigh when I think of you.
"My heart flickers like a candle
"When someone mentions your name."

SCENE 10

(*Small living room below decks–Esmeralda II–interior—nighttime. In the meantime, below decks, Pippo takes a swig from the wine bottle, then walks into the living room, where the guests are playing cards.*)

GENNARINO'S VOICE (*off camera—singing*): "Just think about the fresh snow that falls . . ."

(*One of the guests listens to him sing.*)

ANNA: Who's that singing? Is it Gennarino? My, what a languid voice!

RAFFAELLA: Well, I suppose Communists have a heart as well . . . isn't it so? Hey Pippo, ask your friend over there if Stalin used to sign the order for a mass execution and then break down crying strumming his balalaika all the while.

(*Pippo smiles.*)

PIPPO: Madame, Gennarino's thinking about his home, not Stalin.

CORRADO: That's right, Pippo, don't listen to madame, she's joking.

(*Pippo leaves the room, closing the door behind him. Corrado scolds his wife.*)

CORRADO: Why don't you stop acting like Marie Antoinette? You're dull and vulgar when you start taking the piss out of the Communist Party.
TOTI: You're right.
RAFFAELLA: Now you're starting to insult me? I never! Marie Antoinette!
TOTI: Come on, play . . . I bet one hundred lire . . .
RAFFAELLA: See you.
BUBI: Full house.
TOTI: Yeah, but what's high?
LILLI: Full house, kings high.

(*The others keep playing.*)

RAFFAELLA: They insult me because I won't give in to political terrorism. I don't hide behind a Marxist ideology like you guys do.
TOTI (*snickering*): I'm certainly not hiding anywhere . . . I haven't got a penny . . . I'm just a guest on board.
RAFFAELLA: Mmmmmmmmmm . . .
ANNA: Moralize, my dear Raffaella . . . the world is still in the hands of people who had servants!
RAFFAELLA: Look here, I've never doubted for an instant that Marx had plenty of servants around the house.
TOTI: I've never heard such absolute crap in my life!

SCENE 11

(Esmeralda II—*upper stern—exterior—daytime. It's one of those three P.M. lunches after a long morning at sea. Gennarino is serving spaghetti with an oil, garlic, and red pepper sauce. Everyone takes the first mouthful. Raffaella swallows but then grimaces.*)

RAFFAELLA: Oh no . . . it's overcooked! The spaghetti is overcooked! Why the hell did you let it get overcooked? I just don't understand, it's such a simple thing to look after spaghetti to make sure it doesn't overcook.
GENNARINO: Yes, well, I'm sorry.

(*Raffaella follows him with a dirty look.*)

RAFFAELLA: He's sorry, my foot, he doesn't give a shit. What the fuck does he care?

(*As Gennarino is about to reach the galley entrance, he bumps into Pippo, who is carrying a bottle of wine.*)

GENNARINO (*mumbling*): She's terribly irritable today.
PIPPO: What happened? What was it?
GENNARINO: The industrial whore got pissed off because the spaghetti was overcooked.

(*Gennarino pinches the spaghetti.*)

GENNARINO: It feels just right to the touch.
PIPPO: Well, she really likes it *al dente.*

(*The guests are all busy eating. Corrado tries to take Raffaella's mind off the subject.*)

CORRADO: Oh, really, forget it. It's not too bad.
TOTI: It could be that I'm starving, but it seems delicious to me.
RAFFAELLA: You think it's good, too? Oaky then, you all enjoy it . . . I'll just have to starve.

(*Pippo comes over to the table, carrying the wine.*)

PIPPO: Excuse me, madame . . . you found the spaghetti to be overdone?
RAFFAELLA: What can you do? Gennarino's trying to punish us all . . . probably because we represent the capitalists.

(*Her digging remarks are making the guests a bit nervous. Pippo smiles and winks.*)

PIPPO: You've got to be joking, madame, if it weren't for you people we would be rotting in some stinking factory . . . sweating among those damn machines . . . and we'd get paid nothing.

(*Raffaella keeps it up.*)

RAFFAELLA: Anyhow, as we await the end, the revolution, let's try and make the spaghetti *al dente* . . . at least once.

PIPPO: You're right, madame, (*raising his voice severely*) . . . next time, let's make sure the spaghetti is *al dente*.

SCENE 12

(*Inflatable motorboat—Esmeralda II—deck—exterior—daytime. The bathers are climbing back onto the yacht. A sailor hands them bathrobes.*)

RAFFAELLA: What a fabulous swim! It's just so super! Hey Pippo, come here!

(*Pippo comes running toward her.*)

PIPPO: Here I am, madame. What can I do?

(*Raffaella hands him a parcel containing fresh fish.*)

RAFFAELLA: Here you go, it's fresh fish we just bought from a fisherman on a boat nearby. Let's have a nice fish stew. But try and be a bit more careful and put less hot pepper in it . . . last time we scorched our mouths!

PIPPO: We wouldn't want that to happen again, my beautiful lady.

SCENE 13

(*Galley on board* Esmeralda II—*interior—daytime. Gennarino is sipping his coffee. He can overhear the end of the conversation between Pippo and Raffaella.*)

RAFFAELLA'S VOICE (*off camera*): Mmmmm . . . this time we won't put so much red pepper will we . . .

GENNARINO: Now she comes busting my balls about the red pepper! Fuck it, I'm going to put in a lot of fucking red pepper!

PIPPO'S VOICE (off camera): Whatever madame says.

SCENE 14

(Deck on board Esmeralda II—*exterior—afternoon. Raffaella is alone on deck. Pippo walks up to her.)*

PIPPO: Would you care for a cup of coffee?
RAFFAELLA: By the way, while I think of it, could you change your T-shirts before lunch? You see, they're rather sweaty, and it could be annoying . . .
PIPPO: But certainly, of course, you're right.
RAFFAELLA: Will you bring me a cup of coffee now.
PIPPO: Right away!

SCENE 15

(Galley on board the Esmeralda II—*interior—daytime)*

GENNARINO: Fucking shitty woman! Yessiree . . . I'll change my sweaty T-shirt!

(Gennarino angrily takes off his T-shirt as Pippo tries to calm him down. The other sailor is washing the dishes and having a good laugh.)

PIPPO: What are you doing?
GENNARINO: Now you'll see how I'll change my sweaty T-shirt!

(Gennarino takes an enormous white T-shirt out of the closet. He puts it on furiously.)

PIPPO: Are you going to wear this thing? What the fuck's gotten into you? You gone mad?
GENNARINO: Madame wants me to change my T-shirt!
PIPPO: Come on, cut the crap . . .
GENNARINO: Pour the coffee, hurry! I'll bring that industrial whore her coffee!
PIPPO: Holy Mary save us! This is a real ship of fools!

SCENE 16

(Deck on the Esmeralda II—*exterior—daytime. Gennarino carries the coffee tray across the deck to where Raffaella is sitting.)*

GENNARINO: Coffee is served, madame.

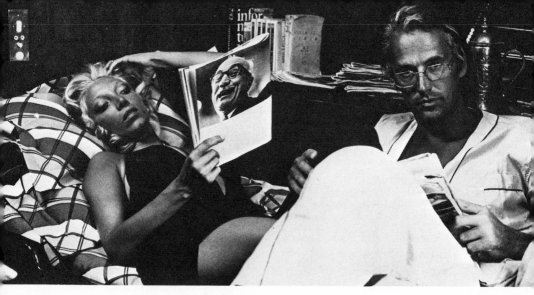

RAFFAELLA: Thanks. What are you wearing. Who do you think you are, a clown?

GENNARINO: Didn't you say we had to change our T-shirts?

RAFFAELLA: 'Scuse me, Gennarino, but are you trying to be funny?

GENNARINO: Funny? What do you mean? I'm the one who's always pissed off.

SCENE 17

> (*Below decks on the* Esmeralda II—*exterior—nighttime. In the small living room the guests are playing poker. Corrado is tired.*)

CORRADO: Good night, darling . . .

RAFFAELLA: Off to bed, angel? I'll join you in a minute.

CORRADO: 'Night everyone . . .

> (*Toti is at the head of the table and isn't playing.*)

CORRADO: You're not playing tonight?

TOTI: With those stakes, I just couldn't afford it.

> (*Toti catches up with Corrado in the passageway.*)

TOTI: Those fools are losing millions of lire!

> (*Pippo is walking down the passageway.*)

PIPPO: Good night, doc!

TOTI (disappearing into his cabin): Good night, Pippo.

PIPPO (to Corrado): Good night, professor.

> (*Corrado disappears into his cabin as well.*)

CORRADO: 'Night, Pippo.

SCENE 18

(*Deck on the* Esmeralda II—*exterior—nighttime. Gennarino is joined by Pippo on deck.*)

GENNARINO: Hey, boss, what's going on?

(*Pippo nudges Gennarino.*)

PIPPO: Listen to this . . . they've really got a great thing going on down there. . . . The husband feels sleepy and leaves his wife to gamble the night away.

(*Gennarino makes a contemptuous gesture.*)

GENNARINO: If that were my wife, I'd kick her ass all the way into bed! What kind of men are they anyway? What kind of shit is this? The men give their wives total freedom and then the women take advantage of them. The husband goes to bed and the wife stays up gambling. Jesus, what is this world coming to?
PIPPO: Tell me, Gennarino, what do you do at night when you're at home?
GENNARINO (aggressively): I go out to drink and gamble.
PIPPO: And your wife goes straight to bed?
GENNARINO: Well, I'm the male!
PIPPO: Well, they just do the opposite to what we do with our wives.
GENNARINO: I know . . . these bastards are ruining our women! Who's going to wash our underwear in the future!

(*Pippo adopts a mysterious air. Gennarino moves closer to him. It's clear that Pippo has a secret to tell. He pulls out two crushed cigarettes from his pocket.*)

PIPPO: Look what I found in the brunette's cabin. . . . I think it's hashish.

(*Gennarino's eyes flash.*)

GENNARINO: I knew something was wrong, they were too relaxed. You think it's hash? Let me smell it.

(*He looks at the cigarette.*)

PIPPO: Well?
GENNARINO (knowingly): This is "mariana."

(*He smells the joints, then studies them carefully. Pippo is very excited.*)

PIPPO: "Mariana"? Have you ever tried it?

(*Gennarino gives him a dirty look.*)

GENNARINO: You've got to be kidding.

(*Pippo grabs them from him.*)

PIPPO: Let's smoke them!

(*Gennarino takes them back.*)

GENNARINO: Smoke? Smoke, my ass! There's a chance you'll like it, then you'll start stealing and you'll end up in prison.
PIPPO: Don't be ridiculous, you're exaggerating. Let me try one.
GENNARINO: No siree . . . I'm going to confiscate them. You go to bed.

(*Pippo is broken-hearted as he leaves.*)

PIPPO: Ahhh, fuck you! For once in my life I had a chance to have an orgy . . . fuck you royally!
GENNARINO: Go to bed, you ass . . . what orgy? He's looking for thrills with six children and a pregnant wife to look after. Go away. . . . What a revolting yacht. . . . They probably think this is a whorehouse. . . . This monkey over here wants an orgy. . . . That fine group below is gambling. . . . If you rub me the wrong way I'm going to send up a flare and the harbor police are going to arrest the whole damn bunch of you!
RAFFAELLA'S VOICE (off camera): While you're emptying the ashtrays, I'm going to take a breath of air. It's too smoky in here.

(*Gennarino moves away quickly. Raffaella is climbing up onto the deck.*)

RAFFAELLA: Ahhh, a breath of air, it's so hot.

(*Raffaella lets down her blond hair and combs it out with her fingers. From the corner of the deck Gennarino begins to sing and play his languid Neapolitan song. Raffaella looks at him for a moment, then walks away annoyed.*)

SCENE 19

(*Deck on the* Esmeralda II—*exterior—early evening. The crew is busying itself with the sails.*)

PIPPO: Hey, let's hurry up with those lines! Move it!

GENNARINO: Cool it, I'm almost ready.

(*The yacht seems to be abandoned. There isn't a soul in sight. Raffaella appears from below. It's clear she has just gotten up. She looks around for the others. Anna, the brunette, is fast asleep on deck. Raffaella calls Pippo in a sleepy, hoarse voice. He comes up to her carrying a rolled-up line.*)

RAFFAELLA: What's the time, Pippo?

PIPPO: It's seven, madame.

RAFFAELLA: Seven P.M.? Oh, shit, damn it! Seven in the evening!

(*Anna wakes up yawning.*)

ANNA: Hey, Raffaella, you're finally up?

RAFFAELLA: Damn it, you should've gotten me up, I've been asleep all day!

ANNA: Yes, but it was six in the morning by the time we went to bed.

RAFFAELLA: Where are the others?

ANNA: They left hours ago.

PIPPO: They took the outboard and went to the caves.

(*Raffaella has pulled herself together and is her normal self again.*)

RAFFAELLA: All right . . . Pippo, put the other outboard in the water. I want to catch up with them and have a swim before the sun goes down.

ANNA: You're going for a swim at this hour?

RAFFAELLA: Well, why not? I'll bring my swimsuit. I'll bring along a sweater too, just in case it gets cold. Pippo, the outboard!

(*Pippo is annoyed. He turns to Gennarino.*)

PIPPO: Gennarino . . .

GENNARINO (off camera): What's wrong?

PIPPO: Lower the outboard into the water, madame wants to go out on it.

(*Gennarino makes a face.*)

GENNARINO: The outboard at this time? It's very late.

(*Raffaella isn't at all happy with Gennarino's tone of voice.*)

RAFFAELLA: Who says it's too late?

(Gennarino lowers the boat into the water.)

GENNARINO (in a quiet voice): Just a shit head.

SCENE 20

(The outboard at sea—exterior—late evening. Raffaella and Gennarino are on the boat. They putter along the coast of the island without getting too close because of the menacing rocks. They head for a promontory beyond which the others are probably having a swim. Gennarino has a moody expression. He is quiet and looks slightly worried. The sun is setting rapidly. Finally Gennarino's professionalism gets the better of him, and he decides to speak up.)

GENNARINO: The current is getting stronger.

(Raffaella doesn't even look at him.)

RAFFAELLA: So?

(Gennarino manages to overcome his irritation at her tone of voice.)

GENNARINO: Well, it's just that the caves are quite a way off and the sun is setting.
RAFFAELLA: So what?
GENNARINO: So nothing!

(And he shuts up. They pass the tip of the island and find that here the sea is much rougher. The island now casts a shadow on what was previously the sunny side of the island.)

GENNARINO: I'm telling you, madame, I think it would be better if we turned back.
RAFFAELLA: Why?
GENNARINO: Just to be on the safe side. It's really all the same to me, but it is getting darker . . .
RAFFAELLA: Don't be silly . . . near the caves the sun will last for at least another half hour. Now, hurry up!
GENNARINO: Well . . . I warned you.
RAFFAELLA: Okay, Gennarino, you warned me, and I'm telling you to go on. . . . You aren't scared, by any chance?

(Gennarino is provoked.)

GENNARINO: Scared? Me?

RAFFAELLA: Well, then, move it. I'm not scared. In fact, I'm having a lot of fun.

(*The wind suddenly pushes the boat farther away from the shore. It's getting darker by the minute but neither of them says anything. The engine begins to miss. Then it stalls. Gennarino leaps to his feet and starts trying to fix the engine.*)

GENNARINO: Goddamn son of a bitch engine! Screwed up! Fucked up asshole! Why us?

RAFFAELLA: Oh, this is terrific, it sounds like the spark plugs got wet.

(*Gennarino doesn't reply.*)

GENNARINO: Fuck the stinking guts of this putrid slut! Fucking whore!

(*He is furious. He tries in vain to fix the engine, which just won't start. Raffaella looks like an irate deity. She looks at him provokingly.*)

RAFFAELLA: Damn it, what are you mumbling about?

(*Gennarino doesn't bother to turn around.*)

GENNARINO: I'm swearing to myself, madame. Don't worry, it's got nothing to do with you.

(*Gennarino proceeds to remove the engine's protective covering. Raffaella is trying to catch a glimpse of the other boat, but there is no one in sight.*)

RAFFAELLA: If we could at least see the other . . . we should be so lucky. Well, what's happening?

GENNARINO: What can I tell you, madame? I just don't know.

RAFFAELLA: Very well . . . But is it broken?

GENNARINO: It just won't work.

(*Raffaella is very annoyed.*)

RAFFAELLA: Well, it was obviously destined that I wouldn't be able to go for a swim today. Try and do something!

GENNARINO: What do you think I'm doing?

(*Gennarino is working frantically. Raffaella looks at him skeptically. The island looks totally deserted.*)

RAFFAELLA: Hell, is there any hope?
GENNARINO: There's always hope, madame.
RAFFAELLA: Mmmmmmmmmmmm . . .

(The sea is getting rougher.)

RAFFAELLA: Listen, is there any gas?
GENNARINO (patiently): Yes, there's gas.
RAFFAELLA: Well, that's it, I suppose we just have to wait.

SCENE 21

(Outboard at sea—exterior—evening. A spectacular fiery sunset
lights up the glass-calm sea. Gennarino continues working on
the engine.)

RAFFAELLA: Fortunately for us the sea's calmed down. . . . But
we're really in fine shape, if only Pippo was here, he knows about
engines!

(Gennarino throws her a filthy look.)

RAFFAELLA: Aren't we getting a bit far from shore?
GENNARINO: I warned you the wind was changing.
RAFFAELLA: What's that got to do with it?
GENNARINO: It's got plenty to do with it!
RAFFAELLA: Anyhow, it's no time to start arguing . . . just try and
fix this thing, will you?
GENNARINO: There really isn't anything to be done.

(Raffaella is beginning to realize that things are worse than she'd
realized.)

RAFFAELLA: What do you mean, there's nothing to be done? You
can't fix it? Oh, Christ, how can you take a motorboat out to sea when
you don't even know how to fix it? If there's one thing that gets on my
nerves it's incompetence . . . amateurs dabbling in professionals'
work. Okay! Okay!

(Raffaella massages the side of her head.)

RAFFAELLA: It's pointless to get nervous. Shit, it's cold, good thing I
brought along a sweater.

(Without stopping his work, Gennarino watches her grab the sweater.)

GENNARINO: Be my guest.
RAFFAELLA: This old sweater stinks!
GENNARINO: Naturally, it's mine!
RAFFAELLA: Oh, pardon me!

(Gennarino tries to start the engine. Raffaella puts on his sweater.)

RAFFAELLA: What a marvelous adventure. Damn it, can't see a bloody thing. Well, what can we do . . . they're bound to pass by here sooner or later.

(A light wind starts blowing. Gennarino's hair is in a mess as he works on the engine with a pair of pincers. Raffaella is all bundled up in a hat and scarf.)

GENNARINO: I sure hope so!

(Raffaella is getting very nervous.)

RAFFAELA: Yes, let's hope so. . . . I'm sure that when they don't see us coming they'll start searching for us.
GENNARINO: I hope so.
RAFFAELLA: What kind of attitude is that to take?
GENNARINO: I hope so means . . . I hope so because the sea is enormous and the currents are strong and pushing us farther and farther away.
RAFFAELLA: Well, then, do something.

(Gennarino puts down his pincers and stops working.)

GENNARINO: I can't see a thing.

(*Gennarino puts the engine back together again.*)

RAFFAELLA: Aren't there any oars on board?
GENNARINO: Yes, we have oars, but where the hell are we going to row to?

(*Raffaella is nervous. In her search for the oars she bumps into something.*)

GENNARINO: Fuck! Let's try and be a bit more careful.
RAFFAELLA: Let's be careful? Listen to him, he's the sailor and I'm the one who should be careful!

SCENE 22

(*Outboard at sea—exterior—nighttime. The outboard is floating farther out to sea.*)

RAFFAELLA: I don't know if you've noticed, but it's nighttime.

(*Gennarino is very calm.*)

GENNARINO: I warned you.
RAFFAELLA: No, my dear, you didn't warn me that the engine would break down. If you had, like hell I would have come out with you. Anyway, here we are, no use crying over spilled milk. They'll come looking for us. Look at that face! By the way, do we have a flare gun?
GENNARINO: No, we don't.

(*By this time it is pitch-black.*)

RAFFAELLA: I knew it . . . you just can't trust anybody nowadays. Well, let's not overdramatize, they'll come and get us.

(*After a brief pause, Gennarino is heard speaking in a quiet tone of voice.*)

GENNARINO: I hope so.
RAFFAELLA: Yes . . . let's hope so.

(*The noise of the sea gets louder and louder and the night gets darker and darker.*)

SCENE 23

(*Outboard at sea—exterior—daytime. The outboard with Gennarino and Raffaella floats on the open sea. Gennarino and Raffaella are fast asleep at opposite ends of the boat. The sea is calm, and there isn't a sign of life. Gennarino wakes up and remembers.*)

GENNARINO: Damn it!

(*He shoves his head underwater, then pulls it out and gives her a disgusted look. He takes off his T-shirt and pants, folds them neatly, and sticks a cigar butt in his mouth.*)

GENNARINO (mumbling): It had to happen to me.

(*Quickly he surveys the boat to see what's on board that might be useful. Using an old knife and a twisted wire, he tries to fix the engine. One of the screws is stuck. He puts pressure on it with the knife and it slips out of his hand and into the water. Like a shot he dives in, trying to rescue the knife before it disappears forever. The sudden splash has woken madame. At first Raffaella doesn't know where she is. Then it all comes back to her. For an instant she is terrified because Gennarino is nowhere to be seen. She feels totally alone.*)

RAFFAELLA: Oh, my God! Oh mother, where is he? Gennarino, Gennarino, help, help, Gennarino!

(*He surfaces just as she is about to have a nervous breakdown. When she sees him she jumps perceptibly. Gennarino is completely out of breath.*)

RAFFAELLA: Having a nice swim?

(*Almost miraculously, Gennarino has managed to save the knife before it vanished forever into the deep blue waters. Gennarino gasps for air.*)

GENNARINO: The knife fell into the water!
RAFFAELLA: What are you saying?

(*Gennarino hangs onto the side of the boat and throws the knife into the bottom.*)

GENNARINO: The knife fell!

(*Gennarino lifts himself up, tipping the boat. Raffaella is nervous.*)

RAFFAELLA: All by itself?

(*Gennarino is beginning to get annoyed. Without answering, he carries on trying to fix the engine.*)

RAFFAELLA: Wonder why we haven't seen anyone yet? Where are we? Shit, you can't see land anymore. What's wrong with those assholes, why didn't they come and look for us? What did they do all evening? The sea may be vast, but it could never be as vast as their stupidity. They're probably still there waiting for us to return.

(*Raffaella takes off the sweater. Gennarino continues to fix the engine.*)

RAFFAELLA: What?
GENNARINO: I didn't say anything, madame.
RAFFAELLA: When do you ever have anything to say!

(*Gennarino pretends not to hear her. Raffaella stretches out in the sun.*)

RAFFAELLA: After all, they're the ones with the yacht, the maps, the radars and helicopters! Why they don't come looking for us is beyond me. The fact is that they're a bunch of incompetent fools, they'd get lost in a glass of water . . .

(*Gennarino continues to work.*)

RAFFAELLA: They're probably very calm, waiting for us to return. Look, leave that engine alone, obviously you're no good at fixing it, so just let it be. You're beginning to get on my nerves.

(*Gennarino tries to start the engine by hand.*)

RAFFAELLA: You're really stubborn, aren't you?

(*Unexpectedly the engine starts up, the boat lurches forward, and Raffaella falls over. Triumph flashes from Gennarino's eyes. He has succeeded.*)

RAFFAELLA: Well, at last it's started. What a stroke of good luck! About time? OK, let's go . . . I'm really thirsty.

(*Gennarino puts on his T-shirt and looks at her.*)

GENNARINO: Which way would you like me to go?
RAFFAELLA: You're asking me?
GENNARINO: I have no intention of taking the responsibility.
RAFFAELLA: Look, for Christ's sake, you're the sailor! How should I know which way to go? Why give me the responsibility? Sailors know which way to go; use the sun, the stars . . .
GENNARINO: Yeah, the stars!
RAFFAELLA: You must be able to do something right!

> (*Raffaella appears to be quite content now. She puts her dark glasses on again.*)

RAFFAELLA: All I ask is that we don't wind up in Africa.
GENNARINO: Let's hope not.

> (*The small boat heads quickly toward its unknown destination.*)

RAFFAELLA: What do you mean, let's hope not? Which way are you going?
GENNARINO: Well, you tell me where we ought to go . . . if you'd rather I turn right, I'll turn right.

> (*Gennarino steers the boat to the right and then to the left.*)

RAFFAELLA: Are you trying to be funny?
GENNARINO: Funny? If you'd rather go to the left, I'll go left!
RAFFAELLA: I find all this rather childish.
GENNARINO: Well, it may be childish, but I just don't want to take the responsibility.
RAFFAELLA: So we're going to go around in circles wasting gas?
GENNARINO: Well, if you're not going to tell me where we go, what do you want me to do, stop? You want to have a swim, sunbathe?
RAFFAELLA (pointing): Let's go that way!

> (*Obediently Gennarino turns in the direction Raffella has chosen.*)

RAFFAELLA: You see, I'm not afraid of taking on responsibility. Shit, I hope I'm right . . . and please don't say let's hope so in that tone of voice.

> (*The outboard glides across the empty sea toward the unknown.*)

SCENE 24

(*Outboard at sea—exterior—late afternoon. The boat is at a near standstill in the open sea. Raffaella is sunburned, and her lips are chapped. Gennarino is trying to fish with his hands. Raffaella follows him with a gloomy look. We can sense her desperation.*)

GENNARINO: A fish!

(*The fish manages to get away. At last he pulls in a tiny one.*)

GENNARINO: I caught you, you dirty little son of a stinking bitch!

(*Gennarino clutches the fish triumphantly, then with a sudden move he bites its head off. He hands a piece to Raffaella.*)

GENNARINO: Here, help yourself, it's a lovely fat sardine.

(*Raffaella nearly vomits.*)

RAFFAELLA: It makes me sick, I'll vomit!

(*Gennarino bites into the squirming fish.*)

GENNARINO: You've got to eat something if you're going to make it through the day.

(*She turns away in disgust.*)

RAFFAELLA: I'll never touch it like that!

(*Gennarino quickly "cooks" it for her in sea water, then sprinkles it with a sauce of salt water.*)

GENNARINO: Try it now, I've put some salt on it. I suggest you try it, because . . .

(*Raffaella is totally disgusted, but she takes a bite.*)

RAFFAELLA: It's revolting!

(*She throws the fish into the water. Gennarino tries to stop her, but he is too late.*)

GENNARINO: Why? Why did you throw it away, I would have eaten it! It took me three hours to catch it and you threw it away!

(*Raffaella couldn't care less.*)

RAFFAELLA: Well, what can you do . . . fasting is good for the figure . . . and it disintoxicates you as well . . . you can ask any dietician!

(*Gennarino looks at her with hatred. Raffaella acknowledges his look and returns one equally full of hate.*)

RAFFAELLA: There's no reason for you to look at me that way, you know. It's a fact that your women, having reached the age of thirty, look like fifty-year-olds. They're worse than Turkish women. Look at that stare . . . of course you should diet!

(*Gennarino can't contain himself any longer.*)

GENNARINO: They're compelled by poverty to be on a constant diet!

(*Raffaella looks at him and replies in a long-suffering tone of voice.*)

RAFFAELLA: Are we going to have to listen to stories about the social injustices you people suffer? Please spare me, Gennarino, you'd bore me to death . . .

(*Suddenly she's on her feet shouting and screaming. A ship is visible on the horizon.*)

RAFFAELLA: Ahoy there! Help! Help!

(*The two jump up and down, shouting, waving, and whistling. Raffaella waves her black skirt, Gennarino whistles as loud as he can. She grabs the whistle from him and starts blowing on it.*)

GENNARINO: Let me whistle, madame!

(*Raffaella throws the whistle into the sea.*)

RAFFAELLA: Help us, help us!
GENNARINO: Now she throws the whistle in as well!
RAFFAELLA: Help, we're shipwrecked! Help us!
GENNARINO: It's useless, the wind is against us and won't carry our shouts.

(*The ship disappears over the horizon. Raffaella collapses, on the verge of a nervous breakdown.*)

RAFFAELLA: Can't we do anything at all? Let's try rowing.
GENNARINO: With this current, we'll get nowhere.

> (*Raffaella cries. For the first time her nerves aren't holding up. It finally dawns on her that this incident may turn into something very unpleasant.*)

SCENE 25

> (*Outboard at sea—exterior—afternoon. The wind is getting stronger. Raffaella is still lying on the bottom of the boat.*)

RAFFAELLA: It's really getting choppy. You're not going to tell me that the weather is changing for the worse, are you? All we need now is a storm. Ah, shit! The cigarettes are all wet!

> (*She throws the packet of cigarettes into the other end of the boat.*)

RAFFAELLA: No gas, no cigarettes . . . well, that's it baby, and amen!

> (*Gennarino is standing with his legs spread wide in the middle of the boat.*)

RAFFAELLA: Can I ask what you're doing standing?
GENNARINO: Instead of talking, why don't you get up and use your body as a sail.

> (*She stares at him as if he were an idiot.*)

RAFFAELLA: A sail, with my body? What are you talking about? You some kind of nut? Do you have any idea at all which way the wind is blowing?
GENNARINO: Don't know.
RAFFAELLA: Just my luck to have been shipwrecked with an asshole of a sailor.

> (*Gennarino isn't quite certain he heard right, but he is mortally offended. He looks at her insolently. Her attitude is the same as that of the aristocracy who were the target of the people who instigated the French Revolution. The boat seems to be going faster.*)

RAFFAELLA: O.K., O.K., let's play sail! If only we knew where this wind was blowing.

> (*She realizes this isn't quite the moment to ask questions and stands up to be a sail.*)

RAFFAELLA: We're going toward the south, aren't we? I hope we're not going to end up in Africa. I've heard stories about that Ghedaffi character, it really wouldn't be too funny.

SCENE 26

(Outboard at sea—exterior—nighttime. It's pitch-black, a storm is blowing up. Raffaella and Gennarino are lying on the bottom of the boat. She's trying to cover up as best she can with her summery outfit. Gennarino is curled up and looks as if he were fast asleep.)

RAFFAELLA: What are we going to do if they don't find us by tomorrow? I just can't face another night under these conditions. . . . I'm feeling ill.

(Gennarino doesn't answer. Raffaella tries to rouse him.)

RAFFAELLA: Shit, being shipwrecked is one thing, but having to put up with this aborigine . . .

(Raffaella continues to tremble. We can see Gennarino's green eyes glinting in the dark.)

GENNARINO (quietly): Boy, does one need a lot of patience.

SCENE 27

(Outboard at sea—island—exterior—daytime. Raffaella is jumping up and down excitedly. It is daytime and the boat is fairly close to an island. Raffaella is overjoyed.)

RAFFAELLA: Land! Land! Look, it's land! Hurry! I wouldn't want the wind to change!

(Gennarino is wide awake. He grabs the oars and starts rowing.)

GENNARINO: Don't worry, we'll be there in half an hour. We just have to be careful of the rocks.
RAFFAELLA: Why, for the boat? These things are used for this very purpose. They were even used for the landing in Normandy. And even the ads tell you they're "practically unsinkable."

SCENE 28

(*Reefs close to the island—exterior—daytime. The rubber out-board has sunk. As the two stranded people head across the reefs, we see the remains of the boat slowly sinking.*)

RAFFAELLA: Well, I'll just have to sue the firm. "Practically un-sinkable," my foot! Ow! Ouch! Ouch!

(*Raffaella is hurting her feet on the razor-sharp rocks, then gets lost in a maze of reefs and can't find her way out.*)

RAFFAELLA: Hey there, help! Help!

(*Gennarino tries as best he can to get her out of the dead end she seems to have gotten herself into.*)

GENNARINO: I'm coming, madame, but you might have a little more patience at a time like this.

SCENE 29

(*The inaccessible cliffs—exterior—daytime. Gennarino and Raffaella are clambering up the cliffs, she with her hat and flowing skirt, Gennarino carrying the bags he managed to save.*)

RAFFAELLA: This is impossible!
GENNARINO: Be careful over there, madame, the rocks are loose and dangerous. Maybe it would be better if I went ahead and had a look.

(*Raffaella is limping noticeably, but she won't let him out of her sight.*)

RAFFAELLA: No, not on your life, Gennarino. You're capable of getting lost and never finding me again. No, my dear, I'd rather come along with you. Sooner or later we're bound to reach a house, a hotel, a road, a highway! Oh, thank God this nightmare is over! You know what I really need now? A nice iced coffee.

SCENE 30

(*Plateau on the island—exterior—daytime. The view of the sea is breath-taking. Gennarino has climbed to the highest point to get a better view of the situation. Gennarino whistles at Raffaella and waves, trying to attract her attention. Then he shouts.*)

GENNARINO: I'm afraid that iced coffee will have to wait!

(*Raffaella can't hear him.*)

RAFFAELLA: What? I can't hear you!
GENNARINO: I said your coffee will have to wait!
RAFFAELLA: Why?
GENNARINO: It just so happens that this tiny island is totally deserted.
RAFFAELLA: Deserted? What are you saying?
GENNARINO: I can't see a soul in sight. I can't see anything at all.
RAFFAELLA: How can it be? We're not in the Pacific Ocean, we're in the middle of the Mediterranean Sea! It's just not possible!

(*Gennarino climbs down the rough path. Raffaella is walking toward him. Gennarino is offended.*)

GENNARINO: Look, madame, why are you like this? I'm not a little boy. If I tell you it's a deserted island, I meant it's a deserted island!
RAFFAELLA: Well, I don't believe you. Who do you think you are, the lookout at Cape Kennedy? I just don't believe it, you're not seeing straight or something.
GENNARINO: I can see very clearly madame, there isn't a soul. It happens to be completely empty.

(*The two are almost face to face.*)

RAFFAELLA: Listen . . . look around you, it looks like the Dolomites. But it could be Sardinia—maybe Sicily, how do I know? Why don't you climb back up there and have a closer look?
GENNARINO: Back up there? No way.
RAFFAELLA: What?
GENNARINO: I refuse to go back up there. I saw very well the first time.
RAFFAELLA: All right, Gennarino, if you're going to be like this . . . why should I trust you? You were the cause of all this! You got me lost at sea! It was your fault the engine broke down! You don't know your way around, and like all Southerners, everything you do is not quite right. Why should I trust you as I would a Swiss? Enough said! It's clear to me at this point that you're totally useless. It's just no use trying to squeeze water from a stone.
GENNARINO: I don't think I understood. What did you say?
RAFFAELLA: Nothing, nothing . . .

(*Raffaella realizes this is not a good moment to argue.*)

GENNARINO: I want to know what you said!

(*Raffaella is getting nervous.*)

RAFFAELLA: I said, it's no use trying to squeeze water from a stone!

(*Gennarino explodes. It's the slave's revolt, the revolution at last.*)

GENNARINO: Listen to me, Lady Raffaella Pavoni Zampetti! You've really broken my cock! I'm going to do what the fuck I fucking well want! Who the fuck do you think you are, you frigging slut!

(*He walks away, head held high, as she looks at him with disbelief. Then she loses her temper.*)

RAFFAELLA: Boor! Peasant!
GENNARINO (off camera): Fuck you!
RAFFAELLA: Rude pig!
GENNARINO (off camera): Fuck you royally!
RAFFAELLA: Rude slob! I'll teach him when we get back! I won't take this from that piece of shit! I'll show him!
GENNARINO (off camera): Ball-breaker!
RAFFAELLA: I'll show you! Now where am I going to go? (She hurts her foot.) Aaaah! Ugly brute!
GENNARINO (off camera): Whore!

(*Raffaella starts wandering around the island far away from Gennarino.*)

RAFFAELLA: Shitty cockroach!

(*Gennarino marches ahead, his sailor cap on his head and his bundle of clothes and things under his arm.*)

GENNARINO: Slut, whore, prostitute and pig! They'll all end up on the gallows one day, that's for sure!

(*Raffaella limps and trips, furious at the world. She's carrying her elegant beach bag.*)

RAFFAELLA: Ugly sailor! Fucked-up jackass! Piece of shit! What else can you call someone like this . . . turd!

SCENE 31

> *(Shots of the island—the shore—rocks—plateau—exterior—day-time. Gennarino is now completely free. He wades in the stream for a while, mumbling obscenities directed at her.)*

GENNARINO: Madame of the Prick! Loose woman! Whore! Slut!

> *(Raffaella is clambering up toward the plateau.)*

RAFFAELLA: Shittiest shithead in the world!

> *(Gennarino is still wading along the narrow, shaded stream.)*

GENNARINO: Great stinker! Queen of the sluts! (He trips in the water and loses his balance.) Fucking cunt! I've had enough! A poor devil can take only so much before the time comes when his balls are really broken!

> *(Raffaella doesn't let him out of her sight, following him at a safe distance.)*

RAFFAELLA: Childish coward! Typical lower-class behavior. Looks like it's really gone to his head. Christ only knows what the hell he wants!

> *(Gennarino stands on top of a rock looking down at the sea, the wind blowing his hair all over the place. Her shouts reach him but he isn't bothered. He's feeling happy and carefree.)*

GENNARINO: You slut! It's all over, Gennarino isn't putting up with your shit any longer, now you're up shit creek!
RAFFAELLA (off camera): Nigger, slave, scum of the earth!
GENNARINO: Now we're going to have a few laughs, Mrs. Pancetti! You're really in for it now!

> *(Gennarino laughs happily.)*

RAFFAELLA (off camera): It's the slave's revolt. He thinks this is the fall of the Bastille!

> *(Raffaella walks along the shore, following him.)*

GENNARINO (off camera): You no-good hooker, you'd sell yourself for a dime!
RAFFAELLA: This prick-face thinks he's Sparticus! Turd!

(*Gennarino looks down from his perch on the rock and laughs heartily.*)

RAFFAELLA (off camera): What a situation I got myself into . . . rude bastard.

(*Raffaella walks along the beach, disturbing the resting sea gulls on the sand.*)

GENNARINO: Scummy dyke! Social Democratic pig-faced slut!

SCENE 32

(*A small, abandoned chapel on the island—exterior—interior—daytime. Happy at the thought of Raffaella being frightened and worried about her situation, Gennarino is busy searching around the island. He discovers a chapel. The door is kept closed by a rusty lock.*)

GENNARINO: Hey, there, anybody home?

(*Gennarino knocks a few times and waits.*)

GENNARINO: There's nobody on this God-forsaken island.

(*He forces the lock, which snaps easily. The door opens. It's a tiny chapel.*)

GENNARINO: Well, naturally *you* would be here . . . when isn't Christ hanging around?

(*Gennarino walks into the chapel and finds a tiny altar with a rustic handmade cross on it and some small religious cards depicting fishermen and fishing scenes. Pensively he touches the few objects left there. An old tin can with some dried-up flowers, a section of a fishing net, pieces of wood.*)

GENNARINO: What's this? Ah, a piece of torn fishing net . . . there's nothing at all . . . oh well.

(*He takes off his T-shirt and makes himself at home.*)

SCENE 33

(*Beach on the island—exterior—daytime. Raffaella manages to pull out a sea urchin, but she hasn't got a clue how to open it so*) *she can eat it. She has to resort to licking it. She looks enviously down on Gennarino.)*

SCENE 34

(Rocks—sea around the island—exterior—daytime. Gennarino is in a wonderful mood, the thought of Raffaella starving to death and obviously being very thirsty is making him more and more cheerful. He catches squid and a lobster. He finds a salt deposit which he scoops up in a shell, then heads back to the chapel with his catch.)

SCENE 35

(Side of a rocky cliff on the island—exterior—daytime. Raffaella is totally destroyed. She's leaning against the rock, tearing pieces of material from her skirt to wrap up her cut feet.)

SCENE 36

(Bend in the river flowing through the small wood on the island—exterior—daytime. Gennarino is lighting a fire and settling down to cook himself a superb meal. Choice ingredients. Roast lobster.)

SCENE 37

(Bend in the river flowing across the island—exterior—daytime. Raffaella is walking toward Gennarino. The aroma reaches her twitching nostrils. She's on the verge of tears. Gennarino is busy eating.)

RAFFAELLA: I want you to know that you're a miserable coward. You can do what you like, but I swear, you're going to pay for this! There's got to be a law . . . failing to help in time of need, or something like that. You sit there stuffing your face while others starve

(Gennarino doesn't even bother to look up.)

GENNARINO: Let's think about what you just said. You see, if there were such a law, wouldn't you agree, all the rich people in this world would be behind bars. But since this law doesn't exist, we see only the poor rotting in jail.

(Raffaella hates him.)

RAFFAELLA: Fucking Communist!

(Raffaella walks away.)

SCENE 38

(A clearing with a leafy tree in the middle of it—exterior—day-time. Raffaella is trying to find some food. She looks for eggs in a nest on the tree. Then she tries tasting the leaves. Starvation has almost gotten the better of her fighting, polemic nature. She's tired and breaks into tears.)

RAFFAELLA: If that ugly black beast thinks he can take advantage of this situation to play the shit, he's got another think coming. With all these goddamn birds there must be some eggs. . . . Fucking shitty nature. . . . I knew it. . . . Power makes these proletarians real bastards. See how they abuse their new-found power! They blackmail, starve and take advantage of you. . . . They're worse than Hitler. . . . That dark-skinned ass . . . If he thinks I'm going to crawl over to him and beg for food he's got another thing coming. . . . I'd rather die.

SCENE 39

(Bend in the river flowing through the wood—exterior—day-time. Raffaella pulls herself together.)

RAFFAELLA: Will you sell me that fish?

(Gennarino carries on eating as if he hadn't heard her.)

RAFFAELLA: I'll pay you whatever you like!

(She cuts a pathetic yet tender figure. She has only a tiny streak of battling nature left in her.)

RAFFAELLA: What are you doing, pretending you can't hear me now? I realize you're a piece of shit, but you're not going to let me starve, are you? O.K., let's be realistic. You've got the bull by the horns. How much do you want—one hundred thousand, two hundred—how much do you want for that damn fish?

(Gennarino doesn't bat an eyelid. Raffaella thinks she's going to die.)

RAFFAELLA: Listen, you're really overdoing things now. I'm feeling ill, I even hurt my foot. . . . I'll give you half a million lire for it.

(Gennarino looks at her. Then, with his mouth full, he answers.)

GENNARINO: You just won't stop insulting me, will you? It isn't pleasant to be the underdog is it? There's a slight hitch in all this . . . this fish just isn't for sale.
RAFFAELLA: Why the hell not?
GENNARINO: Well, just this very minute I decided to behave like you people.

(Gennarino throws a piece of lobster into the fire.)

RAFFAELLA: What have we got to do with it?
GENNARINO: Yes madame, you people burn the apples, oranges and vegetables to keep the price of vegetables and fruits at a certain level. Isn't that true?

(Raffaella's eyes are full of hatred and tears.)

RAFFAELLA: Murderer!

(Gennarino snickers.)

GENNARINO: My dear woman, I'm just plain ignorant and incompetent, the well-organized murderers are you people.

(Gennarino lights up a cigarette with a truly satisfied look.)

RAFFAELLA: You thief, you're smoking my cigarettes!
GENNARINO: Did you or did you not throw them away? The lobster wasn't too tasty. Now, woman, listen to me very carefully.

(Gennarino is nasty and tough.)

GENNARINO: Lesson number one, there is no money to buy the food. . . . If you wish to buy this fish you've got to earn it, do you follow? Now wash my underwear!

(Gennarino throws her a bundle of dirty laundry. She looks at the bundle as if she was ready to burn it.)

RAFFAELLA: Never!

SCENE 40

(Field and small stream on the island—exterior—daytime. But she washes the clothes after all. She's washing the old-fashioned way, beating the laundry against a rock and then scrubbing. She is crying but trying to do her job as best she can. The clothes don't look too clean. Gennarino comes up behind her, carrying a bunch of dried twigs.)

RAFFAELLA: This is really the best I could do. I'm sick, let me have that fish.

GENNARINO: You don't really deserve it, but as long as you say pretty please . . .

RAFFAELLA: Pretty please, Gennarino, come on!

GENNARINO: What do you mean, Gennarino? For you, from now on, it's Mr. Carunchio!

(Raffaella looks at him, then swallows her pride.)

RAFFAELLA: Mr. Carunchio . . .

GENNARINO: That's right, Mr. Carunchio. Now then . . . ah yes, the fish.

(*He throws her a fish, which she starts gobbling down. She swallows mouthfuls of fish and tears.*)

RAFFAELLA: Look, this whole thing is cowardly and ridiculous.
GENNARINO: But on the other hand, madame, I don't have a washing machine here, so therefore someone must wash my underwear. Now, Lady Raffaella never washed a pair of underwear because she's never been the underdog.

(*Gennarino moves away.*)

RAFFAELLA: Now where are you going? Wait for me, I hurt my foot!

(*Raffaella follows him because she is scared of the dark.*)

GENNARINO: Now that Lady Raffaella is the underdog she must learn to wash underwear.

SCENE 41

(*Chapel on the island—interior—exterior—daytime. Gennarino heads for the chapel. He's still being followed by Raffaella.*)

RAFFAELLA (off camera): Wait for me . . . please!
GENNARINO: You know . . . work strengthens man's character, so it stands to reason that it would certainly strengthen a woman's!

(*Gennarino whistles.*)

RAFFAELLA: Mr. Carunchio . . . I don't understand why you won't help me, I really hurt my foot. . . . Look . . . be kind . . . don't be like this. I'm calling you Mister, what more do you want? Stop being so boorish and help me. Where are you going? Oh, look, there's a house!

(*Raffaella has arrived in full view of the chapel.*)

RAFFAELLA: How marvelous, now it's a different story. At least we won't be cold tonight.

(*Still whistling, Gennarino walks into the chapel and closes the door behind him. Raffaella is hurt.*)

RAFFAELLA: What are you doing? Hey, you're not going to leave me out here by myself, are you? It's getting dark, I'll catch my death of cold! Mr. Carunchio, be kind, please!

(Gennarino opens the door and gives her a malicious look.)

GENNARINO: What do you mean? You haven't come up with some strange ideas, have you? Oh, I know you wealthy folk are pretty kinky at times.

(Gennarino smiles. The son of a bitch. This is a bit too much even for Raffaella. She's freezing cold and tired but she's not going to take his abuse. The old battling nature emerges for a moment.)

RAFFAELLA: Oh, I see, so you think that I managed to get myself shipwrecked and end up in this shitty place to wind up in bed with you? Fine example of Mediterranean male that you are . . . ugly animal. . . . I ask you, have you ever seen yourself in the mirror?

(Gennarino's smile freezes.)

GENNARINO: Yes, my dear madame, I *have* looked at myself. What's more, I am very highly thought of by women who have more femininity in one of their toes than you do in your whole being! You and your stinking millions!

(And with this remark he slams the door in her face. Raffaella is beside herself.)

RAFFAELLA: Pig!

(She bangs on the door.)

RAFFAELLA: Rude boor! Filthy nigger! This really had to happen to me, goddamn it! Shit, it's cold!

GENNARINO (off camera): Cover yourself up with leaves, like the swine.

RAFFAELLA: I'm feeling ill, you tiny, ignorant, dark, vain and ridiculous brute! You're everything I've always hated, do you hear? You make me sick! Sick, I tell you! I'll catch pneumonia but I don't care!

(In vain she keeps banging on the door, tears streaming down her cheeks. Inside, Gennarino is enjoying her tantrum. The door never opens and she must go in search of dry leaves with which to protect herself. Eventually she falls asleep huddled up in front of the door, cold and humiliated.)

SCENE 42

(Chapel on the island—exterior—morning. Gennarino opens the door, looks at Raffaella still fast asleep on the doorstep, climbs over her, and goes off to stretch. He watches a crab slowly crawling toward Raffaella's hand. The crab climbs onto her hand, Raffaella stirs in her sleep.)

RAFFAELLA: Maria . . . coffee . . .

(A few seconds later Raffaella opens her eyes and lets out a scream.)

RAFFAELLA: Oh my god! What pleasure do you get from torturing a poor devil?

(Gennarino laughs. Raffaella is traumatized.)

GENNARINO: You? A poor devil?
RAFFAELLA: O.K., O.K., rich devil.
GENNARINO: Come on, let's start working. You've got to understand that if you don't work you don't eat. Off you go, inside and clean.

(Gennarino gives her a light kick.)

RAFFAELLA: Oh, mother, haven't we finished this game? Why are you like this? Isn't our situation serious enough without you adding to it? Why are you making me pay for all the social injustices? What do you get out of it? And listen, when they come and save us, if you've been nice to me, I'll be sure to be nice to you . . . you understand?

(Gennarino is becoming nastier. He grabs her by the hair.)

GENNARINO: Who says they're going to save us? How do you know we aren't going to stay here for two, three, five years? Huh?
RAFFAELLA: I'll kill myself!
GENNARINO: If you want to kill yourself, that's your own business . . . but as long as you want to eat, you've got to work . . . understand?

(He keeps tugging at her hair. She tries talking reasonably.)

RAFFAELLA: Look, you're really hurting me.
GENNARINO: What did you have in mind, that I was going to serve you? Ahhhhh! No, my dear, you're going to be serving me and that's the way it should always be, the woman is to serve the man and not the other way around.
RAFFAELLA: Look, you are really hurting me an awful lot!
GENNARINO: I'll be hurting you even more until you understand who's master! . . . Kiss the master's hand! Kiss the hand! Kiss!

(Gennarino shoves his clenched fist in front of her face.)

RAFFAELLA: Pardon me?
GENNARINO: Kiss!

(He slugs her.)

GENNARINO: You ugly industrial whore! I broke my back for you on that fucking yacht! Last night you were telling me I made you sick . . . kiss! Kiss the master's hand or go away and never come back. I can have no pity!
RAFFAELLA: You're a worm!

(A swift slap across her face makes her fall back.)

GENNARINO: Lesson number one, woman. . . . I can't allow you to insult me anymore . . . get it? Now, disappear!

(Gennarino turns his back on her and leaves her kneeling there alone and desperate.)

SCENE 43

(A large rock on the island overlooking the sea—exterior—day-time. Gennarino is busily trying to make himself a harpoon. Raffaella lowers her eyes. Gennarino doesn't say a word—he merely keeps on with his work. She's waiting. He sticks out his hand.)

GENNARINO: Kiss! Kiss the master's hand! Come on, kiss it!

(Raffaella kisses it.)

GENNARINO: Now you can start working.

(The deal is made. She begins working.)

SCENE 44

(Cliffs on the island—exterior—daytime. Gennarino is fishing. We see him underwater catching tiny fish. He surfaces and hands Raffaella the rudimentary harpoon with the squirming fish. She gives him another harpoon and goes running to a small pool of water covered by leaves, into which she throws the fish. She runs back to the rocks to exchange the harpoon again. She knows she must run fast because otherwise he's going to start yelling.)

GENNARINO: Run, you idiot! Hurry up, run, you stupid bitch!

(Raffaella is slipping on the dangerous wet rocks.)

RAFFAELLA: Hold on, it's dangerous. You don't know how difficult it is to run on these wet rocks. If I'm not careful I'll fall and break a leg.
GENNARINO: When I call you it means you've got to run . . . now shut up!

(He slaps her hard across the face.)

RAFFAELLA: Hey, what's wrong?
GENNARINO: Silence . . . woman, you must stay silent!
RAFFAELLA: What the fuck do you expect me to do? How fucking fast do you think I can run?

GENNARINO: Silence! If I call you it means I need you urgently. Now shut up, you idiot!

> (*The harpoons are exchanged and Gennarino once again disappears underwater.*)

RAFFAELLA: Fine character he's got.

SCENE 45

> (*Clearing on the island—exterior—daytime. Now we see Raffaella fetching water. In an old tin can, which he found God knows where, Gennarino is preparing the fish for the stew. Raffaella hands him the water, then sits down. We notice that her sense of humor and critical nature have given way to an almost animal fear.*)

RAFFAELLA: The water . . .

> (*Gennarino likes this fear, for it gives him strength, he feels in command. To reaffirm his dominance he needs only to raise his hand, let out a shout. To see her gradually losing ground gives him intense pleasure. The fish stew is ready. Gennarino hardly looks at her.*)

GENNARINO: You're sitting, huh?

(*Raffaella is dead tired. She turns pale.*)

RAFFAELLA: Well, why not? I worked like you told me, I earned my food.
GENNARINO: On your feet!

(*Gennarino is merciless.*)

GENNARINO: I want to be served. Did you ever ask me to join you on the yacht? Now *I* want to be served, okay? Tit for tat, my Madame of the Prick.

(*Raffaella sighs deeply, then swallows her pride yet again and starts serving him. Gennarino adopts a facetious attitude. He stares at her.*)

GENNARINO: "The wine is warm . . . the bread is cold . . . the spaghetti is overdone . . . the coffee has been reheated . . ."

(*Raffaella hands him a portion of stew. Gennarino pushes it away.*)

GENNARINO: More, I'm hungry . . . boy did you give me hell seated at that table on the yacht. . . . That's enough.

(*He looks at her insolently.*)

GENNARINO: And you looked at me with such disgust. . . . "You wear sweaty T-shirts, how revolting. . . ." Some salt!

(*Raffaella hands him the salt.*)

GENNARINO: . . . As a result, we felt like animals . . . putrid and stinking, worse than a pig. . . . And so we had to wash them four or five times a day . . . and all for what? . . . because madame felt sick at the sight of us.
RAFFAELLA: Gennarino, please spare me!

(*Gennarino gives her a deadly look.*)

GENNARINO: Gennarino? Who told you you could take the liberty? Mr. Carunchio!

(*Raffaella's eyes are filled with tears; her nerves are beginning to give under the strain.*)

RAFFAELLA: God, what a nightmare . . . Mr. Carunchio!

GENNARINO: And say it without making a face!

(Gennarino has been served. As soon as she has helped herself to the stew, Gennarino begins to play the bastard.)

GENNARINO: Water.
RAFFAELLA: It's right here.
GENNARINO: Yes, but it's warm. . . . Go to the stream and fetch some cold water. You see, unfortunately you must be patient. . . . I like mine chilled, just like Mr. Brezhnev's wine. Run, I'm thirsty!

(Raffaella goes to fetch the water.)

SCENE 46

(Open field and stream on the island—exterior—daytime. She washes the shells they've been using as dishes. He watches her, relaxed as he smokes a cigarette.)

GENNARINO: This is the last of your cigarettes. It tastes best of all! You did throw them away, didn't you?

(She feels embarrassed, but carries on with her chores. He keeps on mocking her.)

GENNARINO: What are you looking at, huh? I can stare at you as much as I like, do you understand, woman? What are you looking at? I'm looking at your ass! Ah! On the yacht you would lie in the sun like hogs showing off your tits! Yes, your tits; as if we didn't exist . . . behaving as if we were animals, not men . . . but I think you knew damn well we were men, and you liked the thought that you were making us suffer. You remember, don't you, you industrial whore? Show me your tits now! Come on, take it off, let's see them! You hear me?

(Raffaella pretends she hasn't heard. She continues to do the laundry in the hope that he will get over his sudden whim. Gennarino kicks her in the ass. She turns toward him, full of indignation.)

GENNARINO: Pretending you don't hear me, huh? Are you ashamed? Madame's embarrassed. Why weren't you embarrassed on the yacht? You liked it then, you enjoyed the feeling that you were making us suffer as we watched you lying in the sun! Upper-class nude females . . . lying there provocatively . . . now, strip!

(There is a sudden look of madness in her eyes as she stands up and, throwing a stone at him in retaliation for this new abuse, screams.)

RAFFAELLA: Disgusting worm!

(Gennarino leaps up and tries to grab her. As she tries to escape, she slips and falls in the water. Gennarino follows her into the stream.)

GENNARINO: At last you've rebelled, so now I have an excuse to beat the shit out of you! Come here!

(He chases her downstream. He catches Raffaella. She manages to escape his clutches, falls, tries desperately to defend herself.)

RAFFAELLA: Help! Leave me you coward!

(Raffaella pulls him by the hair.)

GENNARINO: No one can help you! Stop pulling my hair, leave my hair alone! No, ahhh, not my hair!
RAFFAELLA: You criminal! Help!

SCENE 47

(Sand dunes on the island—exterior—afternoon. The chase continues across the white sand dunes. Gennarino has been waiting for this moment, she escapes, he catches up with her, every time he catches up with her he adds yet another bruise to her body. He kicks her, slaps her, punches her. He sinks in the sand and has to let go of her.)

GENNARINO: Yell! Yell all you want, you ugly cunt, but you won't get away, you've got to pay for everyone else! Leave my hair! Ahhhh, you kick me in the balls? I'll kick your ass in, you dumb Social Democratic whore!

(The two tumble down the other side of a dune.)

RAFFAELLA: Enough!
GENNARINO: I'll say when it's enough!
RAFFAELLA: Revolting, disgusting coward, leave me alone!

(Gennarino's beatings are for all the suffering the "underdog" has gone through in the course of the ages.)

GENNARINO: Hasn't it sunk in yet that you've got to pay for every-thing?

RAFFAELLA: Let go of my skirt! Why do you want me to pay for all of life's injustices? Let go of my skirt! This is a fixation with you!

GENNARINO: A fixation, my ass!

RAFFAELLA: Fuck off!

> (*The chase continues over the sand. It is difficult to run, and they fall, trip, roll all over the place.*)

GENNARINO: You've got to pay for everything!

RAFFAELLA: Look, I give up!

GENNARINO: You give up? No, it's too easy that way!

> (*Gennarino lets her have a terrible wallop. She rolls down the dune.*)

GENNARINO: That one was for the economic crises brought on by you and the likes of you by not paying your taxes and transferring capi-tal to Swiss bank accounts!

> (*Raffaella no longer has the strength to try to escape. She screams and begs for mercy.*)

RAFFAELLA: But what have I got to do with it?

> (*Another punch finds its mark.*)

GENNARINO: That one was for the fact that a poor devil can't be ad-mitted to a hospital . . . though on the other hand that might not be such a bad thing, because if he did he would probably never come out alive.

RAFFAELLA: Why me? I'm not to blame for all the injustices in the world!

> (*Another slap*)

GENNARINO: And that was for the increase in the price of meat, Par-mesan cheese, train and bus fares! And for the increase in the cost of gas!

> (*Another slap. Raffaella doesn't even attempt to protect herself anymore.*)

GENNARINO: That was for the increase in the cost of oil and for the workers being laid off.

(Yet another slap)

GENNARINO: This is for the crappy T.V. programs. (Another slap) This is for the State Tax (Another slap) and this is for that ridiculous automobile tax! And (He kicks her in the ass) *this* is because you have frightened us into a state of subservience!

(Raffaella is lying on her stomach, Gennarino grabs her and starts tearing off what little clothing she has left.)

GENNARINO: Come back! Now the real fun starts!

(Raffaella tries desperately to get away.)

RAFFAELLA: But . . . what are you doing?

(Gennarino crushes her with his weight, he pulls her hair, he is being a real bastard.)

GENNARINO: Now we'll start getting a little more intimate!
RAFFAELA: No!
GENNARINO: Yes my dear . . . I'm going to tear off your panties.
RAFFAELLA: No.

(Raffaella pants.)

GENNARINO: Yes . . . I want to rip your tiny perfumed cunt apart. . . . I want to tear you to pieces! You've never known what a man is really like! I'll show you!

(Sweaty and animalistic, Gennarino stares at her in a curious way. There are sensations beginning to pulsate through their bodies which seem to overcome the feelings of hatred and fatigue. They breathe heavily into each other's faces. They stare into one another's eyes. Then Gennarino crushes her lips with his. She squirms beneath him.)

GENNARINO: You impotent industrial whore! I hate you, but at the same time you turn me on . . . and you know that because you turned me on, on the yacht as well! You ugly slut, I can feel that you want me too, I can feel it!
RAFFAELLA: No!

(Raffaella is beginning to get some pleasure out of this, and Gennarino can sense it.)

GENNARINO: Stay still, there's no hope for you at this point. Have the courage to admit what you felt for me. . . . Confess what feelings you have deep inside your gut. . . . You're moaning like a toad crushed by a cart.

(*Gennarino's eyes have the flames of hell burning in them.*)

GENNARINO: Admit it, admit the desires that are burning you up! Tell me, tell!

(*Raffaella gives in. With her eyes closed, with a moan, she nods affirmatively. She is in sexual bliss.*)

GENNARINO: So it's yes, huh? You bitch! Well, I say no!

(*Raffaella opens her eyes without comprehending. He is the epitome of the triumphant erotic son of a bitch.*)

GENNARINO: I'm the one who says no! I'm nothing but a dark ugly boor, I'm the one you told to change his shirt, I'm the one you called a filthy Southerner, I'm the one who's always been the underdog and whom you said made you sick. It just isn't enough that you say yes! You've got to fall in love!

(*Raffaella sits up. She's furious. He pushes her back down again.*)

GENNARINO: In love, passionately in love with me. You're already a slave, but you've got to become a slave of love . . . you're going to slither at my feet like a worm, begging for mercy!

(*Raffaella listens to him wide-eyed. Each syllable he utters rips through her like a bullet. Suddenly she sees the proletariat saturated with erotic supremacy.*)

GENNARINO: You've got to fall so much in love that your guts will feel as if they were being pressed in a vise! Your passion will be worse than a sickness! I've got to come under your skin, inside your head, into your heart! Into your stomach! I've got to be a god for you . . . is that clear? Passion or nothing at all! Passion or nothing!

(*He leaps off of her and runs into the night.*)

GENNARINO (off camera): You've got to find out who Gennarino Carunchio really is!

SCENE 48

(Small hill on the island—exterior—daytime. Along both sides of the hill the erosion of wind and water has formed a series of gullets where Gennarino is now setting up a rudimentary snare to catch wild rabbits. It's a very simple system. A noose dangles in the gullet. The rabbit puts his head through it, the noose closes around the neck, and the rabbit is slowed down in his escape by the rocks tied to the rope. He then becomes an easy target. Gennarino has set the trap and waits patiently. Raffaella looks at him from a hiding place. He has the patience of a hunter and a fisherman, all the wisdom of a gambler and a fighter. He has the patience to wait. She can feel this and is overcome by a desire to throw herself through that very noose. The wild rabbit has been caught, the stones slow him down, and Gennarino finishes him off by stoning him. He picks him up by the ears, the rabbit twitches, Gennarino raises his precious knife.)

RAFFAELLA: Noooooo!

(She shouts as if it were her own throat being slit. Gennarino slits the rabbit's throat and deftly starts skinning the animal.)

SCENE 49

(Wood and clearing on the island—exterior—evening. Raffaella is carrying wood for the fire. She is very changed. Gennarino is totally indifferent. She stares at him with her enormous, anxious eyes. The rabbit is now a bloody carcass, and Gennarino is working on it, preparing it for dinner. Raffaella is pale.)

RAFFAELLA: I feel just like the rabbit. . . . You killed it! You're cruel!

(Gennarino is rough and ignores her. She moves closer, then crouches at his feet. In spite of everything, Gennarino is obviously happy seeing her at his feet. Raffaella remains squatting next to those dark, dusty, sweaty feet. She looks up at him sweetly and humbly, reaches for his hand and places it on her head in a gesture of submission, to give him the sense of ownership he has been looking for. He lets his hand rest for a moment on her head. They gaze at each other. It all happens between

them with this one gaze, irrational as it may seem at first. He is unable to be as boorish as usual. Her look has mellowed him. He tries to pull himself away from the intensity of the look, which is clutching at his very guts. But it is hard. He tries to concentrate on the spit, but the look beckons. It is impossible to fight with this look. There is more meaning in this look than in a thousand words. The spit is soon forgotten. With her hand she strokes his bristly bearded face. He gently takes her face in his hands. His hands slide gently down her body, touching, feeling, brushing, slowly savoring her body. She shuts her eyes as if she had never felt such wonderful sensations in her entire life. Suddenly he slaps her as hard as he can, then pulls her back into his arms. He lifts her. He lies back, enjoying the feeling of her soft curves against his body. Finally he turns her over on her back and throws himself on her, at last savoring this prime piece of industrial whore that has finally been cooked to the right degree of doneness.

SCENE 50

(Wood and clearing on the island—exterior—nighttime. Gennarino and Raffaella are lying in a passionate embrace on the sand. The waves break against the shore. They touch each other, caress, nibble, and kiss, insatiable in their appetite for one another.)

GENNARINO: You're so beautiful, such a woman! My delicate eel! You succulent piglet, ready to be sucked! You've got to call me sir! Yes, sir, that's what I want you to call me!

(Raffaella stares at him languidly.)

RAFFAELLA: Master! Sir! Beat me, kill me, do what you want with me but just hold me tight.

(Gennarino lies back and enjoys her like a lord.)

GENNARINO: I love the way you talk, it gives me goose bumps!
RAFFAELLA: Love, my love, my love!
GENNARINO: Tell me the truth, did you say the same things to that cuckolded husband of yours?

(The words jolt her back to reality. Nothing was further removed from her thoughts as she lay lost in a physical and psychological

limbo, far from her past and from that other reality.)

RAFFAELLA: Please, I beg of you, don't bring up the past, I don't want to think about it.
GENNARINO: Answer me . . . did you say these things to him as well?
RAFFAELLA: I won't tell you!

(*A vicious slap*)

GENNARINO: A slave never says no to her master!
GENNARINO: What do rich folk say to one another when they're together? How do you make love? You filthy whore! Do you have orgies? What sort of filthy things do you do together? It's a known fact that you rich pigs are always screwing four or five at a time, you're a bunch of pigs and nothing else! I bet you take drugs as well! And here you are with that angelic face . . . tell me, how many times have you cheated on your husband?

(*Raffaella finally reacts to all these insults.*)

GENNARINO (in a provocative tone): Three hundred times, six hundred?
RAFFAELLA: Who the hell has put these ideas into your head? Who told you that if a woman is rich she has to be a slut? Was it the Party?

(*Gennarino lets her have a powerful backhand.*)

RAFFAELLA: That hurt! Why?
GENNARINO: You mustn't mention that word! You musn't refer to the Party in that tone of voice!
RAFFAELLA: Shit! As if I didn't have enough to worry about! The Communist Party's my last thought!
GENNARINO: The Party is sacred institution and you musn't mention it! Where do you think you are, on the yacht? Idiot, the Party is sacred! And you're a whore and I'm going to fuck you! Fuck you!

(*And giving her a little pain and a lot of pleasure, he bangs away happily. She moans and he increases his insults because he feels that she likes them.*)

GENNARINO: Ah! Look at my beautiful lady! Whore! Rich slut! Servant!

(*Suddenly he stops and looks down at her breathing heavily. Raffaella opens her eyes in surprise at suddenly feeling him so still inside her. She twists and turns.*)

RAFFAELLA: Why?
GENNARINO: Because!
RAFFAELLA: Please, don't stop!

(*Gennarino shakes his head.*)

GENNARINO: I like to watch you burning up with desire.

(*Raffaella is still breathing heavily.*)

RAFFAELLA: Darling, please, no!

(*Gennarino looks at her suffering.*)

GENNARINO: No, no, when I'm good and ready! How many lovers have you had? Admit it, how many lovers have you had?

(*Raffaella looks at him. She seems sincere.*)

RAFFAELLA: You're the very first.

(*This is too much for Gennarino.*)

GENNARINO: With that whore's voice! You liar, whore, liar! Whore, whore, slut and liar! Lady, I'm going to fuck you!

(*Gennarino starts pumping away angrily.*)

SCENE 51

(*Wood and clearing on the island—exterior—dawn. It is dawn, the early morning light casts a delicate shadow on the island. The birds sing. Gennarino and Raffaella are still making love, totally consumed by their passion.*)

SCENE 52

(Cliff on the island—exterior—dawn. Raffaella and Gennarino head shakily for the sea, where they are going to look for some food. They wobble like a pair of drunkards. The cold water brings them to their senses. Their nerves are shocked into action once again. Raffaella's breasts are firm, her nipples pointed. Gennarino is overcome once again with desire. He grabs hold of that slithering weak flesh and throws her onto the sand. Once again he's able to nail her.)

SCENE 53

(Cliffs on the island—exterior—daytime. Now Gennarino looks like a haggard old man. The sun is high in the sky. Gennarino goes into the water to try fishing but as soon as he walks in he stumbles and falls asleep underwater. He swallows, chokes, and manages to surface just in time. He is about to call out to Raffaella but sees she is fast asleep, like an angel, on a sun-drenched white rock. With great difficulty he staggers up to the rock and falls down beside her. He is struck by the expression of contentment on her face. A satisfied look comes into his eyes.)

GENNARINO: I may be ready for the hospital, Mrs. Raffaella, but you never looked so satisfied on the yacht! Agnelli! . . . Screw Fiat and all your other companies too!

SCENE 54

(Clearing by the tiny chapel on the island—exterior—daytime. Flowers and vine leaves are encircling and beautifying Gennarino's genitals. He opens his eyes and looks in amazement at the floral arrangement. A pleasant smell reaches his nostrils. Raffaella is coming up carrying an enormous shell on which there is some sort of omelet.)

RAFFAELLA (very sweetly): Darling, are you awake? Seagull egg omelet cooked in rabbit's grease prepared for my most beloved and adored master and owner, Mr. Carunchio! It's the first omelet I've made in my entire life, and it's probably revolting. Oh, my lord, is it revolting?

(Gennarino smiles. He eats.)

GENNARINO: It's almost revolting . . . do I have to consider this as homage?

(He points to the floral decoration adorning his privates.)

RAFFAELLA: What, the omelet?
GENNARINO: The flowers!
RAFFAELLA: Oh, more or less . . .
GENNARINO: See what kind of screwed-up woman you are. A serious woman from my area would never think of crowning it with flowers.

(He lies back to rest. She moves closer to him, sweet and amusing.)

RAFFAELLA: I'm no longer myself. . . . I feel insane, inebriated, as if I had been raped by the Turks, kidnaped by pirates, taken by the sheiks! These are primeval sensations. . . . I'm really confused. . . . I don't know if you're able to understand what I'm saying, but it's been really wonderful for me!

(*Gennarino enjoys the flavor of victory. He looks at her sleepily through half-open eyes.*)

RAFFAELLA: And how was it for you?

(*Gennarino has a condescending air about him.*)

GENNARINO: Well, not bad really!

(*She smiles.*)

RAFFAELLA: Stop joking! Silly idiot!

(*A slap. Violent and unexpected. This time she is really upset because it was the last thing she expected.*)

RAFFAELLA: Ahhhhhhh!

(*Gennarino is somber.*)

GENNARINO: Well, what's all this, we getting personal again?
RAFFAELLA: Well, shit, that's not funny anymore. . . . I was joking . . . after all!
GENNARINO: After all what? What's gotten inside your head? The

woman is nothing but an object of pleasure for the working male . . . that's all you are for me.

RAFFAELLA: In other words, like a whore in a brothel?

GENNARINO: Ahh, I wish . . . those were the days!

RAFFAELLA: Fascist, you sound like a nostalgic Fascist!

> (*Gennarino raises his arm as if to hit her. She moves away rapidly.*)

GENNARINO: Don't ever say that word. Because of those people, blood was shed by members of my family! I can't joke about a thing like that.

GENNARINO: On the one hand, whore can be an insult, but it can also be interpreted as a compliment. . . . Fascists can only be taken as an insult.

> (*She smiles at his compliment. They kiss and hug.*)

GENNARINO: I'm the only one who really understands you!

SCENE 55

> (*Cliffs—exterior—daytime. They have reached the water to go fishing as usual, using the spears. Raffaella gives him a hand. Gennarino goes underwater. As soon as he's out of hearing she can't resist calling out.*)

RAFFAELLA: You son of a bitch!

> (*She waits for him to re-emerge.*)

RAFFAELLA: That was love . . . last night . . .

> (*Spitting out water, Gennarino denies it.*)

GENNARINO: It was an erotic and pornographic session. Love is what one does in bed with one's wife.

> (*He goes under, Raffaella smiles and waits for him to surface.*)

RAFFAELLA: See, you're such moralists, you say that, because you don't have a wife.

> (*Gennarino's head bobs up and down in the waves.*)

GENNARINO: Who said I haven't got one? I have a wife and two kids!

(Raffaella almost has a stroke, who knows why? Gennarino notices the change.)

GENNARINO: What's wrong, does it disturb you?
RAFFAELLA: Oh . . . of course not.

SCENE 56

(Cliffs on the island—exterior—daytime. Gennarino comes back from fishing. Raffaella waits for him, smiling and making a flower chain.)

SCENE 57

(Clearing on the island—exterior—daytime. Raffaella is going fishing, using a line. Lying on the deflated rubber boat, Gennarino watches her as she gracefully runs toward the cliffs. His look is impossible to misinterpret. He is in love. He leans back with a dreamy look. Then sighs contentedly. He thinks about the situation and smiles.)

GENNARINO: Ah, Mrs. Pancetti, on the yacht you certainly didn't have such a satisfied look!

(He shuts his eyes. He is truly content.)

SCENE 58

(Cliffs on the island—exterior—daytime. Raffaella is on the rocks, her hair covered with flowers. A beautiful three-masted vessel glides through the blue waters close to the island. Suddenly she sees it. Her first impulse is one of immeasurable joy.)

RAFFAELLA: Hel . . . ahhh . . . hel . . . !

(The impulse quickly vanishes. The yacht passes close to the island. It most probably won't be stopping, for its bow is pointing away from the land. Raffaella is uncertain—she is torn between shouting out or not. Then she hides behind a rock. From behind the rock she watches as the yacht goes by. If she gave a sign, yelled perhaps, they would certainly hear her. They would see her because the boat is quite close and she is a dark figure against the white cliff. She is quiet and stays still, her wide eyes shining brightly. She waits excitedly for the boat to pass. It's a

gamble, she's leaving things to chance. This is proof of her true sentiment about Gennarino. The yacht becomes a tiny dot on the horizon. Raffaella comes out of her hiding place and laughs like a mad woman. Then she heads for the underbrush.)

RAFFAELLA: Mr. Carunchio!

SCENE 59

(Underbrush and clearing on the island—exterior—daytime. Raffaella races through the underbrush and across the rocks shouting.)

RAFFAELLA: Mr. Carunchio! Mr. Carunchio!

(Gennarino is fast asleep on the deflated boat as she appears out of the brush. She studies him carefully with her enormous eyes. Then calls to him.)

RAFFAELLA: Mr. Carunchio, I love you!

(Gennarino wakes up and looks at her sleepily. He looks at her again because he notices the odd expression of her face.)

RAFFAELLA: Mr. Carunchio, I love you! A yacht passed by and I didn't even call it, in fact, I hid and waited for it to pass!

(As he listens to her, simple and complicated feelings tumble over one another in his mind. He is completely bewitched by this woman.)

GENNARINO: You're mad!

(Raffaella kneels in front of him.)

RAFFAELLA: Yes, completely mad, madly in love with you . . . I'm bowled over by this crazy dream. . . . I've never been so well in my life, I don't want it to end. . . . I love you! Madly!

(Gennarino, as is customary, has an enigmatic look. Then he lets her have one of his terrible slaps. He is always able to catch her unaware, to amaze and hurt her. She was declaring her love, and this was the last thing she expected.)

RAFFAELLA: Owwwww, why?

(Gennarino is cynical.)

GENNARINO: It's for one of two things . . . either it's a lie and therefore the slap was for that, or else, it's the truth and then it's because you dared not to tell me! If a ship passes by, you tell me! You've got to tell me everything, do you understand? I'm the master! I'm the one who'll decide if we shout out for help or not. Have I made myself clear?

> (*Raffaella is really very hurt. She had expected that her insane gesture of love would have been received in a completely different way.*)

RAFFAELLA: Mmmmmmmmm . . .

> (*Gennarino calls out to her.*)

GENNARINO (sweetly): Come over here!
RAFFAELLA (shouting): No!
GENNARINO: Come on, come over here.

> (*Raffaella moves closer. Gennarino takes her head in his hands and touches her forehead.*)

GENNARINO: You've got to understand once and for all that I'm the one who makes the decisions.

> (*Now things are a lot more loving. Raffaella growls lovingly. She looks like a wild panther.*)

GENNARINO: And there's no fooling around!

> (*She growls again. Gennarino smiles indulgently. Gennarino growls louder than Raffaella. Raffaella crouches low and plays kitten.*)

RAFFAELLA: Miaooooooo . . . you hurt me!
GENNARINO: The pain is gone now, isn't it?

> (*Raffaella nods and pouts.*)

RAFFAELLA: Noooooo.
GENNARINO: It still hasn't gone away?
RAFFAELLA: Noooooooo . . .
GENNARINO: So it still hurts? Well, come over here and I'll make you feel a lot better.

> (*Gennarino kisses her. The whole thing becomes a love game. She sighs between kisses.*)

RAFFAELLA: You're such a brute . . . you're always hitting me!
GENNARINO: Well, after we make love you feel better, don't you?

> (*Raffaella looks at him languidly.*)

RAFFAELLA: You aren't a sadist, are you?

> (*Gennarino isn't quite sure what the word means but it has a
> pleasingly foreign and educated ring to it.*)

RAFFAELLA: Ahhhh . . . owwww . . .
GENNARINO: Look at how beautiful you become when I hit you.
. . . Jesus Christ, your eyes look just like the devil's! Two light bulbs
screaming out all the desire you carry within you. Come here, where
are you going?

> (*Raffaella slithers out of the boat, grunting and roaring. Gen-
> narino catches her and overcomes her.*)

GENNARINO: What are you, panther? Snake? Sow? Who are you?

(They make love. A long, tiring love. Then they lie back in the sand, naked and very close to one another. Because of their very opposite natures the erotic feelings between them are especially intense and vibrant. Gennarino's initial sexual desires have now given way to a consuming and passionate love which he attempts to conceal behind a façade of virile boorishness. The fear is that, should he disclose his true feelings, this unreal situation, generated by his finally being able to strike back at the upper classes, would change abruptly. Raffaella's subservience is a direct result of her playing the role of the underdog and the battle which has been going on between them since their landing on the island. A definite masochistic preference on her side has greatly increased her sexual appetite. It's obvious he is afraid that if he eases up on his violent tactics toward her he would risk losing her altogether. Gennarino is frightened that to show his true sentiment, and therefore his unadmitted weakness, would put an end to Raffaella's miraculous love for him. Raffaella is avidly savoring this situation. It is as if she were in suspended animation inside a bubble, without worries, and refuting all thoughts and analyses. Logic, mathematical hypothesis, realistic data, and rationality have become her ardent enemies. Instinctively she rejects them all now that she is in the presence of a wonderful thing: a free love which is to be enjoyed in the same way a butterfly enjoys the spring. Their passionate and exhausting couplings, so saturated with new and wonderful emotions, are constantly in danger of being shattered. The constant fear that this marvelous dream will end, that the Garden of Eden will be lost, makes them strive for the highest peaks of sexual and emotional gratification. They abandon themselves totally to the unusual destiny which has swept them onto this tiny dot in the middle of the deep blue sea in August.)

SCENE 60

(Clearing on the island—exterior—nighttime. They are locked in an embrace beside the crackling fire. Raffaella is breathless.)

RAFFAELLA: My darling, you are the very essence of primitive being, man before he was transformed. Darling, the first, the real man, you know . . . you ought to have been the first.

(Gennarino, who is enjoying her, is suddenly struck by a doubt.)

GENNARINO: The first? You refer to a person as the first when you know that there's going to be a second . . . ah!

(*Raffaella laughs at the way he always interprets things in his own way.*)

RAFFAELLA: The first and only one! What I'm saying is that I'm sorry not to have been a virgin. It was you who should have deflowered me, to have left his mark. Darling, angel, please! Sodomize me, sodomize me!

(*Gennarino doesn't have a clue as to what the word means. Clearly he is struck by the sound of the word. He pretends he hasn't heard. Raffaella insists.*)

RAFFAELLA: Please, sodomize me!

(*Gennarino tries to gain some time. He hugs her, looks around, avoids looking at her.*)

GENNARINO: Well, I don't know . . . I don't really feel like it.

(*Raffaella gets more and more passionate in her movements. She is set on her demand now that she's discovered another virginity*

she can offer up. She wants to offer it up to the person she feels has been her first real man.)

RAFFAELLA: Yes, I beg of you, my love. . . . You're my first man, sodomize me!

(All of a sudden Gennarino is furious. He tears himself away from her and looks at her, full of hatred.)

GENNARINO: Look, you filthy bourgeois bitch, are you doing it on purpose, are you trying to make a fool out of me by using these difficult words? What the hell is this thing you're talking about? What sort of filth are you going on about now?

(Raffaella looks at him in amazement but at the same time tenderly.)

RAFFAELLA: No, no, my darling. I'm sorry.
GENNARINO: Sorry, my ass! Is this the way to talk? Yessiree, I'm ignorant and I'm proud of my ignorance!
RAFFAELLA: Angel, I used that word because it's a very difficult thing for me to try to explain.

(Gennarino is still angry but curious.)

GENNARINO: I don't know the revolting things you people do. What's this thing? Sostromize? Somormize?

(Raffaella is embarrassed.)

RAFFAELLA: Well, to sodomize me would mean . . .

(She turns in his arms and makes the appropriate gesture, making the action quite clear. She looks at him sweetly and maliciously over her shoulder.)

GENNARINO: So that's it, huh? Well, why are you being so complicated. Why don't you just call a spade a spade?

(Gennarino has realized that she is offering the soft cheeks of her posterior. Raffaella smiles.)

RAFFAELLA: My darling, I just couldn't. This is an act of love and it would sound vulgar.

(She kisses him, giggling. Gennarino is sweet and amused.)

GENNARINO: In love there is no vulgarity. Vulgarity is a word invented by you bourgeois!

(He thinks back on her offer.)

GENNARINO: How do these things come into your head?
RAFFAELLA: I don't know!

(He turns her onto her stomach, lovingly yet brutally.)

SCENE 61

(Clearing on the island—exterior—daytime. A shining day. Gennarino and Raffaella are sitting in the shade beneath a tree by the shore. They are wearing white sailor pants and dark T-shirts. Raffaella is mending her torn skirt while Gennarino is fixing a net. We see their laundry laid out to dry behind them.)

RAFFAELLA: Don't give yourself airs of superiority. Only once have I seen such a look. It was a bored child at a party.
GENNARINO: What are these stupidities? Learn to sew, why don't you?
RAFFAELLA: It's a beautiful poem that is well suited to you.

(Gennarino looks at her distrustfully.)

GENNARINO: Bullshit! You starting to talk complicated again? When I can't understand what you're saying, I don't trust you. Ah, imagine, as if one could trust a woman!
RAFFAELLA: Woman! I'm not just any woman now, I'm yours!

(Gennarino is happy to hear her say this, but he isn't totally convinced.)

GENNARINO: Those are very pretty words, but what if we hadn't been shipwrecked? How would it have been between us then? I would have been downstairs and you would have been upstairs. I would have been the poor dark one and you the rich white one. I wouldn't have even crossed your mind. You would have been the grand lady and I would have been the disgusting servant . . . each in their place.
RAFFAELLA: You're being so unfair, I didn't know a thing then. I never loved before in my life!

(Nonetheless, Gennarino is bitter.)

GENNARINO: Let's stop telling fairy tales. Our relationship exists only because we're here. A desperate passion, but here. I'd love to see

Mrs. Pancetti with this peasant walking around Milan. Try picturing it—how much love would be left then?

RAFFAELLA: I'd probably love you even more!

GENNARINO: More? Then you lied when you said that your love was absolute! Let's try and be as precise as possible when we make these statements. Let's not lie, or else I'll get pissed off and kill you.

(*Raffaella laughs.*)

RAFFAELLA: You'll kill me?

GENNARINO: Yes, I'll kill you.

SCENE 62

(*Beach on the island—exterior—daytime. Gennarino and Raffaella are lying on the beach sand. Raffaella has an idea: she starts to take off her wedding band.*)

RAFFAELLA: Let's get married.

GENNARINO: No, that's your husband's. I want something of yours.

(*He touches one of her earrings, a tiny gold loop she has always worn.*)

GENNARINO: I want this.

RAFFAELLA: Ahh, the earring, of course.

(*Gennarino takes it off, Raffaella smiles.*)

RAFFAELLA: Awwww! Shall I put it on for you? Wait a second.

(*Raffaella raises herself onto her elbow and puts the earring on Gennarino's ear.*)

RAFFAELLA: Here we are, Burt Lancaster in *The Crimson Pirate!*

(*Gennarino, who has obviously seen the movie as well, smiles like Burt Lancaster, showing all his teeth. Happy with their private ceremony, they stand on the shore locked in a passionate embrace.*)

SCENE 63

(*Beach on the island—exterior—nighttime. Raffaella sleeps. She is beautiful and totally relaxed. Gennarino looks down at her and holds her in his arms as you would a child. His loving gaze*) *travels across the sinuous lines of her body. Now that there are no witnesses, his love is very clear. A very real, passionate love. As he watches over her he is overcome, like most lovers, by a million fears. Will he lose her? Will they be able to carry on this miracle forever? A deep sigh and a very sad look. He shuts his eyes as if in prayer, asking that this whole situation last as long as it possibly can. Then he holds her closer. The two bodies are huddled up in each other's warmth on the deserted, windy beach.)*

SCENE 64

(A small wood on the island—exterior—daytime. A nest on a tree. Gennarino has climbed up to get his hands on the eggs. He is really playing the role of a pirate, with his earring in one ear, a bandanna around his forehead, and a medallion around his neck. But, most obvious, he has a happy, victorious air about him. There are plenty of eggs. He looks at them and takes about ten. Mother bird swoops down on the thief and flies angrily around him. Gennarino looks at her affectionately.)

GENNARINO: You caught me right in the act, you poor thing. Don't be nervous—I'll take only what we need.

(Gennarino puts back the eggs and takes only two. Smilingly he starts climbing down the tree when he sees a yacht. It's an enormous luxurious boat heading straight for the island. Gennarino strains his eyes. Then he turns beet red. His gaze travels through the bushes, searching for Raffaella. Raffaella is on the beach with a bundle of dried-up wood in her arms. She has seen the yacht as well. She looks up in search of Gennarino. He gazes at her steadily, till their eyes meet.)

SCENE 65

(Small wood and clearing on the island—exterior—daytime. Gennarino and Raffaella meet on the clearing. Her face is flushed from running. He's panting from the climb down the tree. On the other hand, it could be the moment's emotion

rather than simply the exercise. It is a very important moment for both of them. They look at each other.)

RAFFAELLA: Darling, come on, let's hide. Even if they come on shore we can lock ourselves up in the chapel.

(She begins to pull at him. He stands firm. Gennarino has other plans.)

GENNARINO: Did you leave the wood on the beach?

(Raffaella nods her head. Then she is overcome by a terrible fear.)

RAFFAELLA: No, darling, don't!

(Gennarino is very curt and to the point.)

GENNARINO: You say you really love me? Well I want to know the whole truth.

(Raffaella immediately begins to shower him with affection.)

RAFFAELLA: What other proof do you need? The way we are now is as if we were born here. You were the one who said it. The structure of society is such that it could easily change us back to the way we were. The only thing of any importance is us, now, on this island.

(*Gennarino stops her.*)

GENNARINO: No, no, my dear. I want to know if Lady Raffaella Pavone Lanzetti thinks along the same lines as you do.

(*Raffaella is desperate.*)

RAFFAELLA: What does it matter how we were before? What's happened to the two of us is a miracle. It's a once-in-a-lifetime thing. Why go back to the old way of things? It's a deforming, horrible mechanism which will destroy us! Please, let's stay, my love!

(*Gennarino grabs her by the shoulders and looks at her intensely, very much in love with her.*)

GENNARINO: First I need proof. After that, I'll give you anything you want, but first I want proof!

(*Raffaella feels the tears swelling up in her eyes.*)

RAFFAELLA (sweetly): Why don't you believe that I want only you?

(*Gennarino stares at her.*)

GENNARINO: You're frightened, aren't you?

(*Raffaella leans against his chest.*)

RAFFAELLA: Yes . . .
GENNARINO: That's why I want proof.

(*Gennarino leaves her and races toward the beach to light a bonfire. Raffaella watches his dark, lithe figure racing through the golden trees. She sighs deeply.*)

RAFFAELLA: Such a dreadful character.

(*Gennarino is already making smoke signals with a leafy branch. The yacht heads for the island.*)

SCENE 66

(*Deck on board the French yacht—exterior—daytime. The owner walks along the deck followed by a blonde, respectable guest.*)

BLONDE GUEST: The sailor is down in the kitchen eating.
OWNER: And what about Madame Pavone Lanzetti?
BRUNETTE: She's down in my cabin washing, poor dear.

(*A beautiful blonde pops up on deck.*)

BLONDE: Isn't it marvelous, we saved the shipwrecked. These things can happen only at sea!

(*The guests are all sitting around a table on the deck.*)

BRUNETTE: Ahh, the sea opens doors to all kinds of adventures.
A GUEST WITH A MUSTACHE: Yes, it's always such an adventure.
BEARDED GUEST: Yes, that's true, you're so right!
BLONDE: It's so romantic.
BLONDE GUEST: Ah, yes, the sea is the greatest adventure of them all.
BRUNETTE: Oh, the little sailor. Isn't he the cutest thing!

SCENE 67

(*Below decks on the French yacht—interior—daytime. Down in the crew's quarters a meal has been laid out for Gennarino. The owner is in front of him trying to get some particulars on the shipwreck. He chews on his cigar and has a pronounced French accent.*)

OWNER: So how did your shipwreck with Mrs. Pavone Lanzetti go?

(*Gennarino is keeping to himself.*)

GENNARINO: Nothing . . .
OWNER: What do you mean, nothing? It's impossible . . .

(*Gennarino gives him a dirty look.*)

GENNARINO: What can I say? If I tell you it was nothing, it means nothing.
OWNER: But she's the biggest ballbreaker on the Mediterranean. Surely she must have busted your balls?
GENNARINO: Uhuh.

(*The owner insists.*)

OWNER: A lady without her creature comforts? You're not going to tell me that . . .

GENNARINO: Well at first, but then . . .

(Gennarino's expression brightens at the thought of "then.")

OWNER: She calmed down?
GENNARINO: Well, she couldn't very well stay on her high horse forever, so she gave in.
OWNER: Really?
GENNARINO: She was very well behaved.

(The owner is definitely unbelieving.)

OWNER: Never . . .
GENNARINO: She trusted me.
OWNER: She trusted you? Well, that's the best I've heard yet. You deserve a medal! You'll see, her husband will give you one. I called him on the radio and he's on his way by helicopter.

(There is a sound of a helicopter.)

OWNER: Yes, it's the coast guard helicopter. You see it?

(Gennarino is somber as he watches the black dot on the horizon getting larger and larger as it gets closer and closer. His eyes are sad but determined.)

SCENE 68

(Deck on the Esmeralda—*exterior—daytime. Corrado smiles.)*

CORRADO: Thanks, Gennarino.

(Gennarino smiles as well, but he is slightly embarrassed.)

GENNARINO: You're welcome.

(Corrado gives him a paternal wallop on the shoulder. We are on the Esmeralda *with all the orginal guests, who are celebrating the return of the shipwrecked. It is Toti who seems to be the happiest and proudest of all the guests.)*

TOTI: Ah, here's Gennarino, a glass for him!

(A brief attempt at a round of applause is quickly over and the champagne is poured for the toast. The voices and chatter of the guests soon die down. Gennarino and Raffaella gaze at one another intensely.)

SCENE 69

(*Pier in the small harbor—exterior—daytime. From one end of the harbor we hear a loud yell.*)

TUTUZZA: Gennarinoooooooooo!

(*A woman is racing toward the yacht, which has just docked. A young but already aging woman, in the way lower-class women normally are, having been burdened by children and hard work. But she's still pleasing and quite pretty. She has fiery eyes and a passionate temperament she can't seem to contain. Her great love makes her eyes shine. She races across the pier to embrace her husband who has returned.*)

TUTUZZA: Gennarino! My love, my treasure, my darling!

(*Gennarino sees her heading for him like a cannon ball. He has a moment of panic. Then he runs toward her. The clash is violent. She clutches him to her, showering him with kisses and tears. Warm and happy, she whispers broken phrases of happiness.*)

TUTUZZA: At last I can hold you tight, my love!

(*Gennarino feels stared at by the world.*)

GENNARINO: That's enough . . . enough!

(*In fact the guests, as they climb into the car waiting for them, look complacently at the rather pathetic scene, mocking smiles on their faces. Raffaella isn't smiling. She feels rather chilly.*

Gennarino can't take it for too long. He grabs his wife's arm and twists it.)

GENNARINO: That's enough of this! Do we want everyone to see us?

(Tutuzza won't listen to reason. She stares lovingly at her Gennarino. He is a miracle to her.)

TUTUZZA: I thought you were dead! I shed so many tears for you!

(With an icy stare, Raffaella looks at them. Tutuzza covers him with kisses. The guests drive away while Corrado, Raffaella, the owner of the yacht, and Toti walk up to Gennarino and Tutuzza.)

GENNARINO: Well, I'm alive, let's stop this farce in front of all this crowd!

(Tutuzza sees the group coming up to join them and thinks she understands Gennarino's embarrassment. Corrado is the first to shake her hand.)

CORRADO: Madame . . .

(Tutuzza happily shakes the hand of the "commendatore," who presents her to his other friends. Toti is openly overjoyed to be shaking hands with this member of the "people.")

TUTUZZA: Thank you, thanks . . . I'm honored!

(It is Raffaella's turn to be introduced to Mrs. Carunchio. Raffaella shakes Tutuzza's hand. The two women are so radically different. Somehow Tutuzza manages to hold her own against this elegant woman because of her genuiness and her happiness. Tutuzza is happy but, being a woman, she takes one look at Raffaella and finds her hard to swallow. Raffaella isn't able to remain indifferent to those big dark eyes. Gennarino feels torn to pieces. A razor blade seems to be slicing his heart up in little pieces.)

RAFFAELLA: I'm happy to make your acquaintance . . . when I think we might never have met . . . I mean, had they not saved us . . .

(Her attempt at conversation is a bit muddled. Only Gennarino takes it for what it is supposed to imply.)

TUTUZZA: Certainly . . . of course, you're right.

>   *(Anyhow, it's only a moment, because Corrado takes her by the arm and Tutuzza reddens in the presence of all these elegant people. Raffaella and Gennarino are alone. Their eyes meet. Gennarino whispers to Raffaella.)*

GENNARINO: I'm waiting . . .

>   *(Raffaella feels faint, and in that instant Gennarino is happy because he feels that all is not lost, that she still loves him.)*

RAFFAELLA: I know.

>   *(She points to Corrado and Tutuzza.)*

RAFFAELLA: It isn't easy.
GENNARINO: They were there earlier.
RAFFAELLA: She's very pretty.
GENNARINO: I'm waiting.

>   *(Raffaella stares at him and nods. Boldly, Gennarino sports Raffaella's earring. Not far away, Corrado is talking to Tutuzza.)*

CORRADO: Oh, by the way, be sure to give this to your husband.

(He hands her an envelope, which Tutuzza accepts obediently.)

TUTUZZA: Certainly, and thank you, Mr. Pavone Lanzetti.
CORRADO: Thank him again on my behalf, and be sure to let me know if you are ever in need of anything.

(Corrado, Raffaella, Toti, and the owner of the French yacht climb into the car.)

TUTUZZA: Good-bye, gentlemen, all the best!

(They wave good-bye from the car, and they're off. Tutuzza hangs on to Gennarino's arm happily. She is devouring him with her eyes.)

TUTUZZA: I can hardly believe I'm touching you again! The little ones understood everything when they saw me crying. They were leaping around with joy when they heard the news that you were alive!

(Gennarino is slightly moved at the mention of his children.)

GENNARINO: Poor little ones . . .
TUTUZZA: They really wanted to come along.
GENNARINO: You shouldn't have come. Imagine if they'd come too . . . what an embarrassment to have your wife running after you like this. Are they all right?

(Tutuzza smiles.)

TUTUZZA: They're dying to hug their father . . . and so am I.

(They start walking along the quay. She hugs him tightly, then thinks back.)

TUTUZZA: They were so thoughtful, they even reserved a room with a bath at the Hotel Hope, the one over there.

(She points toward the colorful houses near the port. Gennarino isn't taking part in her enthusiasm.)

GENNARINO: The Hotel Hope, where every now and again somebody arrives with a tiny suitcase and ends up shooting himself!
TUTUZZA: What are you saying? There's a nice veranda overlooking the harbor where we can dine at night like two upper-class people. Oh, I forgot, Mr. Pavoni Lanzett gave me this for you.

(Tutuzza hands him the envelope.)

GENNARINO: What is it?

TUTUZZA: I don't know.

(*He opens the envelope and finds a check for a million lire. Tutuzza sees the check.*)

TUTUZZA: Holy Mary Mother of God, a million lire!

(*Gennarino turns green. His hands shake.*)

GENNARINO: How dare he!

(*He lets his wife have a terrible backhand.*)

GENNARINO: And how dare you accept this?

TUTUZZA: He told me it was for you.

GENNARINO: "Give it to my husband yourself," that's what you should have said to him. That bastard—who does he think he is, handing out charity?

(*He's at his wit's end. He starts striding furiously down the street.*)

TUTUZZA: Where are you going?

GENNARINO: I've got things to do.

TUTUZZA: And what about me?

(*Gennarino runs off quickly. His wife tries to keep up with him but then lets him go because she knows him far too well to try to stop anything he does.*)

TUTUZZA: Gennarino, I'll wait for you at the Hotel Hope. Hotel Hope!

(*She has to shout the name because Gennarino is already far away.*)

SCENE 70

(*Jewelry shop—interior—daytime. The shop is a tiny, cheap place. It's the only one in this small fishing village. The jeweler is a fat little man and about as poor as Gennarino, but he feels he's one step up on Gennarino, being a jeweler.*)

GENNARINO: A million lire, I want a ring worth a million lire, a precious stone for an upper-class lady . . . and it must cost a million, not one lire more or less.

(The jeweler hands him an enormous topaz surrounded by diamonds. It's a horrible-looking ring with a cheap setting. Gennarino takes it out of its case and tries it on his pinky.)

JEWELER: Well, here we are, this has twenty diamonds, ordinarily it would cost slightly more, but we can come to an agreement.

(Gennarino admires the ring on his finger. He likes it, he finds it suitable.)

JEWELER: Is it supposed to be an engagement ring?

(Gennarino shakes his head.)

GENNARINO: No, a divorce ring.

SCENE 71

(Veranda at the yacht club—exterior—daytime. On the veranda the guests from the yacht are having a drink. Raffaella stares out to sea with a certain sadness, which strikes Corrado. He's been looking at her for a while and has noticed something strange about her. Corrado loves his wife deeply, their marriage has been a very solid one. His feeling of inadequacy makes him reach out to her, even though he risks getting an abrupt answer in return.)

CORRADO: Are you better now?

(Raffaella pulls herself together and forces a smile.)

RAFFAELLA: I'm okay.

(A waiter comes up to the table.)

WAITER (off camera): Mrs. Pavone Lanzetti, wanted on the phone . . .

(Raffaella gets up.)

RAFFAELLA: The phone . . . it must be my mother, she can track me down anywhere.

(Corrado follows her with his gaze as she crosses the yacht club's gardens toward the telephone.)

SCENE 72

(Yacht club telephone—gas station—exterior—daytime. Raffaella picks up the phone. She expects to hear Gennarino's voice.)

RAFFAELLA: My love . . .

(In fact, it is his voice, and she is terribly excited. Gennarino is speaking from a public telephone from which he can see the yacht club veranda.)

GENNARINO: You just can't do it. You don't have the guts to shout it out to the world. . . . I knew it all along.

(Raffaella is upset.)

RAFFAELLA: Where are you?
GENNARINO: I'm right in front of you, above the harbor at a gas station. . . . I can see you.

(Raffaella looks around. She searches with her gaze among the tiny fishing homes. Way down there on the other side of the street she sees the gas station. Gennarino is inside the station, talking to her and looking up at her.)

GENNARINO: Listen, you failed the test. I don't care, I don't give a damn about anything anymore. Now, listen to me carefully. On the tiny quay over there on the right where the fishing boats come in . . . down by the port, it's the one by the customs office . . . the fourth fishing boat, it's a boat called *Santa Rosalia*. It belongs to a friend. He's offered to take us back to the island. It's leaving in about half an hour, at sundown. I'll wait for you—you'll come, won't you?

(Raffaella listens to his trembling, low voice. Even though she has a tan she appears to turn white.)

GENNARINO: You haven't gotten over it already?

(Gennarino is very tense. His eyes are a pair of slits in his face. He attempts a feeble smile. Raffaella places the receiver as close as possible to her mouth.)

RAFFAELLA: Oh, my love . . . I love you more than ever . . . but so suddenly . . . oh, if only you knew . . . if only . . .

(Gennarino can breathe again.)

GENNARINO: Very well, then, in half an hour I'll meet you at the *Santa Rosalia*. She'll protect us, you'll see, she'll get us back to our island.

RAFFAELLA: What about the others . . . your wife?

(*Gennarino shuts his eyes.*)

GENNARINO: I told you already that nothing matters but you and me. Your husband dared offer me a million, a check for a million, which I wanted to throw back in his face. He wanted to humiliate me with a tip! He has yet to find out who Gennarino Carunchio really is! In half an hour, my love.

(*Gennarino hangs up, sighing with relief. Raffaella looks at the colorful Bardello yacht club. We see her elegant silhouette standing by the phone. She remains by the phone, completely stunned. She shuts her eyes. Something is pulling at her dress. A small boy is looking up at her. A pair of tiny, clever eyes.*)

CHILD: Madame, this is for you.

(*Raffaella accepts the parcel without understanding.*)

RAFFAELLA: Who sent it?

CHILD: The one who was talking on the phone.

(*The child runs off. Raffaella unwraps the greasy paper wrapping. Inside she finds a rose and the ring sitting vulgarly in its box. Raffaella looks at it. The garishness of the ring makes her smile. She's on the verge of tears but manages to contain herself. she looks across the street toward the little houses from where certainly Gennarino is looking at her. In fact, Gennarino has made sure the ring reached its destination. He is proud of his gentlemanly gesture, he's shown her who he is. He's very proud of himself.*)

GENNARINO (to himself): Do you understand, now, Lady Raffaella, who Gennarino Carunchio really is?

SCENE 73

(*Fishing boat—pier—exterior—sundown. The* Santa Rosalia. *The light is getting redder as the sun sets lower in the sky. Gennarino smokes a cigarette as he waits on the quay, very sure of himself. He's stretched out on a pile of nets. Gennarino stares at the long pier where the rich people's boats are lined up and where we see "the yacht" towering over all the rest. He looks far off into the distance and isn't aware of the tiny boy who comes running up to him. He is the same little boy we saw earlier. The child squats down next to him.)*

LITTLE CHILD: Give me a hundred lire.

(Gennarino gives him a dirty look.)

GENNARINO: Why, I already paid you for your services. Did you do a good job?
CHILD: Yes, but give me another hundred lire, because I have to give you something.

(Gennarino is immediately concerned. He searches in his pockets for the hundred lire.)

GENNARINO: What is it?
CHILD: First give me the hundred lire.

(Gennarino gives him the money.)

GENNARINO: Here you go.
CHILD: The lady I brought your package to asked me to give you this.

(The child hands him a note. Gennarino is startled. He grabs the note. The child runs off. He has to strain his eyes to make out her elegant handwriting. He clamps his jaws tightly as if he were trying to crack them. Tears swell up in his eyes, though he tries to fight them back. Suddenly, he starts running like a madman down the pier.)

SCENE 74

(Main pier—exterior—sundown. On the pier a helicopter is about to take off. Raffaella is on board crying. The helicopter begins its ascent just as we see Gennarino running up to it, silhouetted against the heart-breakingly beautiful sunset. He stands on the tip of the pier, reaching out to the helicopter. He shouts like a madman.)

GENNARINO: You fucking traitor! You slut! Damn the day I believed in you! I knew I shouldn't trust the rich, because the rich will always screw you in the end! Industrial slut! You're leaving me all alone . . . alone!

(*The helicopter climbs higher and higher.*)

SCENE 75

(*Pier—exterior—nighttime. It is obvious that Gennarino has been drinking like a fish. He sways up and down the pier.*)

GENNARINO: Sea—you traitor . . . you who were my friend now destroy my very soul. Sea, I spit at thee!

(*A well-placed handbag in the face puts an end to his rantings. It's Tutuzza. Violently, and furious like a raging maenad seeking revenge, Tutuzza slaps him and hits him with her handbag. Gennarino tries to protect himself as best he can, but he's too drunk. He falls down.*)

TUTUZZA: You cheated on me . . . with that slut! The whole world saw you shouting up at that helicopter! Everyone saw you crying out to that whore!

(*Tutuzza is out of her mind with jealousy. Gennarino manages to hit her smack in the face with a powerful punch. She falls and doesn't get up.*)

GENNARINO: Look who's getting bigger than her britches! Stay in your place!

(*Tutuzza keeps on crying desperately.*)

TUTUZZA: You pig, go away! I never want to see you at home again!

(*Gennarino moves off into the night, swaying and propping himself up against a streetlamp.*)

GENNARINO: Don't worry, I won't come home again. I want nothing more to do with you women. That's enough!

(*Tutuzza doesn't follow him.*)

TUTUZZA: Don't forget that now we have divorce in this country!
GENNARINO: Nothing to do with you bitches . . . and if I *really* get pissed off I'm going to jump into the water and drown myself.
TUTUZZA: I was right in voting pro-divorce!

GENNARINO: A slut up there and a slut down here, and what's more the sea is a traitor, how can a man live like this?

(Gennarino leans against a streetlamp. We see his face horribly bruised by his wife's beating.)

SCENE 76

(Pier—exterior—dawn. In the purplish dawn light we see Gennarino sitting on the pier after a sleepless night. Beaten-up and sad, his face all puffed up from his wife's beatings, Gennarino looks out to sea and watches the Santa Rosalia *gracefully gliding across the waters. The boat heads toward the fiery horizon carrying with it all his hopes and dreams. His gaze follows the boat, then he lowers it to the water. Slowly he removes his earring—all that's left of her, of the island, of the adventure he managed to ruin with his own hands. He presses the ring to his forehead, then throws it into the pale waters.)*

SCENE 77

(Ferryboat—pier—exterior—daytime. The post ferry is about to leave the island. The whistle blows. Tutuzza heads for it, dragging an enormous suitcase. She is a dark figure on the almost empty pier. Gennarino is leaning against a mooring. Tutuzza is on the other side of the boardwalk. She glances at him with hatred. Gennarino is a mess from the beatings and green from the booze, ruined by his misfortunes. But he, too, manages a filthy look. She raises her chin and refuses to look at him. Gennarino heads for the ferry as well. One walks on one side of the pier— the other on the opposite side. But they are heading in the same direction. Gennarino moves closer to his wife. As soon as he is near enough he reaches for the suitcase. She pulls away violently. He keeps walking beside her, and though she is putting up a good resistance, we can see she is ready to give in. Gennarino tries once again to grab the case. Tutuzza starts crying and hands it to him. They are two tiny figures, a small couple like so many others on the long, gray pier.)

SEVEN BEAUTIES

SEVEN BEAUTIES

CAST

Pasqualino Frafuso	Giancarlo Giannini
Pedro	Fernando Rey
Commandant	Shirley Stoler
Concettina	Elena Fiore
Don Raffaele	Enzo Vitale
Totonno	Mario Conti
Francesco	Piero di Orio
Mother	Ermelinda de Felice
Carolina	Francesca Marciano
Lawyer	Lucio Amelio
Socialist	Roberto Herlitzka
Doctor	Doriglia Palmi

CREDITS

Written and Directed by	Lina Wertmüller
Director of Photography	Tonino delli Colli A.I.C.
Art Director	Enrico Job
Music	Enzo Iannacci
	(Ediesse Editions—Sugar Music Group)

Running time: 115 minutes

The first American showing of SEVEN BEAUTIES was on January 21, 1976 at Cinema II in New York City.

SCENE 1

(Military train—interior—daytime. Interior freight wagon. Moans are heard rising up from the darkness, which is occasionally broken by the light filtering through the windows and doors of the wagon. The wounded are lying as best they can on heaps of hay scattered around the floor. They are cursing, moaning, and crying as they are jostled around by the swaying movement of the train. Pasqualino sits in a corner wrapped up in bloody, torn bandages. He's wearing a cap and has a pair of field glasses around his neck. The rhythmic swaying includes a light sleep. Beside Pasqualino lies a wounded soldier, moaning and complaining. We see that the train has stopped in open countryside, which is illuminated by the incessant bombings. Pasqualino gathers up all his energy and, driven by fear, races across the open fields, his bandages blowing in the wind. He runs through the pitch-black night like a one hundred-yard sprinter even though he can hardly see because of the darkness. He runs, falls into ditches, and gets up again, driven by his terrible fear. Pasqualino's fear is quite justified as we now see the train burning in the distance, hit by a bomb. Pasqualino is alone in this unknown, dark, God-forsaken place. The freezing wind stirs the branches of the great trees. The sky is starless.)

SCENE 2

> (*Open country—exterior—nighttime. He has no idea where he is running to. During a brief pause he hears a noise in the unknown woods. In the middle of the night, a noise is synonymous with terror. Pasqualino freezes in his tracks; is it man or beast he hears? He tries to move in the dark without making a sound, but as he gropes in the darkness his hands touch something warm.*)

FRANCESCO: Oh, my good God . . . Holy Virgin Mary . . . Oh!

> (*Fear causes the two men to jump back and establish a distance between one another. Pasqualino stands still and assesses the situation.*)

PASQUALINO: Holy Jesus, Joseph, and Mary! . . . You're an Italian!

> (*A brief pause*)

FRANCESCO: Who . . . who are you? . . . Were you on the train?
PASQUALINO: Yes, of course . . . damn this wood and these ditches!
FRANCESCO: You really scared me. . . . The fucking krauts shoot you, then ask "Who goes there?"

> (*At last they touch one another.*)

PASQUALINO: Have you any idea where the hell we are?

> (*They look into the darkness around them.*)

FRANCESCO: It's got to be Germany, that's for sure.

> (*Pasqualino gazes far off into the darkness. In the distance, visible between the trees, the train is still burning.*)

PASQUALINO: In any case, we're better off here than there.
FRANCESCO: That's for sure.
PASQUALINO: That train must be like a furnace. . . .
FRANCESCO: Those poor devils!

> (*Pasqualino looks around, then turns to Francesco with a confidential air.*)

PASQUALINO: Yes, they are poor souls.

SCENE 3

(Wood—exterior—nighttime. We see Francesco's outline in the dimming light of a dying campfire. He sits beneath a large tree. Francesco is a middle-aged man, very thin, with a patient yet ironic expression in his eyes.)

PASQUALINO: The truth is that I don't really have any wounds under these bandages. . . . I suppose I'm considered a deserter; or perhaps something worse.

(Pasqualino has taken off his bandages under Francesco's watchful eye.)

FRANCESCO: Worse, much worse! . . . Simulation of wounds! . . . Whew! I must say you did a good job, though, it really looked genuine.
PASQUALINO: I took them off a dead soldier . . . poor man . . . still, he won't be needing them, and as for me, instead of being in Stalingrad fighting, I'm right here. . . . Let's forget it!

SCENE 4

(Wood—exterior—dawn. A light rain casts a veil over the early morning. Francesco and Pasqualino are marching at a good pace across the woods, their heavy army boots sinking in the moss and the mud.)

FRANCESCO: So I gathered my soldiers around me and I said to them, look, you guys, what the hell are we doing wandering around in these dreadful conditions? Who are we going to kill? Go home, just get out of here! You can't obey people who send you out to fight with poor clothing in a climate where when you blow your nose the snot is crystallized! When you take a crap, you shit icicles! So I got two trucks together, gave each of the lads a permit, and sent them off. Hopefully some of the boys from my patrol have made it out of that frozen hell. As for me, I was to be shot tomorrow morning at dawn—found guilty by some fucking military tribunal. . . .

(The two men have reached a clearing from where they can see a very wide river. It is almost dawn and the light is breaking through the veil of haze which envelops the countryside.)

PASQUALINO: Boy, what an enormous river!
FRANCESCO: It's probably the Rhine, we must be in Rhineland.

PASQUALINO: Where the hell is that?
FRANCESCO: It's still Germany.
PASQUALINO: Then we're still up shit creek!

SCENE 5

(*Wood—exterior—daytime. Through the morning mist we see a large ditch about thirty feet in diameter. A number of army trucks are in the vicinity. The people are ordered to get off one of the trucks. They are pushed into a clearing and told to strip. An SS officer brandishing a whip can be seen walking nearby. The group consists of men, women, and children, all branded with the yellow Star of David. They undress slowly, without tears, huddled next to one another. They put their meager belongings in neat piles–shoes, underwear, and clothes. A family of eight: a middle-aged woman and her husband, an eight-year-old boy, two girls in their twenties, another boy in his teens, and an old lady carrying a baby to whom she whispers gently. The father holds the ten-year-old's hand and softly whispers words of encouragement. The child is having a difficult time holding back his tears. They stare at one another, at their stark naked-ness, their eyes full of tears. The SS guard by the pit calls out to his companion with the whip. The man singles out twenty peo-ple and pushes them toward the gaping hole. The entire family is in this group. As the panoramic camera follows the family, we catch a first glimpse of the inside of the communal grave. The bodies are piled high on top of one another inside the grave. Most of them are wounded in the head. The blood flows freely from one body to the next. Many of them are still alive. They move, they gesture with their hands to show they are still alive. The executioner is sitting with his legs over the edge of the grave, a machine gun in his hands and a cigarette dangling from his lips. A group of twenty climbs into the grave by way of some steps dug into the side of the pit. They stand in single file. Right where the SS guard with the whip orders them to. The naked people stare at the dead and talk to them softly. The executioner stands up, the cigarette still in his mouth. He takes aim and fires two complete rounds from one side of the grave to the other. The bodies drop like stringless puppets. Their eyes open wide, Pasqualino and Francesco stare in total disbelief through the binoculars.*)

SCENE 6

(Wood—exterior—daytime. Francesco and Pasqualino start run-
ning aimlessly through the woods. In the distance they can still
hear the shots. They are pale and distraught at the scene they
have witnessed.)

PASQUALINO: Oh my God, who were they?
FRANCESCO: Probably Jews.
PASQUALINO: Can it be possible?
FRANCESCO: Possible? Certainly it's possible, and we're the allies of
the dregs of humanity.

(Pasqualino turns around in horror at what Francesco has just
said.)

PASQUALINO: How can you say that we're accomplices of those bastards?
FRANCESCO: Did we run out and yell at them? Did we spit in their
faces? No! We're running away like cowards, like the cowards they are!

(Pasqualino listens open-mouthed, then rebels at Francesco's
words.)

PASQUALINO: What could we have done? It would have been a
meaningless suicide. We would have run out, they would have shot us
in the guts and that would have been that! What would we have ac-
complished?
FRANCESCO: No! It wouldn't have been futile. A decent man should
rebel when faced by certain abuses. One should say no; instead I said
yes . . . yes to Mussolini, to orders! To all that shit! In battle I killed
some human beings and I didn't even know why!

(Pasqualino is absorbed in his thoughts.)

PASQUALINO: I killed long before the war started, for personal reasons. . . .

(Francesco is too taken with his own thoughts to comprehend his
companion's suffering.)

FRANCESCO: I killed . . . I was just a son of a bitch!

(Pasqualino talks to himself. A distant music seeps through the
fog.)

PASQUALINO: I did it . . . for a woman. . . .

(*Pasqualino's thoughts begin to take shape until finally they explode into the scene of Concettina at the Peverello Theater.*)

SCENE 7

(*Peverello Burlesque Theater—interior—evening. The camera works its way up Concettina's stretch-marked thighs, adorned by a black garter belt and a patriotic cockade emblazoned with the colors of the Italian flag. Concettina is a strong, lively woman wearing a typical burlesque outfit of the period, her head crowned in a fez. Concettina's song is about the sanzioni, a means of rationing used in war-torn Italy.*)

CONCETTINA (singing):
"Oh, my God, they're sanctioning everything!
The Fascists are sanctioning tea, and they're sanctioning milk!
What else are they going to take away from us?
The more you take away, the more we shall hate you for it, so you better stop sanctioning us. . . .
One thing I ask you, please don't sanction my lover's tool, or all hell will break loose!"

(*The spectators are rowdy, boisterous Neapolitans disapproving whole-heartedly of the performance. In enormous letters above the stage is a sign proclaiming "Economic Self-Sufficiency." Concettina is trying as best she can, considering her girth, to dance as seductively as possible. Behind her, wrapped in the colors of the Italian flag, are two chorus girls, equally fat, who are trying very hard to keep the tempo as they dance across the stage. The audience boos, claps, and jeers but Concettina doesn't let their reaction worry her in the least.*)

CONCETTINA: Hey! What the hell do you guys want?

(*More shouts and jeers from the audience*)

CONCETTINA: Fuck off!
SPECTATOR: Up your sister's!

(*The audience is laughing. Some stand on their seats. More jeers, whistles.*)

ANOTHER SPECTATOR: Show us your ass!

CONCETTINA: Ah, fuck you!
MORE SPECTATORS: Show us your ass!

> (*Concettina lets the audience have a glimpse of her ass, at the same time insulting them with a rude gesture. At one end of the theater there are some steps. A pair of feet slowly, carefully advances down them. We can now clearly see the menacing form. It is Pasqualino. Flared nostrils, half-open, heavy-lidded eyes: his mouth is twisted in a mean grimace and smoke curls out of the side of it. His hands are pushed deep into his jacket pockets. Pasqualino stands still, smoke pouring out of his mouth and nose. Concettina, in the meantime, continues her battle of wits with the public. They still jeer and whistle.*)

CONCETTINA: Up yours, you mother fu . . . !

> (*More laughter*)

SCENE 8

> (*Concettina's dressing room—interior—nighttime. A back room has been turned into a dressing room by partitioning it off with a curtain. It is cluttered with the usual dressing-room debris: powder puffs, patches, make-up, and feather boas. Concettina is no longer as cocksure as she was on stage. She is face to face with her terrible younger brother, her thighs quivering with fear. Pasqualino looks threatening but speaks calmly.*)

PASQUALINO: Concettina, let's be reasonable. Look at yourself, look! Are we pretty? . . . No, we really aren't pretty. . . .

> (*He grabs his enormous sister and forces her to look into the mirror.*)

PASQUALINO: We aren't even that bright . . . we are totally broke . . . as the only man in the family of eight women I have tried to safeguard one thing. . .!

> (*He pushes her against her make-up table.*)

PASQUALINO: Honor! Do you know that to defend this damn honor I am forced to walk around with this?

> (*He pulls out a pistol.*)

PASQUALINO: I want it to be known that we expect respect! Now you see what you've done to me, you ugly cunt! Prancing across a stage showing off your thighs. . . . And it's all because of that bastard that you're singing and dancing in a burlesque!

(*Pasqualino's looks become wilder by the minute.*)

PASQUALINO: Now I'm forced to kill him. . . . I have to shoot him!

(*Concettina bursts into tears.*)

CONCETTINA: For the love of God, Pasqualino, don't kill him! He promised he would marry me. . . . I'm thirty-seven years old, I don't want to die a spinster!
PASQUALINO: Better to be a spinster than a whore! I'll kill him!
CONCETTINA: No! Please! Tottonno will marry me, you'll see! First he'll make me a star; then he'll marry me!
PASQUALINO: A star! Look at yourself, you look like a bald chicken! What star? Didn't you hear the jeers from the audience? You're a disgrace! I'm going to shoot him!
CONCETTINA: No! This is only the beginning, I'll get better. . . . When I get better I'll sign up with the Margherita Theater and Totonno will marry me, he told me so, he loves me!

(Pasqualino stares at the pathetic figure in front of him, her make-up running down her tear-stained cheeks.)

PASQUALINO: You let him know that he has one month . . . one month to make an honest woman out of you! We can't afford to lose our honor . . . is that clear, you idiot? You're the oldest—if you become a slut, what's going to happen to the other seven? Seven sluts? So get yourself married in the next month, or I'm going to tear him to pieces. You can count on Pasqualino's word!

SCENE 9

(Ground floor of Pasqualino's house—interior—daytime. A gilded Madonna under a bell jar dominates the room from its vantage point on the dresser. Pasqualino is using a solid kind of hair wax to smooth down his hair. After a number of applications it begins to resemble a shiny black helmet. All around him the house pulsates with life. The sisters' ages range from nine to thirty. They are all rather ugly and have the family trait of a large nose and frizzly hair. Having combed the youngest one's hair with a delousing comb, the mother is now braiding her hair. The sisters are all keeping busy. Their chores are predominantly concerned with the well-being of the male. One of them is ironing his trousers, another shines his shoes. A third sews on a button and yet another brushes his jacket. Pasqualino is totally absorbed in his grooming. Mixed in with the bustling family activity are the mattress-makers who work in the room, stuffing mattresses and sewing them up again. Concettina is sitting in front of the sewing machine.)

PASQUALINO: Hey, Rosina . . . what about a carnation?

(One of the sisters, whose ass is the size of a barn door, goes rushing off in search of a pretty carnation for Pasqualino's buttonhole.)

ROSINA: Right away, Pasqualino . . . right away.

(Concettina unconsciously starts singing the "sanctions" song. She quickly stops as Pasqualino's deadly look meets hers.)

MOTHER'S VOICE (off camera): How 'bout a cup of coffee?

(Pasqualino walks toward the bureau. On the way he pats a little old lady on the head.)

PASQUALINO: Come on, granny, let's make these mattresses nice and plump!

(*He reaches the bureau, opens a drawer, and pulls out his pistol. He loads it, then stuffs it into his trousers. His mother looks at him disapprovingly.*)

PASQUALINO'S MOTHER: Leave it at home. Why are you looking for trouble?

PASQUALINO: Mother, this will solve our troubles. Those who are feared are respected, and everybody is beginning to respect me. . . .

(*Pasqualino turns toward the women working on the mattresses.*)

PASQUALINO: If you'll excuse us for a minute, this is a family matter.

(*He pulls the curtain across the room. The curtain divides the working area from the living area. The sisters all gather around him.*)

LAUGHTER AND VOICES OF THE WORKERS (off camera): What do you think we care about your family problems?

(*Pasqualino, like a shepherd with his flock, speaks softly and promptly.*)

PASQUALINO: I want you all to watch out for Uncle Nicolino's family, they're a bunch of born cheats—understand?

(*Pasqualino hands his mother a ten-lire note.*)

PASQUALINO: This is for the shopping.
PASQUALINO'S MOTHER: You're an angel.
PASQUALINO: I want you to stop eating bread and onions, buy yourself each an egg. These girls look terrible. With those yellowish faces, when the hell are they ever going to find a husband?

(*The girls giggle.*)

PASQUALINO: Now, remember, let's behave respectably. The first one to get out of line gets her head beaten in by me!

(*Concettina gets the message and looks away. Pasqualino draws back the curtain and heads for the door. On the way he greets all the women and strokes the asses of all the young ones who are intent on stuffing mattresses.*)

PASQUALINO: O.K. girls, let's not get fresh. . . . Have a nice day. . . . Luisella! Why the long face? Give me a pretty smile, come on.

SCENE 10

(*Alleyway and small square—exterior—daytime. Theme song: "Pasqualino." Pasqualino leaves the house and starts walking up the crowded, sun-lit alleyway. Farther on, in the small square by the sea, an old lady is yelling at Carolina and a small boy. She yells at them, then leaves them in tears beside a tiny hand organ on wheels. Pasqualino goes up to them to find out what is wrong. Carolina is a pretty fifteen-year-old with enormous misty eyes. She's wearing bobby socks and is sniffling.*)

PASQUALINO: All these tears, little one, what's the matter? Come on, stop it.

(*Carolina turns to him, her eyes filled with tears. It is clear that the two are friends.*)

CAROLINA: I don't want to go around playing the organ. I'm embarrassed, I have no voice. I can't even carry a tune!
PASQUALINO: What do you care, just shout!
CAROLINA: Yes, but then they make fun of me, they say rude things.

PASQUALINO: Well, don't you know what to reply? If someone is disrespectful, you tell them you're engaged to me. Just repeat these words . . . I am engaged to Pasqualino Settebellezze.

(She smiles through her tears.)

CAROLINA: But it isn't true.

PASQUALINO: Perhaps not now, but in a few years we'll see. You just think about growing up. Fate will take care of the rest.

(Carolina smiles and starts turning the handle, singing softly.)

CAROLINA (singing): "You've got to carry on living, not give a damn!"

A BLONDE GIRL: Robbing the cradle, Pasqualino?

PASQUALINO: Hah, the green-eyed monster!

SCENE 11

(Alleyways, streets, steps of Naples—exterior—daytime. As Pasqualino walks through a sunny Naples, the women all smile at him. A curly-haired blonde sends him a kiss from her balcony. A pantsmaker is working on her doorstep. A woman has a child on her shoulders. A group of dirty urchins chase one another up and down the steps. Two girls sitting on a step wave to Pasqualino. With a sigh he takes off his carnation and gives it to one of them.)

SCENE 12

(The Galleria in Naples—interior—daytime. Pasqualino is now climbing the steps leading to the Galleria.)

NEWSPAPER BOY (off camera): Get your paper!

(Small coffee tables are lined up along one side of the Galleria. A woman is selling flowers. Don Raffaele Scario sits while an old shoeshine man dabs white on his shoes. Pasqualino stands nervously in front of him. Don Raffaele's expression is enigmatic.)

PASQUALINO: But what's wrong, Don Raffaele . . . what's happened? Haven't I always served you well?

DON RAFFAELE: That's got nothing to do with it, my boy. I need people who have the respect of others.

PASQUALINO: What are you saying . . . that I'm not respected?

(Don Raffaele doesn't look at him.)

DON RAFFAELE: What am I saying? Well, when one isn't able to have people respect his family . . .

(Pasqualino is all ears.)

PASQUALINO: How do you mean?

DON RAFFAELE: Why don't you take a nice walk around 3 P.M. Go to the Pallonetto and see for yourself what is happening to your family's honor. . . . He bought your sister a pair of shoes with a red ribbon.

SCENE 13

(Brothel—interior—daytime. We're at the Pallonetto, the lower-class brothel in Naples. In the middle of an enormous room are two rows of chairs. Two large fans rotate lazily on the ceiling.)

DON RAFFAELE (off camera): . . . and he shoved her in there to learn the trade . . .

(At one end of the room a group of whores is waiting for their clients. In the center of the room an old "drag queen" is finishing off the afternoon chores. One of the four whores is Concettina, her face heavily made up. One of the whores lights up as she sees a prospective client.)

WHORE: Look, we already have a client.

(Concettina smiles, then suddenly the smile freezes.)

CONCETTINA: My God, it's my brother!

(Frightened out of her wits, she tries to run away but stumbles in her high heels. Leaping over the two rows of chairs, Pasqualino cuts her off. They are now facing each other. A tense, high noon atmosphere as the two stare at each other. He suddenly starts shouting and beating her.)

PASQUALINO: Whore! Bitch! Whore! Are you happy now that your boy friend has put you in here to learn the trade?

(Pasqualino smashes her about. She tries to get away from his clutches as the other whores try to stop Pasqualino. Women's shouts.)

PASQUALINO: Shame on you! You're a disgrace to our family's name!

(Pasqualino is trying to break away from the whores.)

PASQUALINO: Get off, fuck off!

(Pasqualino manages to free himself from the whores, grabs Concettina, and forces her onto a chair and starts strangling her.)

PASQUALINO: Where is he . . . where? . . . Tell me the truth! Don't try and defend him 'cause I'll kill you, too!

(Concettina gags. Her tongue is dangling out of her mouth. We can see the whites of her eyes as they turn upward. Pasqualino continues mercilessly to strangle her.)

PASQUALINO: Where is that piece of shit, tell me?

(Concettina tries to say something, but she is barely intelligible.)

CONCETTINA: How can I tell you anything if you're strangling me?

(Pasqualino releases his hold slightly.)

PASQUALINO: So that pimp married you, huh?

(Concettina is in tears.)

CONCETTINA: He's over there. . . .

(At last Pasqualino releases his hold and jerks her up.)

PASQUALINO: Go home, go!

(Concettina is upset. He pushes her violently toward the doorway.)

CONCETTINA: I can't go out like this. . . .

(One of the whores kindly hands her a shawl with which to cover her tattered clothes. Concettina grabs it and stumbles toward the door.)

PASQUALINO: Go home! Get out of here!
CONCETTINA: I beg of you, Pasqualino, don't do it, I love him!

(Pasqualino is out of his head now, he shouts uncontrollably.)

PASQUALINO: Fuck you and fuck your love, you asshole. . . !

(He pushes her out the door. He turns away and freezes in his steps. There, at the other end of the room, is "18 Karat" To-

tonno. Two ugly mugs stand on either side of him together with two buxom girls.)

PASQUALINO: Are you "18 Karat" Totonno?

(Totonno pauses.)

TOTONNO: What if I were?
PASQUALINO: If you are, then you're going to marry my sister Concettina!

(Totonno looks at him with contempt, then bursts into a laugh. Pasqualino moves up closer, then speaks in a gentle, almost friendly tone.)

PASQUALINO: Don't laugh, you promised her you would. . . .

(Totonno stops laughing. His face is mean, he's a lot bigger than Pasqualino.)

TOTONNO: Who the hell are you? Never saw you in my life. Piss off, you worm!

(Pasqualino is taken aback by the insult. He moves up even closer, then opens up his jacket, showing his pistol.)

PASQUALINO: Didn't quite catch that last line. . . .

(Suddenly Totonno slugs Pasqualino in the mouth. Taken by surprise, Pasqualino falls down, out cold. Totonno quickly hides the knuckle-duster. To add insult to injury he picks up the dustbin and pours it over Pasqualino's face. Then, taking a broom, he brushes the dirt all over him.)

TOTONNO: There, that will teach you. . . . Have a good day!

(Totonno says good-bye to the people present and walks away like a hero. The three whores who have watched the whole scene rush over to help Pasqualino, who is still out. Kneeling beside him, they try to bring him to.)

WHORE: That cowardly bastard . . .
OTHER WHORE: Look at what he did to him. . . .
"OLD QUEEN" (off camera): Get that bundle of rags out of here, the clients are beginning to arrive.

(Pasqualino slowly comes to. Then, as he remembers what has happened, he stands up suddenly as if he had been bitten by a snake.)

PASQUALINO: Where is that hunk of shit? Where is he?
WHORE: He's gone. Don't think about it.

(Pasqualino trembles with hatred.)

PASQUALINO: I'll have his head . . . that punch will cost him his life!

SCENE 14

(Alleyway—exterior—nighttime. Pasqualino walks up the alleyway where Totonno lives.)

SCENE 15

(Totonno's room—interior—nighttime. A foul-smelling room on the ground floor. A bed, table, dresser, and bedside table. This neighborhood is patronized by the underworld. Totonno is fast asleep on the bed. He wears a pair of shorts and a T-shirt. His clothes are lying beside him. The room is in total darkness except for an occasional flicker of light from the alley. Totonno snores loudly. Pasqualino is standing outside. Quickly he unlatches the window and climbs into the room. He stands still for a moment. A veil of perspiration covers his forehead. He closes the window behind him and turns to face Totonno's ugly body. He is pointing his pistol at him. Silently he goes over to turn the light on, then returns to the bed, the pistol still pointed. Totonno reacts slightly to the light but a second later is back in a deep slumber. Pasqualino looks at him. It is obvious he doesn't want to shoot a defenseless man. He grabs the man's foot and shakes it violently. Totonno kicks instinctively.)

PASQUALINO: "18 Karat" Totonno!

(Totonno's sleepy eyes focus on Pasqualino brandishing his pistol.)

PASQUALINO: Move it! I don't want to kill a man when he's fast asleep! Wake up! It's me!

(Totonno has finally awakened. He's now very much aware. He reacts like a cornered animal. He reaches frantically for his clothes.)

TOTONNO: Holy Mother, good God, you bastard . . . don't shoot!
PASQUALINO: No, not bastard, you called me worm, have you forgotten? Hurry up and find your gun!

(Totonno searches in vain for his pistol. Pasqualino continues with a snicker.)

PASQUALINO: Out with that gun, I need it so I can say it was an act of self-defense.

(In the excitement of the moment Pasqualino accidentally pulls the trigger and shoots Totonno in the chest. Pasqualino is terrorized; Now he's really done it. He closes his eyes, his brow is sweaty, he leans against the window and sighs deeply, then dries his face. He finds it hard to swallow. He takes a closer look at the body, then shies away in horror. Pasqualino goes through the clothes which the corpse is still clutching but can't find a pistol. Totonno has died with an awful expression on his face. He is

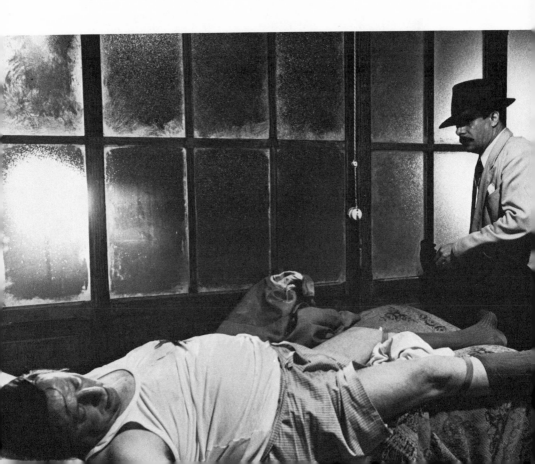

lying across the bed in his striped shorts, his garters neatly hold-
ing up his socks. Pasqualino hears the tune Concettina sang at
the burlesque, then suddenly we are back to the harsh reality of
the mist and the ominous woods.)

SCENE 16

(Wood—exterior—daytime. Pasqualino shuts his eyes in horror
at the memory. Pasqualino and Francesco continue walking
through the unfamiliar wood. They have lost all sense of direc-
tion.)

FRANCESCO: And now where the hell could we be?

(Pasqualino is a few feet behind Francesco. Suddenly his sensi-
tive Neapolitan nose picks up a scent. Like a pointer he freezes
and sniffs the air.)

PASQUALINO: Jesus Christ, the smell . . . it's onions!

SCENE 17

(Wood hunting lodge—exterior—daytime. Pasqualino leaps like
a deer toward a clearing. In the middle of the clearing is a beau-
tiful, square villa. Pasqualino cautiously walks up to the house
and studies it carefully. It looks like one of those fairytale
houses, small and mysterious. The closer he gets to the house,
the more audible is a woman's voice singing to the accompani-
ment of a piano. Pasqualino doesn't know this, but she's playing
a piece by Wagner. Pasqualino peeks in through the front door.)

SCENE 18

(Hunting lodge—interior—daytime. A spiral staircase, vases
filled with beautiful flowers. A magnificent living room, a Wag-
nerian atmosphere. At the piano sits a gorgeous woman clad in a
white veil which barely covers her protruding breasts. A true
Valkyrie if ever there was one. Her sensual body vibrates as she
sings. The scene is a Wagnerian dream come true. Pasqualino is
dumfounded. The room is exquisite. Below a beautiful inlaid
wooden ceiling, portraits of ladies and gentlemen adorn the
wall. The sofa is covered by a wolf-pelt spread. On the writing

table we see a superb bouquet of wild flowers. Pasqualino con-
tinues his search around the house.)

SCENE 19

(The service entrance and kitchen of the lodge—interior—day-
time. The music can still be heard coming from the living room.
Pasqualino comes in through the service entrance and stops in
the doorway. He has found the source of the delicious smell. In
the room there is only a little old lady who is clearly paralyzed.
She is sitting in an armchair with a tiny black dog on her lap.
Pasqualino is starving. He gathers his courage and bows deeply
before the old lady. He walks up to her. She stares at him from
behind her lively little eyes in total disbelief.)

PASQUALINO: Ah, madame, good morning . . . *guten Morgen* . . .
I apologize for coming in without having been invited, but please shut
up. . . .

(On the colorful table we see mountains of food. Pasqualino
heads for it quickly.)

PASQUALINO: Hate to disturb you like this . . . terribly hungry
. . . I Italian soldier . . . you no understand . . . no matter . . . I
foreigner, not *Deutsch.* . . . *Ja* . . . I eat! . . . I come from Naples,
madame . . . Naples! . . . You know where that is? *O sole mio* . . .
tralalalalala. . . . You understand now? Pizza . . . tomatoes on pizza
. . . macaroni. . . . I hungry, now eat much food!

(On the small table next to the old lady there is a soup bowl,
trays, loaves of bread. He lifts the lid off the bowl and is almost
bowled over by the wonderful smell which greets his nostrils.)

PASQUALINO: Ahhh . . . *Deutschen* soup *ja* . . .

(He grabs a ladle and tastes the soup. It's boiling hot and he
burns himself.)

PASQUALINO: *Gut!* . . . very hot, *ja* . . . *gut* . . . madame, you
have no mind if I take some bread, do you?

(Pasqualino's attention is drawn to a stew, which he starts to
stuff into his mouth. Dipping chunks of bread into the stew, he
scoops up the gravy and crams them in as well. All the time he is
talking to the old lady to keep her calm. She is so totally taken
by his audacity that she couldn't talk if she wanted to.)

PASQUALINO: Very *gut* stew . . . reminds me of mother's cooking back in Naples . . . she make *gut* stew *ja* . . . mudder, mudder . . . understand? One never forgets mudder . . . you mudder too. Your daughter playing on piano, she doesn't catch cold playing naked? . . . Hard times madame, war . . . damn war . . . a stew! . . . potatoes! . . . *Kartoffen!* . . .

(*Pasqualino keeps up his frenetic pace; he moves around the table stuffing his pockets and his mouth.*)

PASQUALINO: Madame, I want to take some bread for my friend . . . he is Italian too. . . . No, this I'll leave for you. A little wine . . . to your health, cheers. . . . Ahh . . . pure grapes. I would love to stay on as your guest, and that daughter of yours with that ass . . . must go now.

(*Pasqualino departs with more deep bows. He pats the dog and winks at the old lady, and before he leaves he helps himself to the cheese, hams, and salamis, which he hadn't noticed before.*)

PASQUALINO: Little dog, very cute . . . thank you, madame, may you live to be a hundred . . . a salami, cheese . . . delicious . . . auf Wiedersehen . . . and up yours madame!

(*On tiptoe Pasqualino dashes out the front door and back into the clearing, where he tries to get his bearings.*)

SCENE 20

(*Wood—exterior—daytime. Squatting under the trees, Pasqualino and Francesco are digging into their unexpected feast. The atmosphere is relaxed, reminding one of a pleasant picnic. Good food, good appetite, and healthy air. Suddenly Pasqualino's mouth opens wide, and he freezes. The sandwich doesn't fall out of his mouth as he lifts up his arms in a surrendering gesture. Francesco, who is sitting in front of him, looks inquisitive, then turns to look behind him. Two enormous and mean-looking German soldiers are pointing their machine guns at Pasqualino and Francesco. We see our heroes walking across the countryside pushed on by the two Germans. Panoramic shot of the sky. Music: "The Ride of the Valkyries."*)

SCENE 21

(Concentration camp—exterior—interior—daytime. Oppressive fog and dark skies over the camp. Wagner's "Die Valkyrie" still playing. Through the fog we see the naked multitudes waiting to be shorn, disinfected, and washed. Stacks of bodies, living skeletons walking aimlessly around. Forced labor. Thousands of people. A prisoner hanging from a beam, swinging gently. Barbed wire surrounds everything. Hundreds of naked skeletal corpses. They are being stacked on trucks. Even Dante couldn't have envisioned a "hell" like this one. We see the barracks where they live like chickens in their coop, four to a bunk. Pasqualino is dressed in a prisoner's uniform, his eyes wider than ever. His strength is ebbing away. The beast appears through the fog, enormous and cruel. Her uniform is complemented by shiny riding boots. Like a Wagnerian vision she rises out of the fog brandishing a whip.)

SCENE 22

(Concentration camp barrack no. 23—interior—exterior—daytime. Pasqualino is looking through the bars on the tiny window of his barrack. He looks onto the Appleplatz, where he can clearly see the enormous woman. "Die Valkyrie" still plays. Pasqualino is struck by this awesome creature. All is silent around him. The atmosphere is tense, the bodies are crowded on top of each other, huddled together like animals seeking shelter from a storm. The barrack doors fly open and a group of soldiers storm in, shouting and flailing away with their fists. The soldiers drag them out of their bunks and violently push them out the door. The prisoners who are left behind peek out the window to see what the fate of their companions will be. Pasqualino and Francesco are huddled together in a bunk.)

FRANCESCO: Where are they taking them?

(A reply comes from a bunk below.)

PEDRO: Who knows, it's all very mysterious . . . work perhaps . . . but then again they could be going for a nice cyanide shower, or to the ovens . . . quién sabe?

(Pedro has an extraordinary face, noble and proud among all these ghosts. Pasqualino looks at him, totally bewildered.)

PASQUALINO: How do you know? Who are you?

(Pedro smiles.)

PEDRO: I'm familiar with death, my friend. . . . I'm a failed anarchist, three attempted murders, Hitler, Mussolini, Salazar. The problem was, I wasn't too good with bombs. The Nazis have turned death into a fine art.

(Pasqualino is able to listen to only half of what Pedro has said. He is too frightened to listen, he can't comprehend what is truly happening.)

PASQUALINO: Fuck that slut . . . but what's happening in the world? Since when is the world like this? . . . We let them kill us off like animals and no one lifts a finger? . . . And those Jews, there were so many of them, so shrewd, such cunning people, and the Russians, didn't they have a revolution? . . . Don't these people rebel? . . . It's really my good luck that I should end up in these shitty places!

SCENE 23

(Appleplatz and barrack no. 23—exterior–interior—daytime. In the Appleplatz two prisoners are playing a waltz on their violins. The fog envelops the square and adds an even more unreal dimension to the whole scene.)

PASQUALINO: Jesus, they're playing a waltz!

(*The violins are occasionally interrupted by the shots being fired on those who are either collapsing from fatigue or trying to escape. Pasqualino stares blindly in front of him.*)

PASQUALINO: God, they're like sheep on the way to the slaughterhouse, it can't be, no . . . it can't. . . .

(*He desperately reaches out for Francesco.*)

PASQUALINO: Francesco, I don't want to die! I'm young, I have to live, I haven't had a chance to live yet, my life has been a piece of shit!

(*Francesco looks at him. Pasqualino is desperate.*)

PASQUALINO: I've always had a love of life but I've never been able to live well.

(*Pasqualino's eyes have a determined look about them.*)

PASQUALINO: I can't die like this, I've got to get out of here. I can do it. . . . I've got to find the way to get out of here. . . .

(*Hilde—the Great Beast. Like an evil Buddah she supervises the slaughter.*)

SCENE 24

(*Ground floor of Pasqualino's house—interior—daytime. Pasqualino's mother is sitting on a low chair winding wool into a ball. We have gone back many, many years. The atmosphere is peaceful in this corner of the world.*)

PASQUALINO'S MOTHER: Girls will be girls, Pasqualino, but no matter how wicked they are, if you find a means of looking into their heart you'll always find some goodness.

(Pasqualino stops crying, his face streaked by tears.)

PASQUALINO'S MOTHER: There's even a song that says the same thing.
SHE SINGS: "When you behave like this you are like a cup of black coffee. On the bottom of the cup there is sugar, but the coffee is bitter unless you stir it. . . . So I have to stir you until the sweetness rises up and I can taste it. . . ."

(She laughs and laughs. His mother's laughing face disappears and in her place we see Hilde's menacing look.)

SCENE 25

(Camp—exterior—daytime. The prisoners are being counted. They stand in the freezing Appleplatz, lined up in rows of five. The blockelder counts slowly.)

BLOCKELDER: Eins . . . zwei . . . drei.

(Pasqualino stares at the Beast. He is softly humming the song his mother taught him. In his look we can read passion and sexual lust, we can picture Spanish guitars playing romantically and love-making by the seashore. In his brave attempt to be noticed by the Beast as he tries to seduce her, Pasqualino raises the tone of his serenade. Francesco hears the strains of this inappropriate tune and is convinced that hunger and fatigue have finally gone to his friend's head. Pedro notices Pasqualino's Casanova look and points it out to Francesco. There is no doubt: The madman has set out to seduce the Beast. Pedro finds it hard to believe, but it's true. Pasqualino continues serenading her. Her ruthless stare goes right over the heads of the skeletons standing in the cold morning. During a pause in the counting she hears a few notes of Pasqualino's song. She turns her killer eyes toward the source of this sound which has reached her ears. Pasqualino is tense. He puts his whole being into the gaze. The Beast slowly walks toward him. Pasqualino's feeble voice gets weaker and weaker as she approaches, and eventually it dies out completely. He lowers his lids. He's far too frightened to

continue with this love game. The Beast is almost on top of him now. He lifts his lids and with superhuman effort gives her his most seductive and warm look. She stops to consider the look in these green eyes, but she isn't really interested. Her eyes are diverted to the other prisoners. Even though he was noticed for only an instant, he is happy, it's better than nothing at all. As she walks off, his gaze follows her imposing figure.)

SCENE 26

(Barrack no. 23—interior—nighttime. The naked light bulb, which accentuates the squalor of the room, is never turned off. Pasqualino and Francesco are curled up on the highest berth of their bunk.)

FRANCESCO: You're totally insane!
PASQUALINO: What have I got to lose? I want to give it a go. . . .
FRANCESCO: It's too dangerous! She's a sadistic bitch!

(Pasqualino shakes his head. He is determined to go ahead with his crazy strategy.)

PASQUALINO: I know, but I've explained it to you already. I had a vision of my mother; no matter what a ruthless bitch this woman might be, there's got to be a little sweetness tucked away somewhere . . . perhaps she needs some love. . . . You see, Francesco, I may not have studied, but when it comes to women, I'm something of an expert.

(Francesco replies jokingly, even though he is tired and depressed.)

FRANCESCO: I wouldn't have doubted it for a minute. . . .
PASQUALINO: Want to know what they used to call me back home? Pasqualino Seven Beauties!

(Francesco is amazed.)

FRANCESCO: That's what they called you?
PASQUALINO: Can you believe that? I know I'm ugly. . . .
FRANCESCO: To say the very least! . . . You're revolting!
PASQUALINO: Well, strangely enough, even though I was so ugly the women would lose their heads over me and the people would look at me and ask how I could do it when I was so ugly. They said it must have been because I was charmed, I had the "seven beauties." Do you understand me?

FRANCESCO: No, I don't understand, but I believe it. . . .

PASQUALINO: I'm not bragging, women really like me, or should I say they really used to like me. . . . To tell the truth, I haven't seen myself in a mirror in nearly two years. So, then, seeing that I was pretty ugly in those days, I am rather concerned about how I look now.

(Pasqualino is pathetic in his concern. Tears are beginning to fill his eyes.)

PASQUALINO: How must I look after all these years? My teeth are loose, I can hardly keep my eyes open. I'm skin and bones and I noticed my ass is beginning to sag. Please, Francesco, take a good look at me and let me have your honest opinion.

(Pasqualino raises his head and allows Francesco's wise look to assess the extent of the damage.)

FRANCESCO: You really *are* quite revolting; *I* wouldn't bother!

(Pasqualino is obstinate.)

PASQUALINO: No, I've just got to try it. . . . I want to live, Francesco, I want to have children, I want to see my children's children, and I also want to see my children's children's children. . . .

(Pedro's voice rises up from the lower bunk.)

PEDRO: What's all this shit you're going on about?

(Pedro laughs. Pasqualino leans over and grabs the anarchist by his shirt.)

PASQUALINO: You fucker, how dare you? Who are you to make fun of me?

(Francesco rushes over to split up the two.)

FRANCESCO: Are you mad?

(Pedro doesn't react, he just laughs and lets Pasqualino shake him.)

PEDRO: I've got nothing against you personally, but you really are talking a load of shit.

(Pasqualino lets him go and crawls back into his corner.)

PASQUALINO: Piss off!

PEDRO: You see, the more children you have the more you speed up the end.

(*Francesco is interested by what the anarchist is saying.*)

FRANCESCO: In what way, what do you mean exactly?

(*Pedro stretches out in his bunk and speaks gently.*)

PEDRO: In the thirteenth century there were five hundred million people in the world, in the fourteenth century they were double that number. We are now so shocked by twenty or thirty million dead, but in the next two or three hundred years we are going to be ten, twenty billion. Then you'll see, every corner of this earth will be worse than this camp! Man will start killing for a piece of bread, whole families will be wiped out over an apple. Then the world will end.

(*Pasqualino and Francesco listen attentively, totally absorbed by what the anarchist is saying.*)

PEDRO: It's really a shame because I believe in mankind. A new type of man must hurry up and appear . . . not the type of beast which has unbalanced the harmony of nature up to now, but a civilized man, a man who would be able to find peace and harmony within himself.

(*Francesco is surprised.*)

FRANCESCO: What are you saying? That we must put things back in order?
PEDRO: Order? No, these barbarians here are very orderly. . . . No, we need the shadow of disorder. That is the only hope, man in disorder.

SCENE 27

(*Totonno's bedroom—interior—nighttime. The picture slowly coming into focus is that of Pasqualino shooting Totonno, Totonno reaching for his clothes. Pasqualino moves slowly and disbelievingly toward the bed.*)

SCENE 28

(*Don Raffaele's office—interior—nighttime. An enormous office cluttered with imposing equestrian statues. The only light in the room comes from a lamp on the desk behind which Don Raffaele*) *sits in his shirt sleeves, admiring some figs in a basket. Standing before him is Pasqualino, pale and concerned. Don Raffaele is relaxed and complacent with a serene expression on his face. He has a child's happiness at the unexpected gift of fruit. Using a well-worn hunting knife that must have seen a lot of action in its day, Don Raffaele is busy cleaning a fig. He delicately divides it into four parts and, picking up a slice, sucks the juicy pulp. Pasqualino waits impatiently.)*

DON RAFFAELE: You made a mistake, my boy. You should have waited for him to pull out his gun.
PASQUALINO: I did wait! Five whole minutes, but he just didn't have one. . . .
DON RAFFAELE: You still shouldn't have shot first. You should have put a gun in his hand.

(Pasqualino raises his shoulders in a helpless gesture.)

PASQUALINO: But . . . I only had one. . . .
DON RAFFAELE: Well, you should have gone prepared. You should have brought two! One needs to be prudent in these situations. . . . Prudence is most important. . . . A prudent man goes to the house, throws the gun in his lap . . . "Here, you son of a bitch!" Then, the minute the man has the gun firmly in hand, you shoot him. It's self-defense, a crime of passion, it's only a few months before they let you out, free and respected.
PASQUALINO: Don Raffaele, how could I have foreseen . . .
DON RAFFAELE: A careful man would have foreseen! Now we're in trouble . . . the body must disappear, and you lose the respect you were looking for. You see, to really gain respect people must know what you did, but in this case no one must know about it. . . . He must have skipped town; probably off to America. No one knows. People may suspect, but no one knows for sure. . . .
PASQUALINO: Well, what am I supposed to do, throw him in the sea?
DON RAFFAELE: No, he'll float like a turd . . . and you'll end up in jail like an idiot.
PASQUALINO: That's great!
DON RAFFAELE: What we need here is a little imagination. . . .
PASQUALINO: Yeah! And a hell of a lot of luck!
DON RAFFAELE: My dear boy, anyone can be lucky, but the man

who wants to be better than all the others must have balls! He must do something no ordinary man would have the guts to do.

PASQUALINO: I get it, Don Raffaele. . . .

(Pasqualino helps him on with his jacket. Leaving the massive statues behind, they head for the exit.)

DON RAFFAELE: Relax, sonny. I noticed you're very nervous, calm down.

PASQUALINO: Very calm . . .

DON RAFFAELE: That's why there are men whose names you just hate to mention, and people start trembling . . . do you understand me?

PASQUALINO: I get you, Don Raffaele. . . .

DON RAFFAELE: You're a bright lad, you catch on fast!

PASQUALINO: I understand you. . . .

DON RAFFAELE: Well, I've said everything there is to be said. You now have a chance to become one of those men we were talking about. It's entirely up to you now.

SCENE 29

(The disappearing bodies sequence—underwater scene—daytime. We are underwater. An ugly brute is wearing cement weights in place of his shoes and we see him rapidly sinking to the bottom of the sea.)

DON RAFFAELE'S VOICE (off camera): I told you, the man must disappear. Don't listen to those people who tell you about the infallibility of the American systems. We invented cement shoes for traitors right here in Naples. Those guys in Chicago and New York are nothing but cheap plagiarists.

SCENE 30

(Disappearing bodies sequence—mortuary—interior—nighttime. A corpse lies in its coffin on a table, surrounded by flowers and candles. The undertaker's assistants are dragging a sack through a window. They pull out another corpse which they put in the coffin, side by side with the other. The coffin lid is nailed down carefully.)

DON RAFFAELE'S VOICE (off camera): The double-seated coffin is our invention as well! When you see a funeral procession in Naples you really can't be sure how many corpses are in the coffin. During particularly violent periods they even manage to squeeze three bodies into a coffin. . . . I assure you that all these methods were invented right here in Naples.

SCENE 31

> *(Disappearing bodies sequence—the Fontanella Cemetery. In a corner of this famous cemetery there is a section called the "bone depository" where skeletons have been propped up over the course of the years. Mountains of bones and skulls add to the pleasant spectacle. Little old ladies are dusting the bones. Two men walk in carrying a skeleton which they add to all the others.)*

DON RAFFAELE'S VOICE (off camera): You recall the Fontanella Cemetery? When it was first opened it had about five hundred skeletons. Now the number is in the region of five thousand. Who do you think added the other four thousand five hundred?

SCENE 32

> *(Totonno's room—interior—nighttime)*

DON RAFFAELE'S VOICE (off camera): I want you to come up with something really original. Call me and let me know.

SCENE 33

> *(The scene of the crime—interior—daytime. Three suitcases on the floor, a sack full of sawdust. Pasqualino is in his T-shirt and trousers, apron and cap. He pours the sawdust into a basin under the table. Totonno's body is lying on the bed. Pasqualino moves over to the bed, drinking out of a bottle. He's feeling nauseous, but he is determined to go through with it. The time has come, he stands before his victim and wraps him in a sheet. He suddenly can't go on, he has a fit of hysterics. He bangs his*

*feet childishly on the ground, bites his fingers to the quick, fi-
nally calms down after smashing his head against the wall. He
pulls himself together, drinks the entire bottle of Three Star
brandy, and once again is ready. He lifts the body off the bed.
It's too heavy for him. He lets it fall. Finally he lifts him onto
the "operating" table. Farting noises come from the body.)*

PASQUALINO: Shit, is this fucker ugly . . . prick-face! Listen to
those noises, nothing but a hot air balloon . . . I always said he was
full of hot air.

*(Pasqualino picks up the hatchet, sweating and out of breath
from the effort. He is by now totally inebriated but is still unable to stop trembling. He moves over to the body and raises the
hatchet. He suddenly collapses.)*

SCENE 34

*(Alleyway—exterior—morning. It's the early hours of the morn-
ing. We see a cart being pushed to market. Slowly the alleyway
starts coming to life. As the camera follows another cart we discover yet another alley. Blinds are being pushed open, three
suitcases are lowered onto the street. Pasqualino steps out the
window and looks around. It is clear he is still drunk and feeling
sick, but he carries on regardless. He pulls the blinds behind
him, makes sure no one has seen him, then bends over and tries
to lift the suitcases. To his horror, he discovers he can't lift
them. They are in fact terribly heavy. Pasqualino is terrified.
With a superhuman effort he just about manages to lift them a
few inches off the ground. He's got to make it. He takes three
steps and has to stop. He's sweating, he's out of his mind with
fear. Somehow or other he makes it to the main road. Here he
can at least hail a taxicab or a horse and buggy. A German
shepherd starts following him, attracted by an interesting smell.
The dog is dragging a blind man, who is unable to stop the
animal and must hang on for dear life. Pasqualino looks at the
dog. He feels as though the animal's interest in his suitcase is
going to attract the attention of all the passers-by. He tries to
get rid of the dog with a swift kick. By now he is on the verge of
tears.)*

SCENE 35

(Main road—exterior—daytime)

THE BLIND MAN: Here, Fido, what is it? . . . Why are you pulling? Hey, cut it out, who's there? . . . Who are you? Speak up, what are you up to? . . . Fido, don't pull, I'll fall!

> *(Pasqualino has hailed a horse and buggy and is loading the cases.)*

BLIND MAN: Here, Fido, you son of a bitch! . . . What the hell's wrong?

> *(Pasqualino gives the dog one last kick and gets on the buggy.)*

DRIVER: Where to, sir?
PASQUALINO: To the station . . . fuck off, you goddamn blind dog.

> *(The dog has finally given up but the blind man is insulted by Pasqualino's last comment.)*

BLIND MAN: You filthy son of a whore . . . making fun of a poor blind man!

SCENE 36

> *(The streets of Naples—exterior—daytime. The buggy meanders through the streets of Naples. It is a beautiful, sunny morning.)*

SCENE 37

> *(Station—exterior—daytime. They stop in front of the station. A swarm of porters surrounds the buggy. They fight and scratch each other trying to attract this client. Pasqualino looks at them as if they were a pack of starving rats.)*

PORTERS: Sir!

> *(Pasqualino leaps to the ground and blocks them.)*

PASQUALINO: Don't you dare touch!

> *(The porters are pissed off. Pasqualino unloads the cases and pays the driver. The porters look at him with hatred.)*

PORTERS: Your Highness, we apologize! We won't touch your bags!

(Pasqualino realizes that perhaps he went too far.)

PASQUALINO: Sorry, I can manage on my own.

(The porters look at him in disgust.)

PORTER: Do it yourself, then, you poor shit!

(Having paid, he attempts to carry the three cases, pretending they are as light as feathers.)

PORTER: I really want to see how he's going to manage.

(Pasqualino gathers all his strength and lifts them; his veins are ready to pop. The porters continue to jeer at him.)

PORTER: Hey, look at Hercules . . . peasant! . . . Now he's going to burst, just you wait!

(Pasqualino is furious but realizes he won't be able to make it.)

PASQUALINO: All right . . .

(He turns to one of the friendlier-looking porters.)

PASQUALINO: Do me a favor and carry them for me.

(The porter lifts the cases onto his cart as Pasqualino carefully supervises the operation. The others don't stop teasing him.)

PORTER: Hey look, Hercules has given up . . . that will teach him to be such a smart-ass! You shouldn't help him at all!

(The cases are loaded, the porter smiles and starts moving.)

PORTER: Don't pay any attention to them, where are we going?
PASQUALINO: The train to Rome–Genova–Turin . . . what do they expect, that everyone has money?

(With one hand protectively on the cases, Pasqualino walks into the station.)

SCENE 38

(Cafeteria—interior—daytime. Pasqualino is on the phone. As he speaks he tries to put on his tough-guy act.)

PASQUALINO: Don Raffaele . . . it's me . . . sorry if I disturb at this time but I wanted to tell you that the cheeses have been sent via Palermo, Milano, and Genova . . .

(*He gets closer to the mouthpiece.*)

PASQUALINO: . . . and that's all there is to it. As you said, one needs a little imagination. Everything's O.K. . . . he'll never be heard from again.

SCENE 39

(*Ground floor—Pasqualino's house—interior—daytime. A shout. The door opens and Pasqualino's sisters come rushing in, trying to calm down Concettina.*)

CONCETTINA: That bastard! He killed him! He killed my Totonno! Bastard!

(*Pasqualino leaps out of bed and dives for the window. The police are now in the house.*)

MARSHAL: Stop him! Cut him off in the courtyard! Stop, Pasquale Frafuso, you can't get away, you're surrounded!

SCENE 40

(*Courtyard—exterior—daytime. Like an acrobat, Pasqualino is climbing from one balcony to another, dashing in and out of the hanging laundry. Women are shouting, but no one tries to stop him. The policemen chase him. Having reached the top of the building, Pasqualino knows he's trapped. He grabs hold of some sheets and swings from one building to another across the court-yard. The crowd lets out a shout as he leaps. Pasqualino makes it to the other side. He turns to look at the policemen who have just reached the top of the other building. He is cocky and sure of himself.*)

PASQUALINO: Piss off, all of you . . . you'll never catch Pasqualino Seven Beauties alive!

(*As he turns to run away he falls into the arms of the waiting po-licemen who in the meantime had sneaked up behind him. The marshal looks at him and shakes his head.*)

MARSHAL: You fool!
PASQUALINO: Well, I made a mistake!

SCENE 41

(Concentration camp—exterior—daytime. A group of prisoners have been led outside to see a public punishment. In her fierce Nazi voice, Hilde reads out the order to whip two of the prisoners twenty times for the horrible crime they committed. They dared use some planks of wood from their barracks to make a fire so they could boil some weeds in an attempt to make a soup.)

HILDE (she reads the order in German)
TRANSLATOR: In barrack number five, two men tore up planks of wood, thus causing damage to Reich property. The following prisoners shall be punished by a whipping . . .

(Hilde clicks her heels, turns, and salutes the officers who are about to carry out the order. The two prisoners are stripped to the waist and tied to a sawhorse. The whipping starts. A soldier counts out loud.)

OFFICER: *Eins . . . zwei . . .* (Up to thirty)

(Hilde leaves the area. The spectators watch the grim spectacle. Carefully Pasqualino starts walking back through the ranks of prisoners. Francesco looks at him worriedly.)

FRANCESCO (quietly): Are you insane?
PASQUALINO: Don't break my balls!

(Another prisoner is curious to find out what Pasqualino is doing.)

PRISONER: What are you up to?
PASQUALINO: Shut up!

(Hilde stops to chat with another female officer. They are standing beneath the swaying body of a prisoner hanging from a beam. They offer each other a Nazi salute, and Hilde moves away. The counting continues and we hear the cries of the punished prisoners.)

SCENE 42

(*Passageways throughout the camp. Pasqualino is creeping close to the walls as he follows the Beast.*)

SCENE 43

(*The latrines—exterior—daytime. Some officers are pinning up a list of orders in a hut which serves as a place where the prisoners can read about the day's events. Hilde is watching. She nods approvingly at the officers.*)

HILDE: *Gut!*

(*Her hands on her wide hips, she studies the order for a few seconds. Pasqualino comes out from the latrine, wetting his hands with saliva so as to flatten down his hair and try to give some shape to his moustache and eyebrows. He straightens his cap and gathers up his courage. He walks out of the latrine whistling the serenade and heads straight for the Beast. Pasqualino whistles his tune. Hearing this sound, Hilde lifts her eyebrows. Like a sparrow calling to its mate, Pasqualino beckons the woman. His eyes half-closed and heavy-lidded, he tries to adopt a romantic pose. Hilde looks at him. He flaps his eyelashes romantically, trying to win her. He sighs sorrowfully, as if to say "What can I do—I like you a lot, though I know it's going to get me into trouble." The Great Beast looks at him angrily. Is this little worm making fun of her? The veins in her neck begin to swell. She shouts something terrible in German, then beats Pasqualino on the neck with her whip. The poor man falls back into the latrine shed.*)

SCENE 44

(*Camp—exterior—daytime. Pasqualino is all alone in the camp courtyard. The Great Beast is riding in the sidecar of a motorcycle. Fog envelops the camp. The motorcycle goes round and round. Pasqualino has carried his act this far, and he isn't going to stop. Kneeling, he is a pathetic figure, a human relic, but he attempts to smile and nod in reply to her terrible scowl.*)

Hilde shakes her head. The motorcycle drives away, spraying Pasqualino with mud. In the center of the Appleplatz, *Pasqualino is about to faint. We fade to a distant memory.)*

SCENE 45

(The Galleria—exterior–interior—daytime. We are once again in colorful, sunny Naples. A newsboy is shouting out the headlines from the newspaper he's selling.)

A NEWSBOY: The murderer has finally confessed! Read all about it! It was Pasquale Frafuso who did it! Latest edition! The murderer has confessed!)

SCENE 46

(Prison visiting room—interior—daytime. Detailed shots of the newspaper headlines: "The Neapolitan Monster Has Confessed"; "He Saws His Victim into Tiny Pieces and Sends Him Off in Three Suitcases"; "Horrible Murder in the Underworld"; "The Murderer Confesses to His Crime." Lawyer Cangemini is furious.)

LAWYER: You mean you confessed?

(Pasqualino answers proudly.)

PASQUALINO: Yessiree . . .

(The lawyer throws down his briefcase on top of the papers.)

LAWYER: Boy, what a way to go about doing things! How the hell am
I supposed to do my job? But since when does one admit . . . confess?
You don't give me a chance, damnit!
PASQUALINO: If I must tell you the truth, sir, I am proud of what I
did. . . . I'm a man of honor.
LAWYER: You're a piece of shit, that's what you are.

(Pasqualino is mortally offended.)

PASQUALINO: How dare you! Take that back, you shit!

(Pasqualino grabs him by the lapels.)

LAWYER: Stop it! What do you want to do, kill me as well? Stop it, or
they'll stop our meeting!
PASQUALINO: Take back the "piece of shit"!

LAWYER: Consider it taken back . . . what I really meant was incompetent . . . inexperienced. . . . You see, my boy, this way you ruin yourself, and my good name too, because it's impossible for me to get you off. (*He points to the papers.*) The Neapolitan monster confesses. . . . The ripper tears his victim to pieces. . . . We don't stand a chance unless we take the only way out . . . mental infirmity.

(*Pasqualino has calmed down, but he is suspicious.*)

PASQUALINO: What's that?
LAWYER: You know; you've got to pretend you're crazy.
PASQUALINO: Sir, I'm a serious man. I did what I did to defend my honor. I'm not going to start behaving like a fool.

(*The lawyer looks worried.*)

LAWYER: But what the hell are you going on about? You're mistaken, we're talking about the death penalty, my lad. It's a matter of life or death.

(*Fear—but with dignity*)

PASQUALINO: I won't act the fool!
LAWYER: I'm sorry, because I really wanted to do Don Raffaele the favor, but I can't destroy my liver over you. What the hell do you want from me? What would you like me to do? Look, it's your own business. If you decide to go for mental instability, I'll defend you, but if you choose this "honor" then I'll forget it and let you die "honorably." You can let them in now!

(*Sisters and mother enter the room, noisy, colorful, and cheerful. Pasqualino grabs the bars.*)

PASQUALINO: Mother . . . mother . . . mother!
MOTHER: Darling Pasqualino!
CONCETTINA: Pasqualino . . . my Pasqualino!
PASQUALINO: Mamma!

(*Their eyes full of tears, they try to touch one another through the bars. Concettina moves to one side to speak with the lawyer.*)

CONCETTINA: Any news, sir?
PASQUALINO: Mamma . . . mamma . . . mamma!
MOTHER: Little one, how do you feel? My angel . . . it's been such a long time. . . .

PASQUALINO: How do I feel? Like shit, but what about you all? Is Don Raffaele helping out?

MOTHER: He's so generous with words . . . but so far we haven't seen a penny.

(Pasqualino doesn't understand what she is saying.)

PASQUALINO: But how come . . .

(Pasqualino raises his eyes to look at his sisters. Then they shift over to Concettina, who is talking to the lawyer.)

LAWYER: Concettina, I'll do my best, you know I will. . . . Wow! Do you know, you get better-looking every day!

(Concettina is flirting openly. She is wearing a very fashionable dress, which makes her considerable girth even more obvious. Pasqualino opens his eyes wide.)

PASQUALINO: Not again, Concettina!

(Concettina turns toward him, then raises her shoulders.)

CONCETTINA: Pasqualino, I can't help it!

(The mother tries to explain to Pasqualino.)

MOTHER: Look, your lawyer is one of the best in the city. Don Raffaele suggested we use him. He's expensive and we have no money. Besides, you did it for her and she was already compromised. . . .

(Pasqualino is bitter.)

PASQUALINO: To be compromised is one thing, to be a whore is another!

(From her corner Concettina looks at the lawyer with a warm, sexy expression.)

CONCETTINA: Be patient, sir, do it for my sake. . . .

(Pasqualino is torn apart by this vicious circle of unfair situations.)

PASQUALINO: Isn't life a farce sometimes.

SCENE 47

(Prison courtyard—exterior—daytime. A prisoner is doing exercises to keep in shape. Pasqualino walks around this confined space, too proud to do exercises, which he feels are beneath his dignity. Pasqualino is tortured by the decision the lawyer told him he must make. The prisoner continues his jumping jacks. He turns to Pasqualino.)

PRISONER: Hey, if you don't do some exercises your ass and stomach are going to sag, and then it's going to be too late to do anything about it. Come on, jump! Exercise is a fundamental thing if you want to keep a healthy body. Hup . . . two . . . three . . . four!

(The prisoner slows down. He is intent on watching Pasqualino. Pasqualino's expression has changed. He now adopts an erect and pompous stance, his hands firmly on his hips, his jaw thrust forward. His eyes are those of a madman. The prisoner stares at him. Pasqualino begins speaking in a stentorian voice.)

PASQUALINO: People of Italy!
PRISONER: Who do you think you are . . . Mussolini?
PASQUALINO: . . . . war bestows the seal of nobility . . .

(It's a gross imitation of Mussolini. The prisoner can't believe his ears. Hearing this outburst, the guards start running toward

Pasqualino's courtyard. Pasqualino is really getting carried away.)

PASQUALINO: . . . on those nations who have the courage to face it . . .

(*The prisoners jeer and whistle at Pasqualino's speech.*)

THE PRISONERS (all together): Duce! . . . Duce! . . . Duce!
PASQUALINO: This is a wonderful era for the Italian people as we prepare to send them off to the four corners of the world . . .

(*The guards rush up to subdue Pasqualino, who continues his ranting and raving.*)

PRISONERS: Duce! . . . Duce!

(*The prisoners applaud: Pasqualino is dragged away forcibly.*)

PASQUALINO: Eia eia alala! . . . And up yours!
ANOTHER PRISONER (singing): "Hail, oh great country of heroes. . . . *Parapaponzi ponzi po.*"

SCENE 48

(*Law court—interior—daytime. Pasqualino is in the dock. He is pale and tired, but his expression is one of dignity and pride. His eyes wander around the courtroom. All the protagonists of his story are in the room. Carolina looks at him with sorrowful eyes. She lifts her finger to her lips and blows him a kiss. His mother and seven sisters are there as well. The bailiff reads the charges against Pasqualino. Only now does Pasqualino notice that the elder sisters are all made up heavily and they all in one way or another resemble Concettina. He gives his mother a stern look. With a slight gesture of his head and a flash from his eyes, he asks his mother the reason for his sisters' looks. The mother looks first at the girls, then at Pasqualino. She lowers her head and admits that yes, they have in fact followed in Concettina's footsteps. The girls are embarrassed, and they too lower their heads. Pasqualino is furious. Still using only his eyes, Pasqualino asks his mother the reason. She pulls in her shoulders as if to say, "What could we do?" Lawyer Cangemini is expensive, she gestures with her hands, and therefore we had to find a solution. Pasqualino lowers his eyes. He has been mortally wounded. His honor is now totally destroyed. The bailiff's monotonous voice continues to read the charges. Pasqualino has tears in his eyes as Don Raffaele and the lawyer wink at one another. The lawyers put away their papers. Concettina and the mother are crying. Pasqualino turns to Carolina. Close-up of Carolina's face as seen by Pasqualino. They drag him out of court. He looks back at Carolina.)*

SCENE 49

(Train station in Aversa—exterior—daytime. The train is enveloped in smoke as Pasqualino is led off it by two policemen. He is handcuffed. The surrounding countryside is very pastoral. The farmers turn to look at him. The women take pity on him. Two or three kids follow the prisoner. The two policemen take him into the tiny police headquarters.)

SCENE 50

(Police headquarters—interior—daytime. Pasqualino sits down on a bench. Another prisoner is in the room waiting. The man has a distinguished air about him. He looks like a professor, with his deep eyes reflecting intellectual and spiritual well-being.)

PROFESSOR: Political criminal?
PASQUALINO: No—Pasqualino the Ripper.

(With great insouciance he lights up a cigarette. He offers a cigarette, which the other man declines, then, adopting an attitude of savoir-faire, Pasqualino points to himself.)

PASQUALINO: . . . the Monster of Naples . . .

(He flicks the ash with his pinky, with the air of a man who knows how to play his cards right.)

PASQUALINO: . . . total mental instability . . . twelve years . . .

(The professor is amused by this strange character.)

PROFESSOR: You're fortunate, I got twenty-eight years and four months.

(Pasqualino is curious.)

PASQUALINO: Wow! Twenty-eight years! What the hell did you do?
PROFESSOR: My crime was that of thought . . . in this country that is the worst crime a citizen can commit.

(The professor looks at a picture of Mussolini on the wall.)

PROFESSOR: *He* doesn't like it.
PASQUALINO: So, you're an anti-Fascist. . . .

(The professor smiles.)

PROFESSOR: Socialist.

(Pasqualino looks at him with interest.)

PASQUALINO: The truth of the matter is that I don't know too much about these things. Dad was sort of a Socialist . . . he was also a contract bricklayer . . . bah, as for me I have other interests. . . .

(He points to Mussolini's picture.)

PASQUALINO: . . . as a matter of fact I rather like him . . . after all, he did make some changes . . . he gave us great roads, created an empire . . . foreigners all envy us because we have such a great leader . . . when he appears on his balcony . . . those eyes, that voice . . . well, everyone has great respect for him. . . . Look, before he came people used to spit right in our faces. He really straightened things out, before he arrived everyone was always on strike, things were really in a mess.

(The professor listens patiently.)

PROFESSOR: Sure, he cleaned up the peripheral things, wiped out the labor unions and the class struggle. As a result, the cost of living is twice what it used to be in 1919 and wages have gone down. You say everyone envies us our Mr. Mussolini, but I say to you that it is the bosses who envy him and they alone. The Italian people are still hungry, and what do they get? Nice words from him when he shouts down from his balcony.

(Pasqualino is amazed that anyone should speak of Fascism in this way.)

PASQUALINO: Quiet . . . they'll hear us if you're not careful.

(The professor is sad.)

PROFESSOR: Bless those days of disorder, of strikes . . . now we believe we're strong and hide the disease from ourselves. If it's really true that he's going to lead us into war, you can be certain it will be our downfall.

(Pasqualino laughs.)

PASQUALINO: Now I know why you got twenty-eight years!

SCENE 51

(Women's wing of the Aversa Insane Asylum—interior—daytime. As we watch Pasqualino steal some cigarettes from a bedside table, we can hear his voice explaining off camera.)

PASQUALINO'S VOICE (off camera): So, I'll do ten years . . . then, who knows . . . it's all a matter of getting organized once you're in. . . . I'll work on a doctor, befriend a nurse . . . we Neapolitans are so specialized in the art of getting along . . . if all goes well I can even get myself transferred to the women's ward as an orderly. . . . I'd really be in seventh heaven then!

> (*The bedside table he is stealing the cigarettes from belongs to a little old lady who looks at him inquisitively. Pasqualino bends down to pick up her bedpan.*)

PASQUALINO: Ah, you sly little old dear, you're awake! . . . Let's take a look at your pee . . . hmm, not too good, not enough . . . we have to pee! . . . Pee is life, the more pee, the longer life you'll have!

> (*Pasqualino places the bedpan on his cart and proceeds with his collection. He moves down the rows of beds. A group of nurses walk in with a middle-aged doctor. Pasqualino immediately puts on an expression of misery. He is the poor underdog.*)

DOCTOR (she has a foreign accent): Pasqualino, how are you feeling today? Do you like your job as orderly? Good, work, work!

> (*She gently strokes his cheek.*)

DOCTOR: I'm putting through an application for another psychiatric examination. We'll make it. We must really put an end to all these criminal cases who come to hide in here.

> (*The doctor heads in the opposite direction.*)

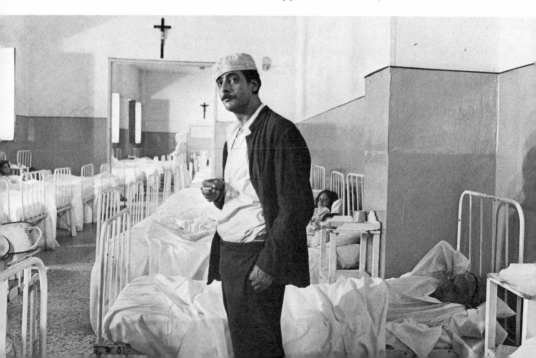

DOCTOR: They really ought to keep them in prison. . . . *Ça va?* And how are you? Sister Josephine, *venez ici!*

> *(Pasqualino drops off the bedpan at the end of the hall, then climbs up some stairs that lead to the corridor where seriously unbalanced female patients are locked up in tiny padded cells.)*

SCENE 52

> *(Corridor—interior—daytime. Pasqualino is attracted to a sound coming from a half-open door. He moves closer to the door, looks around to see if anyone is coming, then peeks in to see who is in there.)*

SCENE 53

> *(Single cell in the insane asylum—interior—daytime. Pasqualino appears in the doorway. A screen blocks his view. He goes out the door for one final check, then comes back inside and shuts the door behind him. Moving around the screen we see a beautiful patient tied to a bed. Her body is arched high off the bed, pointing toward the door, almost as though she thought she could free herself from her bonds and fly out. Her legs are spread apart and her arms are tied behind her. Full breasts protrude from the opened shirt. Pasqualino is suddenly very horny. He moves closer to have a better look. He caresses her, brushes back her shirt. He's hopeful. She looks as if she's enjoying it.)*

THE WOMAN: What are you doing?
PASQUALINO: What do you think I'm doing, I certainly can't walk away from this godsend! It's been months since I had a woman! So, be patient, be kind enough to put out for my sake! . . . If you're quiet we'll get it over and done with nice and easy.

> *(Pasqualino moves closer to her face.)*

PASQUALINO: You horny too?

> *(The woman looks up at him, then shuts her eyes. He kisses her, but she, faster than lightning, bites him ferociously. Pasqualino can't yell out for fear of being discovered. He moves away from her, his lip bleeding. He lets her have a powerful slap.)*

PASQUALINO: You filthy slut!

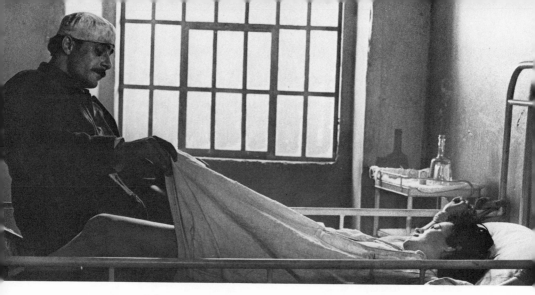

(*The poor woman starts moving around wildly, trying to get away from Pasqualino.*)

PASQUALINO: Stop it . . . shut up . . . you're going to get me into trouble.

(*Pasqualino still lusts after her. He grabs a piece of tape and puts it across her mouth.*)

PASQUALINO: *Now* you'll shut up, won't you?

(*He brutally assaults her. She bucks him like a wild horse. Riding her skillfully, Pasqualino rapes her.*)

PASQUALINO: This insane bitch bites me? I'll make you really insane! Ugly bitch . . . mad slut . . .

SCENE 54

(*Pasqualino is being sprayed by a jet of freezing cold water.*)

SCENE 55

(*Insane asylum cell—interior—daytime. Two orderlies are beating the hell out of Pasqualino. They pull down his trousers, put on a strait jacket and a bib. The scuffle takes only a few minutes. All that is left of the once-proud Pasqualino is a seminude figure, wrapped up like a mummy. They throw him on the specially designed bed for the more "troublesome" patients.*)

FIRST ORDERLY: And thank God you're new here! If you try it one more time . . . !

(Pasqualino is stretched out on the bed, which is much too long for him. This means that the hole provided in the center of the bed for his excretions is at kidney level.)

SCENE 56

(Electroshock chamber—interior—daytime. Pasqualino lies help- lessly on a bed with wires, electrodes, absorbent cotton, and rubber stoppers all over his body. He has a bit in his mouth to stop him from biting his tongue. His eyes and jaws are clamped tight from the pain. A humming sound comes from the elec- troshock machine. The two nurses are totally indifferent to his suffering. They sit beside the bed reading their newspapers.)

SCENE 57

(Padded cell—interior—daytime. It's a tiny padded cell. The only light filters through a poor apology for a window. Pasqua- lino is tied up like a salami and strapped to a bed.)

DOCTOR'S VOICE (off camera): Pasqualino, even though you have committed hideous crimes, you are normal. You can't spend the rest of your days among the hopeless.

(The doctor is perspiring. She sits calmly next to the bed.)

DOCTOR: You really must calm down. You know that the outcome of your psychiatric visit is based on your day-to-day behavior.

(Pasqualino is suppliant.)

PASQUALINO: Doctor, if I remain shut up in here for another eight years I really will be insane when I walk out.
DOCTOR: Look, you've got to resist . . . there is a genuine possibility now that Italy is going into war. That means they will need all the able- bodied men they can get. Therefore we can get you out of here in no time. You just have to be a voluntary, and you can be sure they'll close an eye. . . .

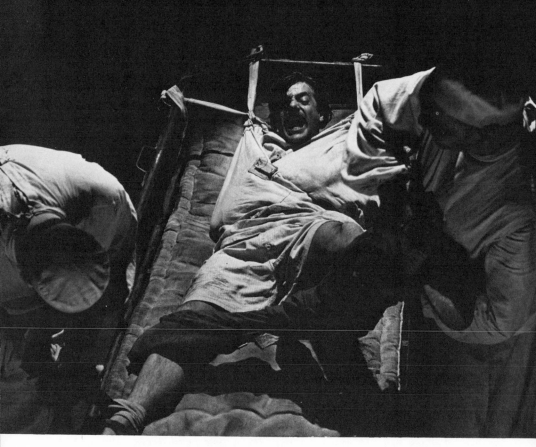

(Pasqualino is all ears.)

DOCTOR: This doesn't apply, of course, to mental cases, but if we can obtain a psychiatric report stating that you are cured, you're off. . . .

(Pasqualino is beyond himself with excitement.)

PASQUALINO: Doctor, for the love of God help me. . . . I want to live . . . is it too much to ask for?

(She looks at him full of understanding.)

DOCTOR: I'll try, Pasqualino, but don't get your hopes up, because I have a terrible feeling that this war is going to end in a terrible blood-bath. . . .

(Pasqualino isn't interested. He simply wants to get out.)

PASQUALINO: Anything is better than this place. I'm ready to do anything, as long as I stay alive.

SCENE 58

*(Concentration camp Appleplatz—exterior—nighttime. His fig-
ure illuminated by the searchlights, we see Pasqualino standing
with his arms stretched above his head in the enormous Appleplatz. His expression is one of fatigue and desperation. His eyes
partially open, he mumbles an old Neapolitan tune. Pasqualino
sings softly "Oh Maria." It looks almost as if the song inspires
him to fight on just a little bit longer. He draws strength from
the words as he sings louder and louder. His thin neck vibrates
from the effort he is putting into the words. He sings as if he
were back in the little town of Mergellina serenading his girl
friend from below her balcony.)*

PASQUALINO (singing):
"Open up your windows, Maria,
"Look down on the street so that I may see you . . ."

(Now he puts his full strength into the singing.)

PASQUALINO:
"Oh Maria, Oh Maria,
"I have lost so much sleep over you . . ."

SCENE 59

*(Hilde's office in the camp—interior—nighttime. The Great
Beast is sitting in semidarkness behind her desk. In front of her
is another female officer. Hilde is talking on the phone.)*

HILDE: (a few lines in German)

*(Pasqualino's singing can be heard quite clearly inside the
room.)*

SCENE 60

*(Concentration camp Appleplatz—exterior—nighttime. Pasqua-
lino is completely out of control and is singing as loud as he
can.)*

PASQUALINO (singing):
"Let me spend just one night with you . . .
"Oh my Maria. . . . I have lost so much sleep thinking

"About you. . . . Oh my Maria . . ."

(*Hilde leans out of her office window, which gives onto the Appleplatz. Her pig eyes glare at Pasqualino. Then she shuts the window.*)

SCENE 61

(*Hilde's office—interior—nighttime. Pasqualino is violently thrown into the room. He falls to the ground and lies there like a dog. Pasqualino looks at Hilde. Like a gambler who has finally made it to the gambling table, he is frightened. But now that all the barriers are out of the way he can play the game to the very end. Pasqualino looks at her lovingly.*)

HILDE: Out . . .

(*The SS "Angel of Death" orders the two guards to leave. She also sends out the other female officer, then turns her gaze to Pasqualino, who's still lying on the floor. Hilde moves over to the edge of the desk and sits on it, letting her enormous leg dangle off the side, nervously hitting herself on the boot with her cat-o'-nine-tails. She studies that small, insignificant crea-*)

ture that looks at her in such a ridiculous way. She speaks to him unexpectedly.)

HILDE: So what's this game you're playing, you slimy macaroni?

(Pasqualino still looks at her lovingly.)

PASQUALINO: Jesus! You speak Italian. . . . Finally I can talk to you! . . . What are you a witch, a fairy? Good God, tell me who you are. . . . You've put a spell on me. . . . From the very first time I set eyes on you I . . . I . . .

(Hilde doesn't move as she listens to Pasqualino. Then she shakes her head menacingly.)

HILDE: What are you saying, you disgusting macaroni?

(She drinks thirstily from a stein of beer.)

PASQUALINO: I love you! I love you!

(Hilde grimaces as she reflects on Pasqualino's words. She picks up her beer off the fully laid-out dinner table. In the brief pause Pasqualino feels as if he's going to die. Behind those inscrutable sky-blue eyes the SS could be deciding his fate. At last she turns to him. Pasqualino keeps on looking at her, full of love. The Beast takes a sip from the black frothy beer, then gestures to him.)

HILDE: Undress . . .

(Pasqualino is disappointed. He can't believe he's heard properly.)

PASQUALINO: Pardon me . . . did you say I had to undress?

(The Beast nods.)

PASQUALINO: Oh, I see. . . .

(He tries to kill time. Only a half-smile is on his face now, almost as if he were reproaching her for this prank. Then he starts to undress. It is an odd striptease. First he lets his trousers fall, but keeps on his top because he has just noticed the pathetic state of his genital organs. He feels they are too ridiculous to show off. He stands before her, naked and skeletal, nodding his head in the way adults nod at children misbehaving. Hilde stands up and slowly moves closer to Pasqualino. She fixes him with her

mean stare, scrutinizing him in all his nakedness. She is an imposing figure in front of Pasqualino. Hilde studies him from head to toe and then, with her whip, moves aside the flaps of his top. The Beast grimaces at the sight, then moves away from him. Pasqualino has managed to live through this humiliating visit. He has kept his head up high. He is still full of inner strength. He smiles at her lovingly.)

PASQUALINO: O.K., O.K. . . . you wanted to have a good time. . . . I'm glad that at least I make you laugh. . . .

(Hilde doesn't turn around.)

HILDE: And you hate me, I know . . . everybody hates me.

(This, in fact, is the first time Hilde has spoken as opposed to giving orders in her thundering voice. To Pasqualino this represents quite a victory. The Beast looks at the portrait of Hitler hanging up behind her desk. Her eyes are full of irony.)

HILDE: You hope to eat . . . you think that with your love you will be able to get food.

(Pasqualino is serious now. He is no longer kidding.)

PASQUALINO: Yes, miss, it's true that I am absolutely starving, but it's also true that the feelings I have in my heart could be impossible for you to understand. Yes, it's true that everyone does hate you, and seeing I have never seen such a shit as you in my life, maybe I ought to hate you, too. But what can I do? Maybe I'm crazy . . . yes, I am crazy, but I believe that you aren't the way you make out to be. . . .

(Pasqualino bursts into tears but continues to talk.)

PASQUALINO: Tell me the truth, who are you really? . . . Tell me.
. . . Maybe you aren't a witch, perhaps you're a victim, yes, you're a
poor victim who is here killing helpless people out of a sense of duty.
. . . Witch? You're not a witch, you're a victim! . . . Just like the rest
of us. . . .

> *(Hilde doesn't bat an eyelid as she listens to Pasqualino's decla-*
> *ration. She keeps on drinking beer.)*

PASQUALINO: You are a real woman . . . a woman! Under that uniform there's rosy flesh, fat palpable flesh . . . mmmmm . . . flesh that
would turn me wild, soft rounded flesh. . . . Yes, you make me crazy.
Yours is a flesh that must be stroked, kissed, squeezed, and bitten. I've
really lost my head over you . . . it may be madness, it may be a sickness, a vice, even, but then, what is love?

(There's no holding him back now.)

PASQUALINO: I'm intoxicated with love, that's why I did what I did.
Now all I ask is one thing. You want to kill me? All right, kill me, but
promise me you'll do it with your own hands . . . with your own
hands, please, miss. . . .

> *(Totally expressionless, she keeps on looking at him. She lights*
> *up a cigarette.)*

PASQUALINO: Touch me, please touch me, and then I can die a
happy man. . . .

> *(Pasqualino is shaking. It's most probably fear but he really ap-*
> *pears to be in love.)*

HILDE: You Neapolitan piece of shit . . . you can't stand up straight
. . . you can't carry on this farce for much longer . . . you want to eat
. . . I know you do . . . all right . . .

> *(Notwithstanding her size, she begins to strip quickly. Her shirt,*
> *skirt, and jacket fall to the ground, and she is left standing in*
> *her military underwear and T-shirt.)*

HILDE: So first you make love to me, then I kill you with my hands
. . . that's what you want, isn't it?

(Slowly and menacingly she moves over to the leather couch where she lies back, methodically hitting herself with the cat-o'-nine-tails. She's a mass of quivering flesh. The Great Beast waits. Pasqualino knows he must perform this time. He wets his lips and closes his eyes. The Beast waits for him to make his move. Pasqualino tries to smile. He reaches out with his thin hand and makes contact with the warm, butter-fed, rosy flesh. Pasqualino's cold hand makes her shudder. She's putting him to the test. She stares intensely at him. With her cat-o'-nine-tails she begins to beat his bony buttocks. Pasqualino bends over, sinking his face into all her flesh.)

PASQUALINO: Be good to me, my love for you is great, but there is very little strength. . . .

(He strokes her, pinches her, sucks at the layers of flesh, trying to get some reaction from that cold, heartless mass. Her icy animal eyes peer at him critically. Pasqualino is calling on all his strength as he puts into effect his whole repertoire of kisses, sighs, grunts, rubbings, kneadings, proddings, playful slaps. He is like a shipwrecked passenger using all his energies to save himself from drowning. He has but a single thought in his head: I want to live. A violent whack on his buttocks puts an end to this fruitless attempt. The enormous Beast towers over the human larva at her feet. In her hands she holds a bowl.)

HILDE: You don't have the strength for an erection . . . here, Naples . . . eat!

(She places the bowl in front of him. It is piled high with bread, sauerkraut, sausages. Pasqualino attacks the bowl. Hilde lights up a cigar.)

HILDE: Now you eat, then you fuck . . . if you don't fuck, you die!

(Pasqualino stuffs the food down his throat. Hilde places a chair in front of Pasqualino, then straddles it back to front. She starts singing.)

HILDE: (Singing in German, a piece from a Wagner opera)

SCENE 62

(Burlesque theater in Naples—interior—nighttime. Satin panties, black garter belts, seductive swaying of bodies which promise unattainable ecstasy. Three young boys peek at the act. One of them is young Pasqualino. This is probably the first time he has reached sexual awareness. Fifi Mignonette is doing the "Indian Dance." As she slithers across the stage she brings to mind forbidden dreams of Oriental odalisques, wanton Eastern prostitutes, their thighs quivering and sweaty as they entice you with their pelvises, then turn you on with belly dances.)

SCENE 63

(Courtyard of a building in Naples—exterior—daytime. A child cries loudly in the sun-drenched courtyard.)

SCENE 64

(Ground floor in a house in Naples, probably the ground floor of Pasqualino's house. Pasqualino and a girl are making love on bales of carded wool.)

SCENE 65

(Stairs in a house in Naples. In a corner of the landing, Pasqualino and another girl are making love standing up. Frantic pulling and tearing of skirts and petticoats being removed.)

SCENE 66

> (*Hilde's office—concentration camp—interior—nighttime. Pasqualino is putting body and soul into this last supreme effort of love-making. The Beast glares at him. Her big hands are all over his face. She's probably amused by the man's strong will power.*)

HILDE: I want to look into your eyes. . . .

> (*So saying, she pries open his eyes. It is a shock to Pasqualino to be facing the SS once again. With his eyes shut he had been using his imagination, but now must face the harsh reality. The look in his eyes is that of the bicycle racer who is about to have a stroke before reaching the top of the hill. Pasqualino doesn't give in. He gets pissed off. This is no way to treat him. He's putting his whole being into this performance. His sense of honor comes forth and from somewhere he finds the strength to penetrate the dark cavern of her body with his ailing dart. The Beast raises her eyebrows as she feels him inside her. Her expression is more one of surprise at the wonderful ways of nature than one of pleasure. Pasqualino collapses. He is nothing but a pile of bones. He has little more strength than a ninety-year-old man. He's nothing but an old rag folded over in half, a heap of misery. He collapses on her enormous body. At least he proved he truly was a man. The Beast scowls at the human larva. With an abrupt gesture she unloads his light body off hers and with a swift kick pushes him to the side of the couch. Hilde gets up. Pasqualino is curled up in one corner. She puts on a military overcoat and moves over to the bar, on top of which are a bottle of champagne, glasses, and a silver tray. She turns on the light and pours herself a drink.*)

HILDE: You make me sick. Your fight for survival is disgusting. Your love-making is disgusting!

> (*Pasqualino remains immobile on the couch, lying in a pool of sweat.*)

HILDE: In Paris there was a Greek who would make love to a goose. He did it for money; he did it to survive . . . and you, you subhuman Mediterranean larva, you even find the strength to get an erection. . . . That's why you will end up the winners of this war . . . you will be the ones who are left . . . you tiny slithering worms . . . no ideals or ideas . . . and us, with our dreams of a superior race . . . it is far too difficult. . . .

(Pasqualino doesn't even raise his head. It isn't over yet. Having drained her glass, Hilde continues.)

HILDE: What is your barrack number? Number 23, isn't it? Well, from now on you will be a blockelder!

(Pasqualino hasn't really understood, or at least hopes he hasn't understood. Pasqualino lifts himself up. He reaches out toward the Beast, who is sitting up straight in a chair, a grotesque figure depicting the abuse of power. Hilde is evil and forbidding. Pasqualino is pale and trembling.)

HILDE: Blockelder, I order you to hand over six prisoners for immediate extermination.

(Pasqualino shakes his head.)

HILDE: Yes! If you don't I'll have the whole barracks executed.

(Pasqualino hopes he hasn't understood what she just said.)

HILDE: Either you hand over six prisoners and the others can eat, and who knows, perhaps even survive, or the whole bunch is going to go up in smoke! It is entirely up to you. . . .
PASQUALINO: You are a ruthless bitch . . . ruthless!
HILDE: You too, my Mediterranean worm, can now play the butcher.

SCENE 67

(Barrack no. 23, corner of the shack—interior—dawn. The pale morning light brightens the camp. Pasqualino, wearing the blockelder uniform, is sitting at his desk studying the list of names to which is attached the future of all the others.)

FRANCESCO: No!

(Francesco's face appears out of the darkness. Pasqualino looks at him.)

PASQUALINO: Yes! That bitch was explicit . . . it's either six, or all of us. . . . These poor devils have already been condemned to death so we may as well save our own skins . . . don't you think?
FRANCESCO: This is nothing but vile blackmail. In this way they are trying to bring us to their level. We must rebel!

PASQUALINO: So we'll all be dead.

FRANCESCO: So be it!

PASQUALINO: Go fuck yourself, Francesco! You can say what you like, but right now I'm in command over here. Now then, I'll take them at random . . . I don't want to know who they are. . . . O.K. numbers eight to fourteen. . . . I just don't want to know who they are. . . .

(*The prisoners' fates are sealed.*)

FRANCESCO: Holy Virgin Mary!

PEDRO: You'll only be needing five men, amigo!

(*Pasqualino looks at Pedro, who is standing in the doorway smiling. Pedro comes forward. He is weak but very cocky.*)

PASQUALINO: Why?

PEDRO: I'll volunteer. . . .

PASQUALINO: You're crazy, why?

PEDRO: I've broken my balls!

SCENE 68

(*Barrack 23—interior—daytime. Two reserve officers are shouting, trying to muster the prisoners into the square.*)

RESERVE OFFICERS: Wake up! Come on, get up!

(*Reveille is being played at a very fast tempo. There is no time to kill.*)

RESERVE OFFICERS: Hurry! You macaronis, you're still asleep, get up, let's move it, out!

(*Everyone goes out.*)

PASQUALINO: Come on, stay in line, let's move it!

SCENE 69

(*Concentration camp Appleplatz—exterior—daytime. A group of SS officers led by a major are inspecting the men. They pass in front of Pasqualino and his group. Orders are being shouted in German. The major gives Pasqualino a quick glance, then moves over to the center of the square.*)

FEMALE OFFICER: *Schnel!*

> (*The square is packed with prisoners, all in single lines.*)

PASQUALINO: 19423, 19623, 19541, 19377, 19535, 19464.
GERMAN BARRACK CHIEFS: (*They repeat the numbers in German, then yell out, still in German*): Let's go, move it!

> (*Pasqualino looks at his comrades. There is madness in his look. The chosen ones are being dragged out of the files. Once the numbers have been read out, Pedro gives Pasqualino a filthy look because his number hasn't been called. He looks away from Pedro and concentrates on the piece of paper in his hands. He reads out the reason for the execution.*)

PASQUALINO: In barrack number 23, prisoners have been caught in the act of contrabanding food and damaging Third Reich property by tearing out planks from the barrack. The punishment for these offenses is that the above-mentioned prisoners will be . . . will be . . . shot. . . .

> (*The barrack leaders read out the order in German. Totally unexpectedly, Pedro dashes out of the line. Francesco cries out.*)

FRANCESCO: Please!
PEDRO: We must put an end to these fears. I've really broken my balls!

> (*Pedro races across the* Appleplatz *like a madman, avoiding the guards who have started chasing him immediately.*)

HILDE: (*She shouts something in German.*)

> (*Whistles being blown. Obediently the guards dart after Pedro. Machine-gun fire. After a moment of hesitation, Pasqualino joins in on the chase. Pedro becomes a symbol of strength and freedom in this pointless race toward the barracks and the latrines.*)

PEDRO: Brothers, I'm going to dive into the shit!
PASQUALINO: What . . . what are you doing?

> (*Pedro reaches the door to the barracks. He turns and shouts out in a victorious voice, his arms raised high above his head.*)

PEDRO: See you soon, you bastards!
EVERYONE CRIES OUT TOGETHER: Stop! Stop!
PASQUALINO: Stop! Stop!

(*Pedro disappears into the latrine barrack.*)

SCENE 70

(*Latrines—interior—daytime. Two prisoners are busy taking a shit over the side of an enormous cesspool. Totally surprised, they watch Pedro dash into the latrine, stop on the edge of the hole, and shout out.*)

PEDRO: "Man in disorder!"

(*He turns and dives into the swirling liquid mass. The guards and prisoners watch helplessly as the oozing mass closes over Pedro's body. Out of breath, Pasqualino stops and stares at the brown liquid closing on this free man's body.*)

GERMAN GUARD (*in German*): Get back to your lines.

(*Pasqualino is not really all there, but a push from an SS trooper brings him back to reality.*)

PASQUALINO: Wait a minute! Stop! Pull him out!

(*A burst of machine-gun fire puts an end to his shouts.*)

SCENE 71

(*Appleplatz—exterior—daytime. Pasqualino is going back to his line. The Appleplatz and its order is now being disrupted by something very unusual. Francesco is in the center of the square. He is heading for the officers, shouting abuses at them, totally absorbed by his hatred and anger. It is this very anger which makes him a free man. He shouts like a raving lunatic.*)

FRANCESCO: Fuckers! Goddamn bastards!

(*The guards have gathered around him, brandishing their billy clubs. Pasqualino dashes toward his friend in order to stop the SS from shooting him. He reaches Francesco, who is still ranting. With all his might he pushes him through the crowd, pretending to be hitting him, all the while whispering in his ear.*)

PASQUALINO: But what's gotten into you! . . . You'll ruin everything this way . . . please, fall to the ground, come on Francesco, pretend!

(Pasqualino hopes to save his friend's life: somehow he thinks he can do it.)

PASQUALINO: Pretend, fall, please, Francesco, fall! No, pretend, goddamnit!

(The other prisoners are nothing but pairs of eyes in the fog, which are being held back by the soldiers. Francesco has no fear. He has cracked. He screams and shouts under Pasqualino's false blows.)

FRANCESCO: I don't have the stomach to continue. . . . I can't do it!

(He grabs Pasqualino.)

FRANCESCO: How bad can death be, Pasqualino? At least you have the satisfaction of having shouted "bastards" in their faces.

(The major gives a sign and two guards grab hold of Francesco and drag him in front of the officer, hitting him with their rifles. Francesco is at this point totally oblivious to pain. . . . He is just angry. The major repeats the order. Pasqualino comes forward, but he hasn't understood the order. Everyone's eyes are pointed at him. The officer pushes him forward toward Francesco. They stand in front of the whole camp. The marshal translates the order into poor Italian.)

HILDE (in German): Stop! Head of barrack number 23, proceed with immediate execution.
GERMAN OFFICER (in German): Hurry up with the execution or it will be a lot worse for you and the others. . . .

(Pasqualino still hasn't understood.)

PASQUALINO: What do I have to do? What is it you want from me?

(The major puts a pistol into Pasqualino's hand, then looks at him and waits. The reserves have let Francesco go. He is now crouched at Pasqualino's feet. Pasqualino looks around. The major has a feeling that Pasqualino hasn't understood his order. He moves up to him and raises Pasqualino's arm, pointing it at Francesco's forehead.)

OFFICER: Shoot! Shoot! Shoot him!

(*Pasqualino can't do it. He is living out this nightmare. He looks into his friend's face and reads desperation and hunger.*)

PASQUALINO: No, I can't shoot him!

(*Francesco is kneeling at his feet, his head on his knees. He whispers.*)

FRANCESCO: Shoot, shoot me. . . . It'll be my freedom. . . . Be brave and shoot. . . . If you don't someone else will, and I'd rather a friend did it. . . . You'll be doing me a favor, shoot. . . .

(*Francesco lifts up his head and looks at his friend pleadingly. Pasqualino isn't able to pull the trigger.*)

FRANCESCO: This is torture. . . . come on, hurry, I can't play the hero for much longer. . . .

(*Pasqualino shakes his head. He just isn't able to do it.*)

FRANCESCO: If you wait any longer I'll pee in my pants, spare me the embarrassment in front of all these people. Please . . . fuck it . . . shoot, goddamn it, shoot!

(Pasqualino shoots. Pasqualino doesn't move. Francesco falls at his feet. The dogs start growling fiercely as the officers move away quickly. Machine-gun fire. Pasqualino doesn't see the look on his comrades' faces as they fall. Panoramic shot of the prisoners all kneeling in silence, their heads lowered as if time no longer existed. . . . Cut to: the pistol which has now been lowered. . . . Cut to: the stillness of the camp. . . . Cut to: the fog and smoke which constantly surround the camp. . . . Cut to . . .)

SCENE 72

(Naples—alleyway near Pasqualino's house—exterior—daytime. A colorful, incredible crowd scene. Old women in church thanking the Virgin Mary. A loud shout.)

CONCETTINA: Pasqualino has come back!

(The sisters leave their escorts and race across the alley, their protruding breasts straining against their tight dresses.)

SISTERS: Pasqualino is back!
MOTHER: Pasqualino is back!
MOTHER AND SISTERS: Pasqualino has returned!

(The camera starts climbing skyward, leaving the whole scene to our imagination; we can hear the sounds of the crowd, but that is all.)

SCENE 73

(Ground floor of Pasqualino's house. We discover Pasqualino's house is now full of postwar trappings—dolls, post cards, American flags. A picture of Pasqualino in an oval frame. Everything is new. Well-being has sunk its plastic roots into Pasqualino's household. Pasqualino has been given a new suit. His mother is pulling it out of the closet. It's a fine, blue, double-breasted suit, far too big for the emaciated Pasqualino. His mother helps him on with his jacket. A silk shirt and a nice new tie complement the outfit. Carolina suddenly appears in the doorway. She is excited and breathless. Pasqualino turns to look at her. She has grown up and is still very pretty though she too has that equivocal, whoreish look. Her excitement is genuine. Pasqualino is clean-shaven, hair waxed back. His face is ravished by the scars of what he has lived through—heavily lined, bags under his

eyes, a gray tinge to his face. It's all so clear. So is the gradual loss of hair and the white hairs which the wax can't really hide. Pasqualino looks at Carolina, then goes up to her and grabs her by the shoulders.)

PASQUALINO: You've become a whore as well?

(Carolina is honest, she can't lie to him.)

CAROLINA: Yes . . .
PASQUALINO: And did you make a lot of money?
CAROLINA: Yes . . .

(Pasqualino is firm and determined. In his first few words we are aware of his neurotic paranoid state.)

PASQUALINO: Just as well . . . Now close up shop, let's get married and start making kids. We haven't got much time. I want lots of them, twenty-five, thirty . . . we have to become strong because we must defend ourselves. Do you hear them out there?

(Pasqualino points to the alley, which is packed solidly with people.)

PASQUALINO: In a few years we'll start killing each other for a glass of water . . . for a chunk of bread. . . . That's why there have to be a lot of us, in order to defend ourselves. . . .

(Carolina doesn't understand. To her he appears insane, but it's all the same. She's happy.)

CAROLINA: I've always loved you. . . . I'm ready. . . .

(His mother smiles as if saying that words have no real importance.)

MOTHER: Pasqualino, what are you saying? Don't worry, just thank the Virgin Mary that you're back in one piece. Don't think about it anymore. It's all over, what's been has been. . . .

(She forces him to look into the mirror.)

MOTHER: Look at yourself, my boy! Look how handsome you are! Don't think about the past. . . . You're alive, Pasqualino . . . alive!

(Pasqualino stares blankly at his reflection in the mirror.)

PASQUALINO: Yeah . . . I'm alive.